THE PENGUIN BOOK OF WINES

Allan Sichel was born in 1900, in Hampstead, where he lived until his death in 1965. He was educated at Oundle and joined the Guards in 1918. In 1921, abandoning the idea of becoming a doctor, he entered his father's firm of Sichel & Company in Bordeaux, as the fourth generation since its foundation in 1883. Here he 'became a portly gentleman whose figure was even admired by French cellarmen, and thereafter,' he said, 'there was nothing to do but go on enjoying wine.' In the Second World War he served in the Intelligence Corps. As head of the family concern he was part proprietor of Château Palmer and owner of Château Angludet, now the home of his son Peter. He left three children and a number of grandchildren. Since, as a young man, he drank claret for breakfast 'to see what it had to say to me', he always lived for and by wine.

D0756847

THE
PENGUIN BOOK OF
WINES

ALLAN SICHEL

SECOND EDITION

with revisions by Peter A. Sichel

PENGUIN BOOKS

Penguin Books Ltd, Harmondsworth, Middlesex, England
Penguin Books, 625 Madison Avenue, New York, New York 10022, U.S.A.
Penguin Books Australia Ltd, Ringwood, Victoria, Australia
Penguin Books Canada Ltd, 2801 John Street, Markham, Ontario, Canada L3R 1B4
Penguin Books (N.Z.) Ltd, 182–190 Wairau Road, Auckland 10, New Zealand

—

First published 1965
Reprinted 1966, 1968 (twice)
Second edition, with revisions
by Peter A. Sichel, 1971
Reprinted with minor revisions 1972
Reprinted 1974, 1976, 1977, 1978

—

—

Made and printed in Great Britain
by Cox & Wyman Ltd,
London, Reading and Fakenham
Set in Monotype Bembo

CONTENTS

NON-EUROPEAN WINES

PART FOUR

PREFACE

I SHOULD like to record my indebtedness to many friends in various branches of the wine trade for the help they have given in vetting the information in this book; also to the commercial attachés of most of the wine-growing countries and to Mr G. S. Foulds and Mr O. B. Powell of the Australian Wine Centre in Soho, and Mr John Dunbar of the South African Wine Farmers' Association in the City. I am indebted to Mr Leslie Klaber for a great deal of information about the Hungarian vineyards derived from his experience on the former estates of his family and an inborn love and understanding of wine. Mr G. U. Salvi has put all his great knowledge of the Italian vineyards generously at my disposal, aided by his son, who on an exploratory oenological trip to Italy on my behalf averaged about two kilometres to the litre of wine, whilst Mr W. J. S. Fletcher has kept me straight on the wines of Portugal and Mr A. J. Cassinello on those of Spain. Mr F. Rossi, the creator of the modern Cyprus vineyards, has corrected one or two illusions from which I was suffering concerning the wines of that island. Mr Frank Egan and Messrs Duthie & Co. Ltd have helped me with information about and samples of Bulgarian wines and Messrs Norton & Langridge, R. & W. Teltscher Ltd and Walter Siegel Ltd have been most generous with information and samples of Rumanian, Yugoslav and Turkish wines respectively. I am indebted to Mr Walter Sichel for a report on recent German wine vintages and to Mr A. J. L. Reuss for one on the present Champagne vintages. M. Galet of Montpellier and Professor Birk of Geisenheim have been kind enough to clear up some technical points about vine varieties and Señor Juan José Fernandez of the Chilean Embassy has taken a great deal of trouble to make the information about the wines of his country as complete as possible.

Finally I should like to thank my assistant Mrs Pamela Vandyke Price not only for her help in the collection of information, typing and correcting proofs, but for the courage and enthusiasm with which she has tackled the tasting of some of the more dangerous-looking wines that have come our way during the last two years.

I have picked the brains of many good friends during the course of my search for information; all, alas, are not mentioned here because it is not possible to classify friends, but to all of them I express my deep gratitude and the hope that they will consider the book has justified their friendship.

PREFACE TO REVISED EDITION

My father having died shortly after the first edition of this book was published, the responsibility of this revision has fallen on myself. Prices have been revised in accordance with present market conditions, the text has been brought up to date with respect to new wine laws, vintages have been reported in accordance with recent tasting notes and other alterations have been made where necessary. The aim has been to produce a fully revised and up-to-date edition, but to conserve my father's original text wherever possible.

I would like to renew the acknowledgements made by my father to many of his friends who helped with information for the original edition, and who have also helped with this revision. In addition to those mentioned above I would like to thank Peter M. F. Sichel for help on the American Wine Section, Gerald Asher for information on lesser known wines and Edward Bidwell for collecting information from various sources in London. Mrs Pamela Vandyke Price has again been particularly helpful, providing additional information and clarifying various points in the original manuscript.

PETER A. SICHEL

INTRODUCTION

THIS book is meant as an introduction to the whole subject of wine, a guide to those who want to be able to enjoy wine without expecting of it either too much or too little.

The factual information which it gives will form the basis of further study for those who want to explore the mysteries of wine-making, wine development or wine-tasting. The reputation of wines, like the reputation of a work of art, depends on the ability of its judges to appreciate it. There is room enough for differing opinions. I have tried to put into proper perspective the mass of rules and regulations, advice and opinions, that have accrued round the subject of wine since, quite recently, it became a popular drink in Great Britain, America and Scandinavia. The principles guiding the selection of glasses, the question of decanting, and the choice of accompanying food are explained; their application is left to the judgement of the reader.

The evaluations of the qualities of different wines that have emerged through the years are no more than the opinions of others, however experienced they may be in the habit of drinking wine, and can serve only as a useful starting point from which each of us must form his own opinion. They are recorded here, and an attempt has been made to classify the principles on which the quality of wine should be judged. The confusion of labels has a chapter to itself and the methods of naming used in different wine-growing areas are explained so that the reader may have an opportunity to interpret the information given on a label and also grasp the significance of any omission.

Although the book does not pretend to be a comprehensive work of reference, information about the origin, production and character of most of the wines found in merchants' lists in Great Britain is given in Part Three. This, taken in conjunction with the chapters in Part Two on the principles to be followed in the selection of wines for differing occasions, will enable the reader to make his own individual choice and to defend it if need be.

From the book as a whole will emerge, I hope, the fact that whilst good wine is a pure product of Nature, the hazards which surround its birth and development are so great that the advice of a reliable wine merchant is indispensable to the really selective buyer. The information given in this book should guide the beginner at least some of the way.

REPRINT (1972)

For a variety of reasons, increases have been notable for most wines in the year following the revised edition and therefore in this reprint the reader should assume a rise in all the prices quoted throughout the text.

REPRINT (1976)

Since the first edition of this book, enormous changes have taken place in the world of wine. Even in subsequent reprints, there have been radical alterations as regards certain technicalities of wine-making, additions to wine regulations and laws and, inevitably, changes in the prices of all wines. But wine lovers throughout the world continue to find the advice given throughout the pages of the *Penguin Book of Wines* essentially sound, and the author's approach to wine has been recognized as a classic of wine literature. The present edition does not, therefore, attempt to update the text as regards names and prices but remains as it was for the first revised edition, with some slight alterations, so as to preserve the original format and character of the whole.

PART ONE

CHAPTER I

PRINCIPLES OF WINE-MAKING

ACCORDING to the Wine and Spirit Association of Great Britain, wine is defined as: 'The alcoholic beverage obtained from the juice of freshly gathered grapes, the fermentation of which has been carried through in the district of its origin and according to local tradition and practice.' This definition leaves out alcoholic beverages made from other fruit or vegetable juices, and it leaves out wine made from dehydrated grapes shipped to foreign countries and there manufacture into wine. It acknowledges tacitly that the benefits which wine brings and which are contained in the whole grape, in its sugar content, its juice, including water, its skin and the whole of its pulp, spring from the soil in which the grape is grown. It acknowledges too that these benefits are due to natural qualities in the grape which have never been explained fully and that there remains a mystery about wine which scientists have so far been unable to penetrate.

In addition to the direct benefits of the soil, the quality and character of wine are influenced by the natural ferments or yeast cells which at the time of full maturity form on the outside of the grape skins ready to get to work as soon as the grape is crushed and the sugar content is released. Ferments, like the soil, vary from place to place. This is the basic principle on which all wine is made – the yeast or ferments, which are organic cells, feed on the sugar contained in the grape, breaking it down into alcohol and carbon dioxide, they in their turn being killed off by the alcohol they have produced.

It sounds simple enough, but in fact the process is very complicated and there are many things that can go wrong. The yeast cells, for example, can work only within a fairly narrow temperature range; they die or become inactive if the outside temperature is too cold or if the heat generated by their own activities rises above a certain level. If the fermentation ceases before a proper balance is achieved between alcohol and sugar, the wine is left with a vulnerable sugar content which sooner or later will be attacked by other bacteria from the air, such as the vinegar bacteria or rarer ferments, and these will leave the wine with an unpleasant taste. Other hazards also threaten well-made wine, hazards which depend on practical considerations. Even the cask in which the wine ferments may have a harmful effect. For its proper development and protection young wine must be stored in scrupulously clean oak casks or in vats. These are expensive to buy and difficult to maintain. One faulty stave in a cask or vat can spoil the whole content, for wine is very sensitive to outside influences and immediately takes on the taste of a rotten stave or even the smell of a dirty cellar. Storage is a real problem to the small peasant proprietor, who makes a large proportion of the world's wines. Through all the stages of the life of a wine, until it is safely bottled and stored in a cool cellar, the human element influences the final quality. Man is midwife to the new-born wine and the perfect conditions which he tries to provide for its formative years cost money and the care it demands costs time. The small proprietor may have a limited amount of each at his disposal.

In general, red wine is made from black- or dark-skinned grapes and white wine is made from white or yellow grapes, though there are important exceptions, such as Champagne, which is largely made from the dark-skinned Pinot Noir. The juice of nearly all wine-producing grapes is light yellow in colour and is tinted by the colouring matter in the skin of the grapes at the time of fermentation. Therefore, broadly speaking, red wines are fermented in contact with their skins, whilst white wines are not. In all cases, however, when wine with any pretensions to quality is made, the stalks are removed from the fruit before it is pumped or shovelled into the fermenting vat, because the stalks are bitter and contain a large amount of astringent tannin. The popular conception of barefooted workers merrily trampling the grapes is largely inaccurate today. Most fine red wines are not made from pressed grapes at all, but from grapes broken during the process of 'de-stalking', in which they are either pressed by hand through a kind of wooden trelliswork bench, or mechanically rotated in large cylinders. In either case the skins are broken and much of the juice runs out. The juice and the broken grapes are then pumped into vats and ferment together. It is not until the fermentation is over, after five or six days, that, the newly made wine having been run off, the skins with what juice remains are shovelled out of the vat and put under the press. The resulting wine, rich in tannin and known in France as the '*vin de presse*', is normally kept apart until the final ensemble, or blend, is made

With white wine the process is different, since the skins do not go into the fermenting vat. In this case the grapes coming in from the vineyard are pressed in modern presses and only the juice pumped into the vats or casks in which it ferments, carrying with it the ferments from the outside of the skins. Four or even five pressings are made, so the last two should not be used for quality wine.

In the case of red wines all the natural sugar of the 'must', or unfermented juice, is converted into alcohol and gives a wine containing from 10 to 14 per cent of alcohol by volume and a variety of salts, minerals and various acids in minute quantities which in time play their part in producing a flavour and bouquet characteristic of the vines from which they come and the soil in which they grow. White wines are different in this respect. The grapes from which they are made produce a juice richer in sugar than the red grapes and in certain soils are capable of producing a juice very rich indeed in sugar. Since the ferments die in a heavy concentration of alcohol, it is in general not possible to ferment out any liquid to more than 14–15 per cent of alcohol and then only with a very careful control of fermentation under ideal conditions. Rich white wines, therefore, stop fermenting when the alcohol has reached the region of 14 per cent and the sugar remaining from the must is left in the wine in a stable condition and gives to the wines of Sauternes, Barsac, Monbazillac and some fine German wines the characteristic sweetness for which they are famed.

In many vineyards throughout the world the art of the wine-maker has been used to adapt this natural product to a form more pleasing and to a flavour more attractive to man than Nature unaided can produce. Not all regions which have a climate in which the vine can flourish have the soil that produces the delicacy of flavour essential to fine wine. These varying processes will be recorded and explained in a later part of this book and it will be seen that, however the wine-maker adopts the process of wine-making, wine always remains the pure fermented juice of the grape.

Wine is sometimes called a 'living thing'. This is justified in the sense that it is in a continual state of development under the influence of both its organic and inorganic components, besides being affected by the action of oxygen in the air during its life, both in cask and in bottle. The changes that it undergoes are highly complex and their effects never exactly predictable. Some of the sickness to which wine is liable can be cured or prevented, some difficult stages of its development can be eased, but the general maturing of a fine wine that Nature has endowed with the ability to achieve an individuality of flavour and aroma cannot be controlled or influenced. This perhaps justifies its description as a 'living thing'.

During its development, wine must get rid of impurities and of the insoluble particles formed by the chemical changes which take place. These natural changes take their time and cannot be hurried without upsetting other less obvious changes that are taking place at the same time. Therefore the process of wine-making continues for one, two, three or even more years in cask whilst the natural process of clearing-up is going on. This involves the removal of the wine from the deposit it forms, some control of the oxygen it gets and general attention to its well-being. It is a highly skilled business, often best carried out by the grower, relying on an instinct developed through generations.

Wine can suffer from unexplained sicknesses as well as from the better-defined weaknesses and these are still very often best treated by the man who spends his life tending his vineyard. I have many times seen instinctive treatment of various kinds successfully applied by Head Cellarmen and many times seen the application of modern scientific products which in curing one weakness induce another. With wine as with human beings, Nature, given the opportunity, is often the best healer.

CHAPTER 2

THE APPROACH TO WINE

WINE-DRINKING is no occult art to be practised only by the gifted few. Indeed, it is not an art at all. It is, or should be, the sober habit of every normal man and woman burdened with normal responsibilities and with a normal desire to keep their problems in perspective and themselves in good health. It is meant for those who have the courage to enjoy the rhythm of life, not for those whose pleasure lies in exaggerating its miseries. Neither is it a panacea, meant to kill pain by dulling the sensibilities; it is a food for the body and mind from which a human being can draw the strength that will enable him to use to the full any gifts with which Nature has endowed him. It changes no one; it will not turn a creative artist into a scientist, a musician into a painter or a poet into a businessman. It will enrich each. It can be beneficial to everyone and enjoyed in varying degrees according to individual pockets and palates.

Those who wish to study the developments and refinements of wine should ignore the ponderous pronouncements of the pundits. There is no need to be challenging and aggressive in order to cultivate a palate for the finer qualities of expensive wines. Understanding is much more likely to come to the hopeful and modest student who has the courage to be ruthlessly honest with himself. One or two glasses of light table wine – that is unfortified wine – taken at lunch and dinner, will soon form a basis on which to judge quality. It is unnecessary, in order to enjoy wine, to have any technical knowledge of vineyards or vintages. This will come later, quite naturally, and serve gradually to narrow the field of choice to those types of wine which the individual palate prefers. A good wine merchant, choosing the wines of a new vintage for laying down, will generally indulge in what is known as a 'blind' tasting; that is to say he will taste wines from a row of bottles with their labels turned away from him, so that he may not be prejudiced by the reputation of any vineyard or by the price that is being asked for the wine. Often, year after year, he will find that he has selected the majority of his wines from certain specific areas and rejected others which his competitors will choose.

He has been following his own individual taste and will gather around him customers who have the same taste as himself. The student will be wise to take advantage of the wine merchant's experience as a guide to his studies, whilst leaving to his own palate the responsibility for his final choice.

The importance of the individual choice cannot be overstressed, and the first rule for the student of wines is to trust his own palate – to believe in its physical ability to record as many sensations as anybody else's. In the course of time he will become more perceptive in his interpretation of the sensations his palate reveals. This does not imply any change in the recording machine of the palate, but it does mean that the brain has by training become more sensitive to the messages and is better able to detect harmonies or disharmonies.

The second important rule for the student is that he must have the courage to change his mind. As experience grows and perception becomes keener, his taste is certain to change and wines which at first pleased may now bore or actively displease. Since there is no absolute standard of perfection, quality must always remain relative and its appreciation personal. The best wine is the one which, in the opinion of the majority, is better than any other, perhaps a wine in which it is impossible to imagine improvements, yet about which no one is qualified to say 'Nature cannot improve on this'. Wine must, therefore, be approached with an open mind, a readiness to accept it as it is, a readiness to listen to the opinions of others and a determination of each to accept the judgement of his own palate. Wine gives opportunities for exercise to that which it feeds. The sense of taste and of smell will quite quickly discover all that a cheap young wine has to give, and if the student, having solved one mystery, is encouraged to take on something more difficult, wine will give him the opportunity of developing his critical abilities step by step, gradually, until he reaches the expensive realms of matured old wines and meets flavour of such delicacy and subtlety that even his trained palate, and his enhanced perception, cannot respond at one time to all the scintillating facets of flavours that are presented. This is the appreciation of fine wine to which a sensible and patient approach can lead any normal student, and it means that the pleasures of drinking wine are endless.

At this point wines may be said to acquire a recognizable personality, and their origin, that is to say their vineyard and vintage, are of practical interest. The enthusiast who has developed his palate sufficiently to recognize these characteristics, and this is not nearly so difficult to do as is generally thought, is now able to indulge in the popular social exercise of astonishing his friends by recognizing wines by their tastes. One further condition only is necessary. He must have a good memory. Without it he cannot hope to shine at dinner parties. This, of course, should in no way affect the pleasure he gets out of wine. Discussion about the quality or character of wines at this level on social occasions is like discussions about music, poetry, painting or people. It is a curious fact that as far as wine is concerned these discussions never seem to become heated. The last word generally goes to someone who, in an attempt to describe the personality of the wine, hits upon so fantastic a piece of imagery that his opponents are reduced to silence. This stimulus to the imagination is one of the characteristics of wine.

CHAPTER 3

ASSESSMENT OF QUALITY

YOUNG WINES

IT does not follow that because degrees of quality are difficult to assess, it is also difficult to decide what is a good wine and what is not. Anyone can do it by paying attention to those factors which are common to all good wines. In order of importance these are: absence of unpleasant flavour, honesty of production, soundness of construction, purity of origin and positiveness of character. After that the arguments start.

A positive character may be pleasant or unpleasant in varying degrees, suitable or unsuitable to the mood and palate of the taster or the accompanying food. Consider for a moment the 1929 Château Haut Brion. There are some who think it is the best claret they have ever tasted and others who find it undrinkable. I know of no wine with a more positive character, but the only dish I can think of as an accompaniment is a Meringue Chantilly and no claret was ever meant to accompany a Meringue Chantilly. Like all problems connected with the final assessment of the qualities of wine, this is entirely a matter of personal taste.

The first problem is to decide whether a given wine is a good one or a bad one.

First, then, has the wine an unpleasant taste? Presumably all wine has an unpleasant taste to people who dislike wine, so that 'unpleasant' in this context means unclean, bitter, sour, acid, tasting of extraneous matter such as cork, wood or yeasts, or tasting astringent. An acid wine is generally one made from unripe grapes, a bitter taste generally indicates a badly constituted or incomplete wine, a sour wine is on its way to turning into vinegar because of its poor constitution or maltreatment. A cork or wood taste can come from cork or cask, and a taste of yeast means that the effects of the last fermentation have not been properly removed by 'fining' or filtering. There is also a taste of twigs sometimes apparent in cheap wine, which indicates a badly made wine. It may be badly made through ignorance or greed. This particular taste, often associated with that of tannin, comes from the *vin de presse*, which may be added to the *grand vin* in order to give it the tannin necessary for its conservation in bottle. In some cases amongst the cheaper wines this *vin de presse* is the product of grapes and stalks pressed together, giving a dark red, astringent and stalk-flavoured wine. If this is added to the main wine in excessive quantity in order to make as much *grand vin* as possible, the result is a bad wine with an unpleasant taste.

Wine so easily takes up the tastes and smells around it that a multitude of faults are covered by the description 'unclean'. In general, the unclean taste comes from one of three sources. It may come from rotten grapes being gathered at the time of the vintage (particularly easy to do if the weather is wet during the gathering), in which case the unclean smell or taste is of the mouldy, musty kind. It may come from poor treatment of a perfectly good wine during its early life, perhaps by the use of stale clarifying media, or by imperfect racking-off of the lees that form after a wine has been clarified, in which case it resembles that of decaying vegetable matter. Lastly, it may come from a wine having been left too long in contact with air. This occurs for different reasons. A wine loses volume in its oak cask for the first year of its life and if the loss is not made good, the wine in the cask is oxidized by the oxygen in the air. Sometimes hazards of shipping make this inevitable; sometimes it is due to carelessness in the bottling cellar, sometimes carelessness in the shipper's storage cellar: the result is a sort of metallic taste which can be safely classified as unpleasant. There are, too, various illnesses to which young wine is prone. Many of these give an unpleasant taste, and if the wine is not properly looked after or cleansed after the sickness has departed it will retain this taste and must be considered bad wine.

The second criterion of good wine, honesty of production, is less easy for the inexperienced to assess. A wine that has not been produced honestly has been interfered with for one of two reasons: either because, Nature having defaulted in some respect, man has found a means of remedying or at least of hiding the defect, or because someone has decided that it is possible to improve on Nature's methods. In this first case, the remedy is generally sugar, which can both supply Nature's deficiency in a poor year and hide its effects – such as the acidity of immature grapes or the weakness in alcoholic strength that comes from grapes with a weak sugar content. The addition of sugar to the 'must' or unfermented grape juice is generally allowed, provided that the natural sugar content has reached a certain level. It is not allowed if there is not sufficient sugar to produce the minimum degree of alcohol required in its particular region – about 10 per cent in cheap areas. This is logical, since it limits wine to the beverage made from the juice of the grape whilst allowing the vintner to reinforce it. Sugar added to the unfermented juice in the above manner is intended to ferment with the juice and increase its alcoholic content. Since all the added sugar is fermented and turned into alcohol it does not affect the sweetness of the wine. The addition of sugar can in no sense make a harmful beverage and in fact the risk of a great deal of sugar being added is largely eliminated by the regulations governing wine-making in different countries. Too much sugar will upset the 'balanced' taste of a wine, and give it a dull, neutral taste.

There is also unnatural wine produced by the grower who believes, sometimes quite rightly, that his wine is unattractive to the public and who tries to imitate the qualities of successful wines of his region. Unfortunately, this practice is widespread and widely accepted. Such wines range from those in which the fruit acidity necessary to their balance has been artificially stimulated, to those which have been concentrated in order to increase the intensity of their flavour – even flavourings of various kinds being added. The main reason for criticism of these methods is not that they spoil the taste of the wine – often they do indeed make a palatable drink out of something that would not otherwise taste well – but that they falsify wine to the extent that the taster, not recognizing the falsification, might consider the wine to be of a higher quality than it really is and, in the case of the finer wines amongst which these malpractices are unfortunately not unknown, be led to expect development and improvement in bottle which in fact will not take place. It must be wellnigh impossible for the beginner to discover these faked wines when perpetrated by experienced wine-makers. It is not of prime importance that he should recognize them for what they are – they will not harm him – but since they cannot develop in a normal manner they will mislead him and disappoint him in the end.

There are two ways in which the persistent student is likely to come to a proper assessment of such wines. Firstly, by the test of time – if he drinks nothing else, he will become bored with the sameness of the flavour and the lack of any sort of intriguing quality. Secondly, if he drinks other wines at about the same price, he will sooner or later find one which has the indefinable hallmark of purity – perhaps the subtlety of flavour nearly always missing in faked wines, and above all a clean-cut invigorating quality about the taste and a harmony that combines bouquet, aroma and taste into a positive character.

The other three standards suggested as a basis of assessment are concerned with the relative qualities of sound wine and not with the assessment of basic purity. Soundness of construction, purity of origin – that is to say, the characteristic of the district from which a wine is alleged to have come – and positiveness of character are more difficult to define and yet in many ways are easier for the student to recognize. Broadly, recognition of these qualities is a matter of experience, and mistakes can do no harm to the student who is not discouraged by temporary setbacks. A mistake at this level will not launch the student along a false trail of investigation as a mistake in the elementary stage could do.

It is likely that the majority of wine-drinkers will enjoy and benefit from their habit throughout their life without bothering about the finer points of assessment of quality. A knowledge of sound, cheap wine will quickly reveal the superiority all the way up the scale of finer wines matured in bottle. At its best the attraction of fine wines is obvious to a beginner. This is particularly true of white wines and of the fortified red wines, such as port. For the student who likes to know just how much he has the right to expect from wine the analytical approach is important and in the long run more rewarding.

Soundness of construction, then, is important in a fine wine – by which I mean any natural table wine from a good district and generally available (1970) from about 70p a bottle – because it is an indication of the wine's ability to survive long enough in bottle to develop all the qualities which its origins make possible. A soundly constructed wine must be well balanced; the acidity (that is to say the infinitesimal quantities of various acids present in the grape or produced by fermentation, which give liveliness to the wine) must be sufficient, unobtrusive and recognizable more by the effect of its presence than by any taste of acidity; the degree of alcohol must be sufficient to ensure the conservation of the wine but not so high that it will predominate when the wine gets older. Alcohol does not change in bottle, but other elements in the wine are gradually broken down to give the delicate flavour of matured wine and leave the unchanged alcohol more noticeable. This can give an impression of excessive dryness on the palate.

The flavour must be complete and register on all parts of the palate, whilst the weight of the wine must be sufficient to give the impression that is has something on which to live during its maturing period.

Purity of origin matters most to the serious student who wants to collect wines, or found a cellar, or simply assure himself that he will get the kind of wine he likes when buying a bottle at a time. The origin of a wine has the same kind of importance as the pedigree of a horse or a dog. It is an indication that certain flavours and characteristics of weight, aroma and development can be expected. The origin becomes an essential part of the student's vocabularly. Experience alone can bring the ability to determine the purity of origin. That it must be considered in the assessment of quality will, I think, be generally accepted, but it becomes really important only amongst those rare fine wines which are made at the best vineyards in good years. Amongst the lesser categories the finer characteristics of their various origins are generally not well developed.

Positiveness of character is an attribute of fine wines well known to exist but very difficult to explain. It is an indication of strength, of constitution and of health, of promise to fulfil its destiny according to its origin and of its readiness when matured to be judged by its peers. The individuality achieved by wine is no small part of its attraction; it is inconceivable that good wine should develop an unpleasant character with age, so that a wine that has successfully passed the other four tests of quality must have its rating advanced if, in addition, it has individuality of character.

MATURED WINES

Having acquired through some diligence and a moderate outlay the habit of assessing the quality of good pure wine that is young and comparatively cheap, it is necessary to work out some rough rules for the judgement of matured wines. Most wine-lovers will have plenty of opportunities of exercising their palates on wines between the two extremes of the very young and the fully matured. If some standards can be acquired through a little experience of the two extremes, the average in-between wines will more easily fall into their proper place.

The factors which make for quality in young wines are in the main factual and universal in their appeal, those applying to matured wine are comparative and personal. To attempt communication of the pleasurable experience associated with the tasting of fine wine is to risk falling into those very errors of exaggerated claims and description which this book has sought to counteract. So let it be said at once that I believe wine to be one of Nature's means of revealing perfection. This, and no less, is the standard by which the qualities of great natural wines can be measured, and since perfection cannot be defined, the beauty of wine must be measured against individual conceptions of perfection.

There are other tests on a more practical plane which demand standards of quality rare enough to delight the enthusiast and to provide the palate with a high degree of sensual pleasure.

The two main attributes of really fine wine are the subtlety of its flavour and the subtlety of its bouquet. There is no unanimity of opinion about which is the most important. Amongst some wine lovers the sense of smell is more developed than the sense of taste, and although the two are closely connected they are, in the first approach to a wine, two distinct sources of messages to the brain. Like an orchestra true wine must be a harmonious whole, but it is made up of many complementary flavours, as an orchestra is of instruments, which give the whole a scintillating effect as first one, then another, takes fleeting possession of the palate. This is what is generally meant by the subtlety of flavour that characterizes all great wine; it is the intriguing quality which leaves the palate always searching. The same applies to the bouquet, though to a lesser extent, for while the same momentary impressions are present, the general effect is to invite the palate to taste and the drinker expects to find on the palate a fulfilment of the pleasure promised by the nose.

Additional marks must be given for breed – which is connected with purity of origin. There is more to breed than the badge of authenticity which enables the drinker to assess future behaviour from his knowledge of other wines from the same district. There is the thrill of finding a perfect specimen and there is the satisfaction of finding a wine which conforms to the drinker's idea of what it should be. In many ways a half-developed Château Latour of a good vintage, full in body and with the flavour of cedar wood so prominent in this wine when young, can give nearly as much pleasure as the same wine fully matured, aromatic and perfumed, in which this characteristic taste is far less prominent. For this reason also, the breed, or characteristics, of the vineyard is important.

The consistency of the wine is the third guiding factor. Matured wine should be soft and caressing to the palate and its primary taste should be fragrant and refreshing. The colour too should be crystal-clear, varying in tint according to origin and age. For those who like to indulge in the exercise of spotting origins and vintages, colour can be a useful guide, particularly in red wines. But it can also be misleading unless the spotter has a good knowledge of the peculiarities of different vintages. Red wines get lighter in colour as they age. The purple of the young wine changes to ruby and then to brick red as various changes, organic and inorganic, take place during its development in bottle. The changes in colour are best seen at the edge of the wine when the glass is tilted and held against a white background. But not all wines start off with a deep purple colour – it depends upon the vintage – and not all wines develop at the same rate in the bottle. In fact it would be true to say that it is seldom that two vintages, or even two wines of the same vintage, develop at the same rate. The only thing that is certain about colour is that in red wines it tends to lighten as the wine approaches its decline and in white wines it darkens. Colour, then, may indicate how near a wine is to its end but not necessarily how far it is from its beginning. The colour should please the eye, should be clear and lively, but so far as red wines are concerned can be of little more help in assessing the quality of a wine.

White wines, which are both more fragile because they contain little or no tannin (a great preserver of red wines) and more sensitive in their colour reactions because these are not obscured by the strong tints that come from the skins of dark grapes, can reveal faults through their colour, but cannot by this indicate quality. Colours vary from the greenish tinge of Chablis, through the straw of Rhine wines and Graves to the rich golden tints of Sauternes and other sweet white wines. As they become really old the sweeter wines take on a brownish colour, which personally I do not find pleasing to the eye but which nevertheless may be present in wines of astonishing bouquet and flavour. Any indication of dullness in the colour of white wines, or any hint of a metallic tint, are bad signs.

Within certain rather wide limits, then, it is possible for anyone to assess the extremes of quality without being able to value any wine precisely. For this, more experience of the flavours and characteristics of wines is necessary. Some, particularly wines from the more southern and therefore hotter areas, have peculiarities of taste due to the way they are made, or the soil from which they come. The beginner, or even the experienced drinker, may on first acquaintance find some of these so strange that he classifies them as unpleasant. The *vin jaune* of the Jura in France, made in a special way, does not please everyone, and some fortified wines like Marsala, grown on the volcanic soil of Sicily, have a taste which some people never come to like. This does not mean that they are bad wines. The taste of both is clean and natural, and the wine cannot be condemned because of it. Some experience is, therefore, necessary even at the early stage of determining good wine from bad. Whilst everyone has the right to reject for his personal taste, indeed has the duty ruthlessly to do so if he wishes to acquire a knowledge of wine, only experience can give the right to condemn.

No one should be put off by the flowery and extravagant language sometimes used by enthusiasts to describe their impressions. Painters, sculptors and musicians also sometimes express their interpretation of a scene, object or event in a seemingly meaningless and extravagant manner, but no one is prevented by this from enjoying works of art that he understands. So with wine everyone is entitled to his opinion and to express it if he can find anyone to listen. The audience may be bored or impressed. The wine will not be affected.

CHAPTER 4

TASTING

ATTITUDE OF MIND

TASTING is largely an attitude of mind. On the whole the functioning of the palate is automatic and there is little that anyone can do to improve it except to give it practice. There is, as will be seen, a certain amount of elementary practical knowledge which helps in the efficient use of the palate, but it is not nearly so important as the attitude of mind of the taster. This, after all, is logical enough, since the physical palate receives the coded message but the brain deciphers it. In other words everybody tastes individually and interprets according to his experience.

The opinion of the taster reflects his own standards and his own critical ability. Tasting is a challenge to the mind and it is important that the mind or brain shall be in good working order. To be receptive the mind must be tranquil and undisturbed. No one would attempt to taste the difference between a 1952 and a 1953 Lafite whilst watching the 2.30, just as no one would try to listen to a symphony concert with a road drill operating outside the window. Even the hope of identifying the wine and adding glory to one's reputation as a taster must never interfere with one's attitude of calm, relaxed attention.

This tranquillity is not easy to achieve. It is quite impossible at a crowded public tasting or in a private competitive tasting with earnest 'spotters' discussing the characteristics of the wine they have tasted and comparing notes. For example, a hint that one of the wines tastes of wood may be quite enough to distract the receptive mind so much that it registers 'wood' with every wine tasted. Perfect conditions are needed for the tasting of fine wines, but are by no means necessary for the enjoyment of lesser wines, or even for great enjoyment of fines wines under the normal conditions in which they are usually tasted. There are different degrees of tasting, and the practical enjoyment of wine does not demand the same high degree of concentration and analytical gustatory examination that is required of the professional trying to judge the future of a young wine, or of the advanced collector-student wanting to perfect his knowledge of the vagaries of wine. Wine is meant to be enjoyed in its matured state when most of its flavours are well defined and its shape rounded and softened. Then, tranquillity of mind may well take second place to a sympathetic atmosphere. The present object, however, is to discuss the mechanism of wine-tasting, and if the rules of perfection seem to be too austere let it be remembered that they are offered only as a standard and by no means as an absolute requirement for the enjoyment of wine.

In addition to a quiet and receptive attitude of mind and a sympathetic atmosphere, the physical well-being of the taster is necessary; without this a concentration of the normal faculties becomes impossible.

There is also a psychological approach which I have found helpful. Wine is a mysterious liquid in a continual state of change, and its first fundamental and overwhelming characteristic must be its purity. The taster should try to compare that first fleeting impression on the palate with whatever picture of its origin experience or imagination has implanted in his mind. The sunny vineyards, the ripened grapes, the juice flowing from the presses, the actual pressing, all or any of these may vividly impress the mind with the idea of a fragrant wine. The mind that holds for a split second the picture of the raw material and the finished product is more likely to achieve a first rough classification than the one which waits passively for the whole message from the palate. The palate will produce it in time, but it is a great help to start off at the right level. Despite the emphasis on receptivity, there is a certain active quality that, at the moment of tasting, is indispensable to sound judgement. This concentration of memory on past experience is not incompatible with a high degree of receptivity; it is in fact a means of acquiring it. During those few seconds in which the wine is held in the mouth and the palate being asked for its message, this same concentration is maintained. As experience grows the mind automatically compares the present picture with former experience of young wines that have developed, it becomes in time just as possible to foresee the future of a wine as it is to recognize its past. In fact, given the experience of matured wine, it is, I think, rather easier, since the elements that make for development in bottle are sometimes easier to assess than are the flavours that indicate origin.

THE EYE

The eye plays a part in the judgement of wine. It is difficult for the normal person to extract full pleasure from a glass of wine without seeing it. The tastings which are sometimes described as 'blind' are not undertaken by blindfolded tasters but are tastings in which the labels of the bottles have been hidden in order that the taster shall not be influenced by names or prices.

Examine the clarity of the wine in the glass by holding it up to the light. A bottled wine may have thrown a deposit in the bottle during the normal development process, and some of the deposit may have been transferred to the glass by careless decanting or pouring. This will obscure the taste of the wine in the glass but is not injurious to the wine itself. This matter is dealt with more fully in the chapter on decanting.

Assess also the liveliness of the colour. It is possible for a wine to be quite clear of deposit or floating particles and yet for its colour to be dull, like the eye of a sick animal. A healthy wine has a look at once of liveliness and repose which to the student soon becomes a promise of a fragrance of taste.

SMELL

Before the wine reaches the mouth, it should be smelled, not only because in unfortunate cases the smell may be a warning not to taste at all, but because the nose protrudes from the face and, whether you like it or not, you are going to get the smell of the wine before you get the taste. Besides, it is better to deal with each element of taste as it is presented in an orderly manner and not to be in too much of a hurry to get to the best bit at the end. Indeed, there is no assurance that the end will be as good as the beginning, so concentrate on each delight as it is revealed.

The nose may reveal all sorts or things, good or bad. Any un-unpleasant or strong foreign smell is a bad thing, whether it be musty, or sour, or of decaying vegetable matter, sulphur, bad eggs, green twigs, yeast or apples. Decisive smells like these upset the harmony which is the hallmark of fine wine, and any wine which presents them must be rejected. At the same time, it must be accepted that a smell of sulphur is very often present in very cheap white wines, which have to be specially treated in order to survive the rigours of the journey and bottling. They are not 'fine' wine even in its widest sense.

Musty Smells

The commonest unpleasant smell is one of the musty group. This embraces the smell of cork, of old wood, of fungus – but not the sweet smell of mushrooms or truffles which are sometimes found in healthy wine. The description 'corky' is too often indiscriminately applied to all this group and yet it is quite easy to distinguish. It is simply a smell of corks. A single wine cork of good quality has very little smell when new, and to discover whether a wine is 'corked' or not it is better to smell the wine than the cork. The smell of cork in wine is often transmitted by the faulty cleaning of a perfectly good cork.

A musty, woody smell differs from that of cork. It approaches more a vague mouldiness and is generally caused by a faulty stave in the cask in which the wine was shipped.

A slight smell of fungus is sometimes apparent; this is often due to overripe grapes which have ripened during the summer heat but have then been exposed to rainy weather during the time of the vintage. It often takes as long as four weeks to complete the grape harvest in a given area or vineyard and a few days' rain on ripe grapes is enough to start a process of decay which may eventually give a taste to the wine. It is not considered by all connoisseurs to be an unpleasant smell and its effect depends upon its strength. It cannot, however, be denied that it obscures the fragrance which should be a quality of all fine wine. A more pronounced smell of the same kind is sometimes found in very old wines and in this case presages its early disintegration. Wines that have reached this stage, however, often have other qualities of bouquet and taste to compensate for the smell of age.

Clearly there is one important difference between the corky smell and the rest of the musty group. A wine smelling of cork may well be, in fact is likely to be, the only bottle affected in the whole bin or case. No one can be blamed for it. No one can be blamed either for the smell of age, but woodiness is inexcusable, since both importer and bottler should have noticed it and the shipper should have noticed the unsound stave in the cask which gave the taste to the wine.

Acid Smells

A sour smell indicates a wine made from unripe grapes. It is unlikely to be met with in Great Britain, where such wines are not imported. It is not quite the same as the vinegary smell which is sometimes met with and which reveals a wine which has been infected by the vinegar ferment and is in the process of turning its alcohol into vinegar. This is one example of the nose warning the mouth what to expect. Such a wine is lost. There is no method of bringing it back to health. Both these smells are different from a clean, slightly acid smell sometimes found in young wines. This is the type of smell found in fresh fruit juices and represents the 'fruit acidity' necessary to the development of all good wine. If it is detectable on the nose it must be further examined by the palate proper in order to determine whether or not it is present in excessive quantities. It is present in all wine, but the degree to which it is acceptable depends on the other elements with which it will eventually combine to form the bouquet and give liveliness to the wine.

A wine will sometimes in its youth have a smell of freshly sawn matured wood. This is a fault derived from bad treatment or from being lodged in an inefficiently prepared cask. It is a clean smell. In proper quantities it is not noticeable on the nose, in excess it may stay with diminishing but still obtrusive effect in a wine for the rest of its life. The importance of its distracting quality varies in direct proportion to the age of a wine. In a young red wine there is a chance that it may disappear altogether as the wine matures.

Other Smells

There is a smell that comes from inexpert or careless treatment of the wine in its youth, the smell of decaying vegetable matter, of a nice clean compost heap which does not, however, go well in wine. It may come from lees, or deposits, left in the wine, or from the wine being left too long on its lees. The wine is not permanently damaged but needs further care from the wine merchant.

Then there is a rotten-egg smell, universally disliked and probably caused by an accident during the cleansing of a cask, or perhaps by the use of stale materials during the fining or cleansing of the wine.

A smell of fresh green twigs comes from wine made from grapes damaged by a hailstorm; the bruised wood of the vine gives its taste to the grape, its juice and its end product.

The smell of sulphur fumes will be easily recognized by everybody. Sulphur is an important element in the preservation of wine and in the sterilizing of casks. It is present in wine in various forms but is generally noticeable only in its gaseous form and, being volatile and unattached, quickly disappears.

A wine that smells of yeast has, in fact, dead yeast cells in it and has not been properly cleansed after its last fermentation.

A wine that is starting to ferment and contains live yeast cells often has a smell of rotting apples. A smell of fresh apples is a different thing altogether and forms part of the bouquet of various white wines from widely separated areas.

The student need not let this formidable collection of smells discourage him from training his palate. They are included only so as to forewarn him of the more prominent smells – as opposed to bouquet – which he may meet over the years. Above all he should not go in search of them, but stubbornly cling to the first rule of tasting – tranquil receptivity. If a wine then says 'green twigs' to him, he will know what it means and be sure that he has not imagined it.

Everyone will adopt the smelling technique that gives him the best results. For myself, I have found that, having warmed a glass of wine in my hand – even white wine needs a little warming if it is to be analysed rather than enjoyed – and swilled the wine round in the glass to release the ethers and neutralize the smell of the glass, short sharp sniffs, with the mouth very slightly open, give me the best results.

BOUQUET

The unpleasant smells have been recorded at some length for the benefit of the student who enjoys the critical examination of wine, particularly of young wines, but the general wine-drinker is concerned with the pleasant fragrances which wine is capable of giving and which are one of its main attractions. They are far too numerous to list, and will be dealt with more fully in the sections dealing with individual wines. They are produced by a combination of soil, grape, weather and time, and the possible variations are for practical purposes infinite. The technique for discovering them has been described, but the degree of pleasure they give to the taster is entirely a personal affair.

In light wines, known as 'table wines', the bouquet develops as the wine matures in bottle, whilst in some fortified wines, such as sherry, it develops during the maturing process in cask. All spirits, such as whisky and Cognac, become static once they are in bottle, but they are matured for many years in cask and during that time are capable of developing beautiful and subtle bouquets. The one characteristic common to the bouquet of all wine is the smell of old matured wine after it has spent some years in bottle. There is an element of decay about it and a suggestion of sweetness and softness. It is sometimes present to excess when an old bottle has been just opened, and it is then known as 'bottle stink'. It is easily recognized but less easily described. It disappears with aeration and provides one of the reasons for decanting old wines.

The efficiency of the palate can be improved by the use of this simple technique. Personally I have found that my palate tires very quickly, but also recovers quickly. First impressions then become very important. The sensitive parts of the palate are the tip of the tongue, the sides of the tongue, the soft palate and the gums. The roof of the mouth, or hard palate, is used by the tongue as a board against which to squeeze the liquid or solid that is being tasted. Following the rule of dealing with tastes in the order of their appearance, the first intake is a very small amount of liquid on to the tip of the tongue, the second a larger intake for the sides of the tongue and the hard palate, and the released aroma for the soft palate. The gums seem to react mainly to tannin and I am not conscious of having much help from them in anything else. The peculiar sucking noise made by the tasters is the effect of sucking a little air through the wine after it has been warmed in the mouth to help the release of its ethers. The masticating movement of the jaw, probably an effort to squeeze the wine between the tongue and the hard palate, is quite unnecessary, since it is possible to manipulate the tongue without disorganizing the face. The contemplative listening look that often spreads over the features seems to be inspired by the computer mechanism of the brain decoding the message it has received from the palate.

THE PALATE

A wine that has passed the nose test without losing any marks leaves the field open for the palate test, with perhaps some promise of great pleasure to come if an attractive positive bouquet has been revealed. It is not always that the taste of a wine lives up to the promise of its smell, because characteristics such as softness and completeness may be lacking. The real tasting, after all, begins when the wine is taken into the mouth. The first impact is on the tip of the tongue from the first small intake of wine, and from this a great deal is learned about its structure – strong or weak in constitution, fat or thin, full or light-flavoured, hard or soft. This tip of the tongue stage of the tasting is primarily an analytical exercise for those wanting to dissect the wine in order to estimate its qualities and future; it need not be indulged in at the dinner table. The qualities and flavours already present are better revealed at the next stage, when a larger quantity is taken into the mouth. Now is the time to enjoy the wine. The strength warms the palate, the softness caresses it, and with the warmth of the mouth the full aroma is released and is tasted particularly by the sides of the tongue and by the soft palate.

The aroma is roughly speaking the smell of the taste, whilst the bouquet is the impersonal collection of smells given off by the wine, mostly the product of the maturing process, and recognized by the nose alone. The one is a projection, the other the very substance itself. At the same time, the shape becomes apparent – round or angular, streamlined or lumpy, long or short – and the particular flavours that come from the species of wine and the soil on which it was grown are released by the warmth of the mouth. As it is swallowed, the very sensitive soft palate comes into direct contact with the liquid and unnoticed nuances of flavour become apparent and linger in the mouth after the wine has disappeared down the throat. People speak sometimes of its short farewell or its lingering farewell, terms which may sound a little far-fetched but which seem to me to describe very well the taste of freshness which good wine leaves behind it. If it were possible to end here this description of what the taster may expect to get from a glass of good wine, enough would possibly have been said to induce anyone to try to acquire a knowledge of wine and enjoy the scents and flavours and soothing effect on the palate that it can give and that everyone can recognize. But it is not enough, because wine has more to give the taster, and it is in the elusive, subjective regions that the trouble begins and the wine snob comes into his own.

It is no good denying that there is a mystery about wine. The image it conjures up in people's minds is strictly individual and

cannot be put into words. The wine snob insists on words. There is
no need to be put off wine-drinking by these public announcements
of personal impressions. This does not mean that wine cannot be
freely discussed in sympathetic company. But it must be discussed in
a subjective manner, with a full realization that the impression it
makes and the picture it evokes is a purely personal one and worthy
of respect only in so far as the honesty and experience of the taster are
worthy of respect. James Thurber's classic example of snobbishness:
'It's a naïve domestic Burgundy without any breeding, but I think
you'll be amused by its presumption' is a good indication of the
sort of pontifical nonsense that may well discourage the honest
student from pursuing his studies, though, improbable as it may
seem, one cannot say that it does not represent a true impression left
on a particular mind. One can only maintain that it is too vague and
woolly to be of the slightest interest to anybody else. The impression
left by a fully matured wine of great breeding, made in a good year,
may well be beyond the descriptive powers of the ordinary man.
Each may enjoy the wine to the same extent, but only the master of
words be able to describe his impressions. 'The peace of a sunset, the
warmth and scents of a summer evening, the soft caress of strong and
sensitive fingers', applied to the 1953 Château Lafite, may seem high
flown, but at least it is a description of the impressions made on the
taster in terms that can be understood.

Part of the pleasure of good wine is the stimulus it gives to the
imagination and it would be wrong to ask the taster to remain
objective and critical when enjoying wine in the company of others.
To what extent he should express himself must depend on his company. There is a certain life in the picture evoked by the description
of the 1950 Château Margaux as 'a remarkably pretty girl in a short
evening dress'; it reflects the pleasure of the taster. But it could probably have been described just as accurately as 'a pretty and attractive
wine, but lacking dignity'. Is there any reason why it should?

CHAPTER 5

ACCESSORIES: CHOICE OF FOOD AND WINE

THERE is much confusion about the conditions necessary to enjoy wine. Wine is undoubtedly very sensitive, but it is protected against most of the dangers that threaten it by the grower, shipper and merchant. There are, however, precautions which can be taken by the drinker to ensure that it is presented under the best conditions. The greater the true quality, the more important these become.

Wine drunk as a thirst-quencher or wine and water mixed can be enjoyed just as well in the stable as in the salon, in mugs as in glasses, in a smoke-laden bar as in the clean air of a tasting-room; it can be drunk with abandon and enjoyment in the midst of the noisiest and most irrelevant conversation, and it can be enjoyed with the proverbial pneumatic drill going in full blast outside the window. But fine wine cannot reveal itself under these conditions and needs more careful presentations if it is to be fully enjoyed. The rules are adaptable, simple and logical.

FOOD

Even the quite vague conventions governing the selection of wines to accompany food are capable of variation within wide limits. If the attempted definition of those limits made here seems itself to be too vague the reader should bear in mind his right to his own opinion in all matters of taste. It should be possible to experiment appropriately within the limits indicated. A conventional guide is added for the benefit of readers who lack the time for experiments. Wine can either blend with and extend the harmony of flavours in a good dish, or it can contrast with and emphasize those flavours at some cost to its own individuality.

Food can be, and often is, used to intensify the flavour of good wine, but being the less subtle of the two in flavour rarely has to sacrifice anything of its individuality in the process.

In the selection of fine wine to accompany food, since wine is the more vulnerable of the two, it is generally helpful to select a wine that will not be overwhelmed by the food. Spicy foods will kill fine claret or Burgundy, they demand a spicy wine like an Alsatian Gewürztraminer or Château-Chalon from the Jura or even a strong-flavoured fortified wine like sherry or Marsala. Sometimes simply a sweet white wine such as Sauternes forms a pleasant contrast to the impact of the spicy flavour on the palate. Eggs seem to neutralize the taste of most wine, but egg dishes such as omelettes go well enough with any medium-quality red or white wine, whilst remaining unsuitable with delicate fine wines.

Strong-flavoured meats like game demand wines with an intensive rather than subtle flavour. Butchers' meat is perhaps the ideal background for any wine, but whereas all red wine seems to blend well with the flavour of meat, sweet white wines do not. Dry white wines on the other hand can suit meat very well and particularly cold meat. There are, of course, innumerable exceptions in the realm of *haute cuisine*, when the subtle flavours may well in their turn render the dish vulnerable to coarse wine and demand a wine equally refined in its flavour. It may be red or white, but it must be fine. The choice once again is personal. Poultry, by the same rule, because it is gentle and straightforward in flavour, is an excellent accompaniment to delicate red wines, and still for the same reason it goes well and will not spoil the taste of dry or medium-dry white wines.

Sweet white wines come into their own with sweets or with fresh fruit. Many people very understandably like old red wine with fresh fruit, but with a rich sweet a red wine can only hope to sacrifice itself as a sauce, with profit to the dish, and die in the process.

Fish in general, although light and delicate in flavour, does not seem to harmonize with red wine. There are many exceptions to this and the rule is not absolute. The student will gradually find out for himself and may find that some of the lighter red wines and rosé wines go well with fish like salmon, in which a fishy taste is not as prominent as it is in some white fish. There are many who think that light red wine goes well with grilled sole, but in general white wines, dry and lively, are the best choice, especially the Moselles of Germany and the Rieslings from Alsace.

Fortified wines follow the same rules, but because of their high alcoholic content and intensity of flavour are not very suitable for drinking throughout a meal. An old sherry is an excellent accompaniment to turtle or other rich soups. It also tastes very well *in* the soup, when its ethers are released by the heat and its impact on the palate is consequently more immediate than it would otherwise be.

Port, old or young, tawny, crusted or vintage, Madeira, and the richer sherries fit in well at the end of a meal with a pudding or sweet or fruit. Cheese, like meat, is an excellent background to dry wine. All mild cheeses are good for bringing out the flavour of red wines, light or fortified, but very strong cheeses demand generally a strong fortified wine, which is able to defend itself. There is a well-established harmony between the flavours of wine and cheese.

It will be agreed that the governing principle that emerges from the above is the harmonious blending of compatible flavours in food and wine. It is, however, possible to go further than this. Any competent chef knows that harmonious flavours can be created from a blending of contrasts and this, too, is a possibility in the marriage of wine and food. Gourmets, for example, have always disagreed about the best wine to drink with *foie gras*. A rich Sauternes represents the blending of compatible elements, but in the opinion of some the resultant harmony is too rich for their taste, whilst a dry lively red wine blends very well and the two contrasting flavours form a less rich and equally harmonious whole.

Sparkling wines can generally go through any meal. Rosé wines also fit in with most dishes, but since they are generally served cold, go best with light meals and salads.

The only wines which are sometimes difficult to obtain are really old, sweet table wines, such as Sauternes and Barsac, and fine Palatinate hocks. These often develop an attractive nutty taste which harmonizes well with any rich dish. Old sherry and Madeira are more easily obtainable than a twenty- or thirty-year-old Sauternes or Barsac.

ORDER OF SERVING

Like all rules connected with wine-drinking, the rules governing the order of serving wine are nothing more than common sense and are variable according to personal taste.

It will be obvious to most people that if you clog and tire your palate by tasting a sweet sugary wine that leaves a strong taste behind after it has been swallowed, you will not be able to taste a light, delicate and subtle wine afterwards. This elementary principle,

Meat	Red wine and dry white wines.
Game	Strongly flavoured red wines such as Burgundy, and intensely flavoured dry white wines such as German wines.
Fish	Dry and medium-dry white wines: Bordeaux, Burgundy, Muscadet, Alsace and German wines.
Eggs	Nothing.
Omelettes and egg dishes	Medium-quality red or white wines but not fine wines.
Poultry	Any light red wine up to finest quality and medium-sweet white wines.
Sweets and fruit	Sweet white wines or fortified wines, red or white, Champagne, Alsatian Traminer, particularly with melon, pears, etc. Fine Sauternes with peaches.
Puddings	Fortified red or white wines.
Cheese	Any wine, with some regard to the strength of flavour of different cheeses and the matching strength of the accompanying wine.

combined with a knowledge of the wines to be drunk, is all that is necessary in order to determine the order of service. When dining in a restaurant where the host has no personal knowledge of the wines it is safest to rely on the following rules in consultation with the wine butler.

Serve dry wine (red or white) before an obviously sweet wine. Other things being equal, serve a white wine before a red, because its appeal is more direct and it prepares the palate for the more subtle flavour of the red wine to follow. The rule is variable – it depends in part on the accompanying food and is subject to the overriding 'dry before sweet' rule. All white wines are slightly sweeter than red wines, so that logically they should be served after and not before red wines, but if the sweetness is not such as to leave a lasting impression on the palate it will not interfere with a better quality, more intensely flavoured, red or white wine to follow. Despite the exception, the rule is practical, because if a white wine were to follow a red wine successfully, it would have to be of such a quality that no red wine would taste well after it. A rich Sauternes or Tokay or strong-tasting German wine can be a perfect culmination to a meal with wine, but even the finest vintage port will not taste its best after such wines.

There are other exceptions to the main rule of serving dry before sweet. When rich dishes – such as *foie gras*, already mentioned, or smoked salmon – are served at the beginning of a meal, dry wines may be considered a less suitable accompaniment than sweet wines. Full-flavoured Alsatian Traminer with the smoked salmon is, for many, a combination which justifies the breaking of any rule. It limits the choice of the red wine to follow to those with direct appeal and well-defined flavour, such as a young wine from one of the Beaujolais villages or a matured Burgundy, or a wine from the Rhône valley, or a fine Bordeaux wine from the heavier areas, well matured – and expensive.

The next rule is 'young before old', for the clear reason that old wines develop an intensity of flavour which is lacking in young wines. This may seem strange at first sight in some cases and I have often heard the argument that it would be better to serve an old claret before a young Burgundy. In practice, however, the rule nearly always justifies itself and the reason is that in general the more obvious flavour of a young wine, however 'big' it may seem to be, has a quicker impact on the palate and is more superficial in character than the penetrating, more intense, more gradually revealed flavour of a matured old wine. As usual the rule has to be applied with common sense.

No light table wine, however old, will taste its best after a young rich fortified wine, such as port. The majority of the fortified wines are so treated with the express purpose of retaining some of their natural sugar so that they are sweeter than table wines, and the rule 'dry before sweet' applies. It may be said in most cases to take precedence over the 'young before old' rule.

In France there are many who like to end a meal with a medium-dry Champagne. Personally I can do without the rather high acidity of this wine at the end of a long meal accompanied by wines. I have, however, sometimes derived great comfort from one of those very old, gracefully dying clarets, long past their best, that are too weak to fit in anywhere else.

In a critical comparative tasting of wines designed to analyse and discover any weaknesses, it is better to begin with red wines. They have more to give and are generally more subtle than white wines, and it is better to taste them with a fresh palate.

TEMPERATURE

Simple rules about the temperature of wines are evolved from two basic facts. One, that an important part of any white wine's attraction is its refreshing quality, and two, that the most important part of a red wine's quality is its bouquet and aroma.

White Wines

A white wine in consequence should be chilled just sufficiently to make it refreshing, and to counteract the initial impact of a dominating sweetness. This should develop in the warmth of the mouth together with other less obvious flavours. Sweet white wines, therefore, need a little more chilling than dry white wines, but no wine should be so cold that it needs an overlong stay in the mouth before revealing its flavour. In the winter, cellar temperature is generally sufficient contrast to a normally warmed dining-room to ensure a pleasant refreshing quality. Fine old white wines, such as expensive hocks, white Burgundies or really old Sauternes, wines which have so much to give in bouquet and flavour that their refreshing quality becomes relatively unimportant, need very little chilling and can, like the very dry wines, often be perfectly appreciated if drunk direct from a cool cellar.

Red Wines

Red wines, being generally dry, do not need chilling: on the contrary, having lain in cool cellars so that the necessary changes from youth to age can take place slowly and thoroughly, they need bringing to a warmer temperature so that the ethers produced by these changes can become sufficiently volatile to be released from the wine and produce the bouquet and aroma which are the results of its development. They, in their turn, must not be overheated so that the aroma disappears before the wine is taken on to the palate. The temperature of a comfortable dining-room is about the right starting point to prepare the wine for its full development in the mouth.

There are a few exceptions to this rule applying to red wines. Port shippers recommend the chilling of tawny port when drunk as an aperitif and Beaujolais growers maintain that their lighter wines, drunk when a few months old, taste better slightly chilled. This bears out the principle that wines whose main contribution to the enjoyment of the drinker are their refreshing qualities should be chilled. A white wine chilled too much will recover its taste and bouquet in a warmer place, but a red wine warmed to excess can never recover the flavour that has escaped. The over-cooling of a wine deadens its taste, immobilizes it, but the heating of a wine starts chemical reactions and at the same time gives it a new taste, a taste of cooked wine which no more disappears when cool than the taste of cooked meat disappears when cold. A certain amount of care is therefore necessary when taking the chill off red wine. It is better to underdo the operation than to overdo it. A wine that has not been sufficiently encouraged before it is poured out can very quickly be warmed to the right temperature in the glass by the warmth of the hands round the bowl.

Ideally, the bottle of red wine should be left in room temperature for twenty-four hours before drinking. In practice this is seldom possible and a quicker method becomes necessary. Whatever method is employed should avoid one fatal condition – that of exposing one side of the bottle to direct heat so that one part of the wine becomes overheated. In other words, don't place the bottle in front of a coal, gas or electric fire, but place it in warm air which surrounds the whole bottle. The warm air stream from a convector heater, the warm air surrounding an ordinary hot-water radiator or any other place where the air is warmer than usual is a suitable gentle medium. The warmth must be gentle, like that applied to a human patient suffering from shock rather than the doomed lobster. The simultaneous gradual warming of the whole bottle, as opposed to one side of it, will also prevent the setting up of currents in the bottle which can disturb the deposit sometimes formed by matured wines.

A white wine that has been chilled will probably come to no harm if, unused, it is put back in the cellar or warmer resting place, but a red wine that has been allowed to reach room temperature should, if possible, be drunk without being allowed to become very cold again. It is not likely to be at its best if de-chilled a second time.

DECANTING

Apart from the pleasure of looking upon old wine with its beautiful colour in a fine crystal decanter of cut or plain glass, there are three very good reasons for decanting. The first and fairly obvious one is that it removes the wine from the deposit which has formed on the underside of the bottle during the process of development; the second is that it gives the wine a chance to breathe after its long sojourn in the bottle; and the third is that it allows the wine to get rid of any unpleasant smells which it has a acquired in the process of development during many years. All fine red wines, and some white wines, do throw off a deposit during their development in bottle. Sometimes, as in the case of port, this adheres to the glass of the bottle, but generally in unfortified wines it remains loose and settles at the bottom of the bottle so long as this is at rest. If the position of the bottle is changed, the deposit will float into the wine only to settle again, more or less quickly according to the weight, when the bottle is once more at rest. The first object of decanting is to remove the wine from the deposit so that it can be freely moved about at the dinner table. It is, therefore, poured into a clean container.

The second reason mentioned for decanting stems from the fact that wine largely develops in bottle through the action of the oxygen contained in the wine at the moment it is put into bottle. The length of time it needs to get full benefit varies with the vintage – it may be two years or fifty years. Most wines are drunk before they have had a chance to develop fully, and the added stimulus of fresh oxygen acquired during the process of decanting enables them to reveal within an hour or two qualities that would take some years in bottle to acquire, though it must not be thought that a very young wine can be successfully 'matured' simply by decanting it several hours before drinking. Wines which are at their best benefit from the physical action of being gently poured into a decanter also because the volatile elements responsible for the bouquet and aroma lying dormant are released by the movement, just as they are to a lesser degree by being swilled round in the glass.

The third reason for decanting applies to wines that have been so long in bottle that the slow process of disintegration has started. They have often retained the pleasant characteristics of fine wine but these are obscured by the smell of decay, known sometimes as bottle stink. If this smell and taste is too far advanced the wine is lost and there is nothing to be done. But if it is not, it will quickly disappear with aeration and leave the wine clean on nose and palate. Wine in this condition, however, is vulnerable to a further dose of oxygen and should be decanted only at the moment of drinking.

White Wines

In the case of white wines, which are seldom considered in the discussions about decanting, the position is a little different but the results still important. White wines divide themselves roughly into two main groups: the rich, luscious wines with a high degree of alcohol and a lot of sugar, stable but sometimes lacking in the acidity which makes for a long life; and the drier, less alcoholic wines, with little sugar but containing a higher relative acidity. These are again subdivided into the more expensive, well-balanced wines, which develop rather like red wines, and the cheaper, artificially slightly sweetened wines which are maintained in equilibrium by the use of sulphur dioxide. These last two sub-categories benefit from decanting, the one because it enables the naturally developed wine to breathe and reveal itself, and the other because it allows the free sulphur to escape and leave unobstructed the bouquet and taste of the wine. The first group, the rich, luscious wines with a high alcoholic degree, may benefit or not depending on their degree of acidity and their state of maturity. On the whole I would say that, except in the case of some of the finest German *Spätlese* and *Auslese* wines and the fine French Sauternes which have a delicate aroma to release, this group benefits least from decanting.

How to Decant

The mechanics of decanting are not difficult and the operation can be carried out equally well from a bottle that has been reposing in either the recumbent or the upright position. The important thing is that the bottle shall have been in respose, so that the deposit is collected in one place. The decanting of an old wine should be carried out slowly and carefully, because the shock of movement, changed temperature and sudden access to the oxygen of the air can have an immediate and detrimental effect. Ideally, an old wine should be carefully taken from the bin forty-eight hours before it is needed and slowly changed to an upright position so that the deposit which has formed on the lower side can, after some hours in the upright position, slide down the side of the bottle, without mixing with the wine, and eventually settle in the narrow space between the punt, the indentation at the bottom of most bottles, and the side, where it is to some degree trapped. This action of standing the bottle upright has the additional advantage of allowing the air bubble that has formed on the top side of the recumbent bottle to pass through part of the wine and settle under the cork of the upright bottle. The wine benefits from this and if so treated need not be decanted more than an hour before being drunk.

The difficulty, however, arises that a bottle should stand up at least forty-eight hours before being decanted to give the deposit time to settle at the bottom of the bottle, and this amount of notice is seldom available. If the decanting is to take place direct from the bin, all that is necessary is to move the bottle carefully and, without changing its position, place it in a bottle basket and there draw the cork. The best type of corkscrew for this operation is one of those double-action screws which enable the cork to be withdrawn gradually. The sudden withdrawal of a cork creates a vacuum which can cause a lot of wine to spill from a bottle lying in a basket.

The capsule (the seal covering the cork) should be removed from the neck sufficiently far below the lip of the bottle to prevent the wine from coming into contact with it when poured, and the lip of the bottle should be carefully wiped with a clean rag to remove the encrustation that will have formed around it. The bottle is then ready to be lifted out of the basket, still in the recumbent position, for the decanting operation.

In order to be able to see the deposit, which will gradually move towards the neck of the bottle as it is tilted, use a candle or an electric torch. Stop pouring when the deposit reaches the neck.

Decanting Port or Other Crusted Wines

For fortified wines bottled in opaque bottles, or which have formed a firm crust on the side of the bottle, it is necessary to change the method, because the light will not penetrate the glass of the bottle. In these cases the classic method is to place a candle at eye-level between the eye and the wine as it leaves the bottle. The reflection of the light on the wine will be diminished as soon as any deposit is mixed with wine. In the case of old vintage or crusted port, however, where the deposit is either firmly fixed to the side of the bottle or is in the form of large 'bees' wings', the wine can be decanted without the help of a candle by pouring it through a silver wine sieve of fine mesh specially made for the purpose. Only in emergencies should muslin or linen be used to filter wine, and then it must not be new but old and washed very thoroughly in clean water. Above all do not use detergents.

The question of how long a wine should be decanted before drinking is always open to discussion and depends entirely on the character and degree of maturity of the wine. It is impossible to lay down exact rules. No wine is ever spoiled by being decanted too late, since it quickly makes up for the error by being allowed a little extra time in the glass. A period of about two hours is safe for young, robust wines, whilst more delicate wines are safer with a shorter period of about an hour. Wines over thirty years old are safest decanted just before being served, or served carefully directly from a decanting basket. For very old wines, whose exact state of development is unknown, the ideal solution is to stand them up forty-eight hours before use, as already described, draw the cork an hour or so before serving and serve carefully from the bottle.

CORKSCREWS

Any good corkscrew can be used for drawing the cork from an upright bottle. Every corkscrew, however, is not a good corkscrew. The real menace is one made like a gimlet with its point in the centre, a sort of central solid shaft with flanges. This has the effect of boring the centre out of the cork and leaving very little purchase for the screw. The good screw should be about 2¼ ins. long and consists of slightly flattened but not sharp metal, twisted four to five times and ending in a point which is in line with the twist. Looked at from the end, such a screw will be hollow, a length of metal twisted around space. The screw should be inserted into the cork near the edge and directed to penetrate the cork diagonally, emerging at the lower opposite edge. As the cork is drawn, the wrist should be gradually turned about a quarter of a turn. There is the third type of corkscrew especially suitable for extracting old, tight-fitting corks. It is in fact not a screw at all, but an extractor, consisting of two parallel flat pieces of metal, slightly uneven in length, which with a little practice are easily inserted between the cork and the bottle. It grips the cork firmly and will extract it easily if the quarter turn of the wrist is applied at the moment of pulling. Even if the corks are not very tight-fitting, this instrument can be used with particular advantage on old bottles when the cork is liable to break; some care is necessary to avoid pushing the cork into the bottle and a little practice and technique may be required. The secret is to wiggle the flat sides between the cork and bottle and not to push directly.

The most troublesome of corks are generally old vintage port corks, firstly because vintage port lasts a very long time in bottle and the corks get very old, and secondly because of the particular shape of the port bottle neck, which allows the lower end of the cork to expand to a greater width than the narrow part of the neck above it through which it must pass when extracted. These old corks are therefore quite likely to break. In extreme cases of very old wines, it is often impossible to get the cork out whole and some experts resort to the removal of the rim of the bottle itself with the cork. This can be done by holding the horizontal bottle firmly in one hand and striking the rim with a sharp blow of the back of a heavy knife directed parallel with the bottle. The corkscrew should be first inserted in the cork. A little practical instruction is desirable before attempting the operation. Pieces of cork are always successfully dealt with by the silver wine sieve already recommended for wines in which the deposit is of the large bees'-wing type, so that even if the cork breaks or crumbles in a vintage port, the pieces which fall into the wine in the bottle will be prevented by the sieve from getting into the decanter.

GLASSES

Too much is written about the appropriate glasses for different wines. There is one perfect glass suitable for all wines. It is a glass that holds about one sixth of a bottle when full, made of thin crystal, standing about 6 ins. high in all on a base of about $2\frac{3}{4}$ ins. diameter with a stem $2\frac{1}{2}$ ins. long. The bowl is tulip-shaped, about $3\frac{1}{2}$ ins. in depth with a diameter of about 3 ins. in the middle and tapering to $2\frac{1}{2}$ ins. at the lip. This is the most suitable shape for red or white table wines, fortified wines or brandy. It is not wrong, either, for sparkling wines, although for these I have a strong preference for the conical glass often used in Champagne. Traditionally, a rather shorter, squatter glass of un-tapered shape, like half a sphere, is used for port. There may be something to be said for not concentrating the already powerful bouquet of vintage port by the use of a tapered glass. A smaller glass than the all-purpose glass mentioned above can be used for sherry or port, which are generally drunk in smaller quantities than table wines.

The basic requirements of a glass are that it should be big enough to allow a reasonable quantity of wine to be served without filling the glass more than two-thirds full, shaped so that the bouquet can be properly presented to the nose, wide enough for a fairly broad stream of wine to be taken into the mouth and straight to the sensitive sides of the tongue, and with a stem so that the wine can be gently swilled in the glass to release all the aroma. Needless to say, the glass must be scrupulously clean, not washed in detergents nor dried with a detergent-contaminated cloth. Lastly, glasses should not be stored upside down or in an airless cupboard for long periods – they easily acquire a fusty smell of wood from new shelves.

There are other glasses used for particular wines because of tradition and long association. The long-stemmed hock glass, for example, is to me one of the most clumsy contraptions imaginable for holding wine, particularly as the bowl is often too small and sometimes coloured so that the clarity and colour of the wine are hidden. This is a relic of the olden days when wine in the bottle was often dull. Since the first quarter of this century advanced techniques have assured the brightness of bottled wine. Rather stumpier coloured glasses, smaller and thicker, are used in many countries for drinking the young wine of the year in public places. They are adequate and suitable for this purpose.

Special-shaped Champagne glasses can also justify themselves by their festive appearance, and although the conical shape already mentioned seems to combine a perfect presentation of the wine to the palate with a gay atmosphere, the hollow-stemmed, flat-bowled glass, allowing bubbles to rise in a steady stream and spread throughout the bowl, is undoubtedly festive and is traditional.

Very large glasses are sometimes used for fine wines in French restaurants. They vary in shape but are all designed to concentrate the bouquet. In many cases the extra aeration which the wine gets because of the large surface exposed to the air enhances the bouquet and the flavour. Nevertheless, oversize glasses should be used with discrimination and never for very old wines which have become vulnerable to large doses of oxygen. They may well disintegrate within a few minutes. These glasses are generally used by restaurateurs as a kind of status symbol to indicate that a fine old wine is being served, whereas in fact they are more suitable for fine young wines which have not had time to develop all their qualities in bottle. They help the presentation of fine wine which has been decanted too late, as inevitably happens in restaurants. Large glasses are admirably suited to display the bouquet and flavours concentrated in spirits such as Cognac, but I must personally admit to a sense of unease at the sight of fine red wine nestling in an inaccessible position at the far end of several square inches of glass.

ATMOSPHERE

A brass band can be heard above most conversations but a fine orchestra demands silence and concentration if it is to be enjoyed. Having taken the trouble to provide perfect conditions for a fine wine to do itself justice, it is only reasonable that a little attention should also be given to the conditions under which it is to be drunk. Wine speaks in a low voice, sometimes in whispers, and the attention of the taster must be concentrated if the many nuances of smell and taste are to be recognized. It is therefore a good thing in any company if a reasonable majority of those present is inspired by an equal love of wine. There is no need for ritual silence or solemn approach, but there is no room either for distracting conversation during those moments of analytical tasting that occur from time to time when fine wine is being discussed. Above all, there must be an atmosphere of leisure and repose. A sympathetic, receptive approach should unite the company and any suggestion of challenge and competition be avoided.

SMOKING

Ideas about smoking with wine have changed since the days when vintage ports and clarets drunk at and after dinner represented the majority of wine drunk in Great Britain. Today, when probably ninety per cent of the wine consumed is young wine drunk on all kinds of occasions, it has become customary to ignore the rules about smoking. This is right and sensible in a great many cases. The obvious qualities of young wine are not spoiled by tobacco smoke. It is, nevertheless, still a fact that the taste of tobacco or the smell of tobacco smoke kills the delicate taste and aromas of fine old matured wine. Everyone is, of course, at liberty to please themselves, but no one has the right to spoil the pleasure of others by obscuring the bouquet of old wine with the smell of tobacco smoke. It becomes a matter of common courtesy not to smoke in a room where others are enjoying fine wine. There are many instances quoted of professional tasters who find their palate refreshed by a cigarette during a long tasting, but the cigarette is smoked outside the room in which the tasting takes place, so that the atmosphere in which wine is tasted remains as pure as possible. There are exceptions, such as smoking with sherry and other fortified white wines, which lose none of their attraction from an accompanying taste of tobacco. Old matured red wines, however, wines which are worth the time, trouble and expense of keeping in order that they may have the opportunity to develop over the years the delicacy and finesse of flavour and aroma of their true quality, cannot fight against the pungency of tobacco smoke.

THE IMPORTANCE OR UNIMPORTANCE OF AGE

There is a trite little phrase used in wine-drinking countries to the effect that 'Wine is like a man – age makes the bad ones sour and the good ones better', which means, I take it, that with time the truth is revealed. The majority of wines can probably be enjoyed when young, but the pleasure given by a finely bred wine when it is young does not compare with the pleasure it can give when it is fully matured. Since only experience can determine whether a wine is likely to reveal great qualities when old, it is clearly the province of the wine merchant who has studied his subject to advise on the question of wines fit to be laid down for maturing. A great many attractive wines, both red and white, are best drunk when young, but there are some great wines, mostly from Bordeaux, Burgundy and Oporto, which cannot justify the high prices at which they are sold unless they are given a chance to develop their qualities slowly.

Equally, there are finely bred wines which, because of hazards attendant on their birth, are so lacking in some of the usual characteristics of their breed that they never can attain perfection, and there are lesser breeds which, because of the bounty of nature during the year they were born, achieve such balance and proportion that they retain the simple charm of their youth for many years and are in the end more attractive than their distorted betters. Age is no panacea for the lack of qualities due to the accident of birth, but in wine at least it is a necessity for the full development of inherited character and individuality. In general it is true that red wines improve more with age than do white wines, possibly because so much of the charm of white wines lies just in that freshness and fragrance of youth that age destroys. Yet many who admire and enjoy the majesty of fine Rhine wines still prefer to drink Moselles while still young and fresh. It is, as always in wine, a matter of personal taste and the mood of the moment. Although there is probably a high degree of unanimity about the attraction of old hock and young Moselle, there is much disagreement about the attractions of age in other white wines. The fine wines from the Graves district of Bordeaux and from the generous soil of Sauternes and Barsac develop an enchanting bouquet and delicacy of flavour with age, although to many people these attractions are outweighed by their quality of direct freshness and uncomplicated flavour when young.

CHAPTER 6

WINE NAMES

BASICALLY, all wines are named geographically, that is to say, the label states the origin of the wine in terms of wine-growing areas. In the United Kingdom the law also requires that the country of origin should be stated clearly, a useful and indeed necessary safeguard against the confusion which can arise from the borrowing of French place names by other countries and European names by other continents.

Large production areas such as the Rhine, Moselle, Bordeaux, Burgundy, Jerez, Oporto and Champagne, to take a few examples, produce an infinite variety of type and quality within their boundaries. It is therefore necessary, if wine is to be recognizably defined, to know more than its general area of origin. Furthermore its quality and character will depend on the year in which it was made, the grapes and the type of soil on which they were grown, as well as the time at which they were picked. This important information is given in varying detail on all wine labels.

As a rule, the finer the wine the greater the amount of information given, as, for example, with the finest German hocks, which are described by the vintage, the village, the vineyard, the grape, the time of picking and finally the grower or the shipper. Sometimes even the actual number of the cask in which the wine was made is used by the German growers to differentiate a particularly fine cask from its fellows. The great French wines usually need no more than the name of the property on which they are grown and the official controlled appellation name to which the district in which they are situated is entitled by law.

At the other end of the scale are wines of good quality made in large areas, such as the Côtes du Rhône, but varying little one from the other. They, and wines like them, are not known by the names of individual properties but by the appellation area only, with a shipper's name and perhaps a brand name if the shipper finds this desirable.

Labelling customs vary in different countries in the detail they give and the order in which they give it, but the basic information given is common to all wines. The table at the end of this chapter illustrates the principle used in wine-naming and its application in various countries and districts.

Reference hàs already been made to the complicated nature of German wine description. The reasons are further explained in the section dealing with Germany.

In wines such as Bordeaux and Burgundy, it is the soil and the blend of grapes used that are primarily responsible for the varieties of character and quality of the wine produced. The soil varies from area to area and the proportion in which the few authorized types of vine are planted vary from vineyard to vineyard, so that the area and the vineyard become the important factors to be revealed on the label. The effects of the weather during the productive period of the vine each year from May to October are of paramount importance to all light or 'table' wines, and the vintage is therefore usually also stated on the label. Some of the finest wines made are the result of the blending of wines from different vineyards, as for example Champagne, which is identified by the name of the shipper responsible for the blend, and may be either a vintage or non-vintage. Port is another high-quality wine in exactly the same position. Like Champagne shippers, port shippers from time to time decide that a particular vintage is good enough to be presented to the public as it is, without blending with other vintages, and put on the market a 'vintage year'. Not all port shippers choose the same year, nor necessarily do the Champagne shippers. Sherry is the one high-quality wine which, because of the manner of its production, cannot be described as a vintage, and except for rare old bottles, mostly of an experimental nature, no vintages will be found on sherry labels.

Cognac, like all spirits, develops only in cask, and once put into bottle does not change so long as the cork remains sound. A vintage on a bottle of Cognac can, therefore, be very misleading unless it is accompanied by information about the length of time it has been kept in cask before bottling and where it has been kept. New regulations strictly controlling the use of vintages on Cognac have now come into force and in the future vintages on Cognac labels will give a true indication of the maturing of the spirit. Spirit gradually evaporates if kept in cask and since Cognac takes something like twenty years to develop its full qualities in cask, a great deal of the contents of the cask may have disappeared by the time it is bottled. If it has been kept in the cellar of a grower or merchant, there is always the possibility that the loss has been made up each year by the addition of a younger wine. This may not necessarily harm the quality but it must change it. The safest place of all to keep Cognac in wood is in bonded cellars under the surveillance of H.M. Customs, whose regulations forbid the filling-up of casks. In addition, therefore, to vintage and name of shipper, which are the indications of its initial quality, it is comforting to see on a Cognac label some such information as 'landed in year X' (preferably the year after it is made) and 'bottled in year Y' (preferably about twenty years later).

Finally, there are wine-producing areas both in Europe and elsewhere whose wines are mostly grown on an unvarying type of local soil. They need no complicated system of area, parish and vineyard to describe them, but are generally described by the grape from which they are made, by brand names, by description of type, or by borrowing the well-established names of traditional viticultural areas, such as Burgundy, Sauternes, claret and sherry, whose type they are supposed to, and often do, resemble, but whose quality they do not always attain. It will be noticed from the table of examples (pp. 60–66) that the *species* of grape is only used to identify white wines. The rule is not universal – some North American red wines are described by the grape species and also some Dominion wines. The names of the grower, shipper or blender may be replaced by the name of the importer. From the drinker's point of view, it is essential that someone should be responsible for the wine in the bottle. An anonymous label is about as satisfactory as an anonymous letter.

Many wines are labelled with brand names, that is to say names which have no reference to the origin of the wines and must not give the impression that they represent a vineyard. They may be made-up names like 'Vinedo', or imaginary descriptions like 'Bel Enclos' or 'Partners Reserve', but they must not be preceded by any description such as Clos or Château or Domaine that could give the impression that they represent an existing vineyard. They are generally used by exporters to identify wines which would otherwise be entitled only to the name of a primary or large secondary area such as Bordeaux, Sauternes, Graves, etc. They are used freely to describe the fortified wines such as port and sherry and are the only means open to distillers of Cognac and whisky to describe their products if any identification other than the name of the distiller or blender is required. Their main purpose is to give the brand owners freedom to blend wines if this is

EXAMPLES OF HOW VARIOUS WINES ARE IDENTIFIED

Wine group or Primary area	Vintage	Viticultural or Secondary area	Village	Vineyard	Grape	Brand name, character or other relevant information	Grower or blender or shipper or merchant	Notes
FRANCE								
Alsace	1969		[Seldom given]		Riesling	[Certain qualities occasionally given]	Grower and/or shipper	Vineyard names are seldom used, although there are a few. Very fine quality is sometimes distinguished by a description such as 'Special reserve'.
Beaujolais	N.v.					[Brand name sometimes given by shipper or merchant]		The best wines are usually distinguished only by the name of the commune, although there are a very few individual estates which bottle their own wines.
Beaujolais	1969	Brouilly	[Occasionally given]				Shipper and/or grower	
Bordeaux	N.v.					Cave Bel Air	Shipper and/or merchant	Many classed growths are frequently bottled only at the château, in which case the words
Bordeaux	1966	Médoc	Margaux	Château Palmer		3ième cru classé	Château bottled or	'Mise en bouteilles au

Region	Vintage	Appellation	Commune	Château/Vineyard	Grand cru	Château bottled or shipper	
Bordeaux	1900	St Emilion		Château Monlot-Capet			...on label and cord and sometimes on capsule. But these wines can also be of excellent quality when bottled in the U.K.
Burgundy (white)	1969	Côte de Beaune	Meursault		Casse Tête	Shipper and/or merchant	The majority of Burgundies are not domaine bottled or French bottled at the time of writing. This is why the name of the shipper is of additional importance and relevance.
Burgundy	N.V.				Réserve de l'Abbé	Shipper and/or merchant	
Burgundy	1967	Côte de Nuits	Nuits Saint-Georges	Les Perrières		Shipper	
Burgundy	1966	Côte de Beaune	Corton		Cuvée Docteur Peste, Hospices de Beaune	Shipper	
Champagne	N.V.				Cordon Rouge	G.H.Mumm [shipper]	Brands may be the names of firms existing in name only and registered by a trading firm. Various terms are used by Champagne shippers to identify wines for the U.K. market – dry, very dry, etc. The various Cham-
Champagne	1964				Dom Pérignon	Moët et Chandon [shipper]	

Wine group or Primary area	Vintage	Viticultural or Secondary area	Village	Vineyard	Grape	Brand name, character or other relevant information	Grower or blender or shipper or merchant	Notes
								pagne establishments may also make 'luxury' wines, designated by special names, e.g. Dom Pérignon, Dom Ruinart, Réserve de l' Empéreur etc.
Loire	1969	Muscadet	[Only occasionally given for estate-bottled wines]			Brand name often used in conjunction with names	Grower and/or shipper or merchant	Muscadet is both the name of a grape and the whole area, within which there are subdivisions. The grape Muscadet is used here exclusively.
Rhône	n.v.	Côtes du Rhône				Réserve des Mousquetaires	Shipper and/or merchant	Very few single vineyards are named on Rhône wine labels, although a few are beginning to be known.
Rhône	n.v.	Tavel				Rosé	Shipper and/or merchant	

GERMANY

Region	Vintage	District	Village / Vineyard	Grape / Quality	Name	Shipper	
Rhine	N.V.				Liebfraumilch Ballerina	Shipper and/or merchant	The finest hocks and Mosels are sometimes identified by a cask number, e.g. Fass No. oo (hocks), or Fuder No. oo (Mosels). The German wine law is currently formulated but undergoing revision, so that the exact use of terms that are permitted on labels is not strictly defined at time of writing. In general, wines of all categories above the ordinary are made with the Riesling grape on the Rhine and Mosel, although if an ordinary wine is made with the Riesling, this may be indicated.
Rhine	1969				Liebfraumilch Blue Nun	Shipper	
Mosel	1966	Saar	Kanzem Kaltenberg	Auslese		Owner and shipper	
Rhine	1967	Rheingau	Johannisberg Klauser Garten	Riesling		Graf von Schönborn [owner] and shipper	

Wine group or Primary area	Vintage	Viticultural or Secondary area	Village	Vineyard	Grape	Brand name, character or other relevant information	Grower or blender or shipper or merchant	Notes
ITALY								
Tuscany	1964	Chianti				Ruffino, Riserva Ducale	Shipper and merchant	The laws of Denominazione di Origine Controllata were formulated in 1963 and at time of writing 83 Italian-bottled wines possess this certificate which is shown by a special label.
PORTUGAL								
Port						Type – i.e. ruby/tawny, and, often, brand	Shipper	
Port	1955					Cockburn [shippers]	Shipper or importer or merchant	
Table wine – e.g. Vinho verde		Minho		Vineyard, estate or brand name given			Shipper	Portuguese table wines usually rely on indication of area and their shipping name. Vinho verde is always bottled in Portugal and bears the label of the par-ticular...

				Shipper	
Sherry			Isabelita Bristol Milk	{ Shipper	Sherry and port often bear a brand name in addition to that of the shipper and importer. In the U.K. wines of sherry type from Australia, Cyprus and South Africa etc. must bear the name of their country of origin before the word 'sherry' on the labels.
Table wine N.V.	Rioja	[Estate sometimes given]	Escorial	Shipper [grower with the finer wines] and, often, merchant	Spanish table wines often bear a name indicating a similar style of classic wine – e.g. Spanish Chablis, Spanish Burgundy etc.
SPARKLING WINES N.V.	Usually but not invariably given		Brand name and, usually, method of making	Shipper	Wine made by the Champagne method in France will have the description 'Méthode Champenoise' on the label. Other wines will have the description 'Produit en cuve close', which means 'made in sealed vats'.

Wine group or Primary area	Vintage	Viticultural or Secondary area	Village	Vineyard	Grape	Brand name, character or other relevant information	Grower or blender or shipper or merchant	Notes
ORDINAIRES						Brand name, style and, sometimes, alcoholic strength	Shipper or merchant	The country of origin must be indicated on the label.
SPIRITS								
Cognac		Grande Champagne				Brand and indication of quality	Shipper	Vintages on Cognac are now only legal if the spirit has been stored under strictly controlled conditions. A bottle that purports to contain a vintage Cognac should be labelled with the date of the brandy's bottling, as well as of its vintage. Vintage Cognac is not allowed to be sold now in France.
Eau-de-vie						Name and sometimes brand	Shipper	

necessary to maintain a regular type, quality and price which the variation in vintage might otherwise make impossible. Wines known by brand names rarely carry a vintage.

NOTES ON WINE NAME CHART

1. According to French law the label of a controlled appellation wine must bear the name of the appellation and the words 'Appellation Contrôlée'. In the United Kingdom the last words are not obligatory. In the vast majority of cases the controlled part of the appellation is the viticultural area, e.g. Saint-Émilion, or the village, e.g. Margaux. In Burgundy, however, the controlled part of the appellation often applies to the vineyard itself as well as to the village, e.g. Clos de Vougeot is controlled, as is Vougeot, the village in which the vineyard is situated. In these cases the label often bears the name of the vineyard and not that of either the village or the viticultural area. Only the essential information according to French regulations has been included in the chart. There is no reason why the shipper or importer should not include additional information if he thinks it necessary.

Brand names are generally imaginary words sometimes designed to evoke an image of the character of the wine, e.g. Beau Soleil. They are not allowed to be qualified by such words as Château, Clos, Domaine, etc., that might create the impression that they represent existing vineyards.

2. The information on German wine labels is given in a different order from that usually adopted on other wine labels. It is a logical order, starting with the wine-growing area and working down through the vineyard, the grape, the quality of the grape and sometimes to an individual cask number or a limiting description such as 'Cabinet Wine'. The word 'Cabinet' is at the sole discretion of the grower and fixes the standing of the wine in the hierarchy of his own production. It is not a universal standard controlled by law, such as *Auslese*, etc. In the above chart the columns have been numbered to show the order in which the respective descriptions would appear on a label.

Estate bottling is indicated by the word *Wachstum* (growth) followed by the name of the owner of the vineyard and the words *Original-abfüllung*.

Wines bottled by a shipper or wholesale merchant are described either as in *Abfüllung Johan Schmidt* or as in *Kellerabzug Johan Schmidt.*

Grape description is as follows:

Spätlese: a general late gathering.
Auslese: selected bunches gathered late.
Beerenauslese: selected grapes gathered late.
Trockenbeeren: selected grapes gathered even later.

In addition the words '*Feine*' or '*Feinste*' (fine or finest) are sometimes used by growers to qualify further the last three descriptions listed above.

Naturrein. All wines described by the above grape descriptions or by the name of a grape must be made from the natural, unsweetened juice of the grapes gathered in the vineyards. Lesser wines are allowed to have sugar added to the must before fermentation in order that they may acquire the requisite degree of alcohol by fermentation. If this facility has not been made use of the word *Naturrein* (natural) is sometimes added to the description of lesser wines.

Liebfraumilch is in fact a national brand. It defines a type of wine and within certain wide limits can be blended from any vineyard in the Rhine wine area or can be the product of a single vineyard. The name is thought to have been first applied to wines from the Liebfrauenstift vineyards at Worms.

(The law governing the naming and labelling of German wines is being revised and was still under discussion at the time of going to press. See pp. 180–81.)

CHAPTER 7

THE STORING OF WINE

THE time necessary for the full development of wine varies between three and twenty years and in quite a number of cases is more than twenty years, as, for example, the 1945 clarets, which may in some cases need forty years, and many vintage ports and other fortified wines which develop much more slowly than table wines. It is a matter on which the advice of the wine merchant must be taken. It is wise always to allow a recently moved old wine to rest at least three months if it is to recover fully from the effects of being shaken up. Newly bottled wine needs six months to adjust itself to the new conditions it is experiencing in bottle after the freedom of the cask. It often goes through a phase which wine merchants refer to as 'bottle sickness'.

There are five factors to be considered after you have decided to lay down wine and to store it. They are:

> Temperature of storage space
>
> Darkness of storage space
>
> Cleanliness of storage space
>
> Freedom from vibration
>
> Length of time the wine is to be kept

The importance given to the whole matter depends on the type and quality of the wine to be stored.

Temperature has a direct and immediate influence on the organic and inorganic changes that take place during the maturing period. Light quite quickly affects the colouring matter in wine. Cleanliness can affect the taste; movement the progressive development over a period, and time the achievement of final perfection. For the great majority of wine-lovers who can only hope in these enlightened days to find storage space for wines to be consumed within a year, it is obviously the first two points that are of real importance. The fourth point, that of freedom from vibration, will exclude chests of drawers or similar pieces of furniture which shake or disturb the wine every time they are opened to withdraw a bottle. A little ingenuity and adaptability can generally produce space suitable for keeping wine, even in a modern flat. A brief glance at the notes which follow will establish the guiding principles, and enthusiasm will do the rest.

TEMPERATURE

The regularity of temperature is more important, within limits, than the actual temperature. To some extent wine can adapt itself to conditions, but it is important to avoid violent and sudden changes of temperature. The temperature influences the rate at which wine develops and, as already mentioned, it must develop slowly to achieve its best. The colder the temperature, the slower its development.

Avoid in the 'dispersed' cellar direct heat and violent changes of temperature. A room which may be at 60° F. during the summer and warmed up to 65° F. gradually during the winter months is no great danger, but if wine is kept under these conditions for any length of time it is as well to keep an eye open for shifting corks. A rise of several degrees can cause the wine in the bottle to expand and this may slightly dislodge the cork. When the temperature falls the wine will shrink again in volume and leave a space under the cork which is filled by air and can over a number of years tend to spoil the wine. The cork, left unmoistened, will gradually shrink and a subsequent expansion of the wine increase the ullage in the bottle by seeping through the space left between cork and bottle neck.

Low temperatures are required for white wines that are to be kept over a period of years. From 45° F. to 48° F. is ideal. Normal room temperatures up to 60° F. will not damage most young white wines kept for three to four months. Red wines laid down for development over years will generally do best between 50° F. and 55° F., but here again temperatures of up to 60° F. will do no harm to light wines not intended for long-term development.

Wine should be stored away from direct daylight if it is to be kept for several months, and in no case should it be exposed for more than a few days to the direct rays of the sun. The active rays of sunlight have an immediate and upsetting effect on the natural development of wine.

Any sort of continuous or sudden movement or vibration is bad for the development of old wine, though it is comparatively unimportant to young wine kept for limited periods. Apart from the general disturbing effect, it will stop the sediment formed from settling peacefully on the underside of the bottle. Young wine not intended for lengthy maturing in bottle is not affected by general movement or change.

CLEANLINESS

Wine in bottle is fairly well protected from the effects of extraneous smells, but it is still vulnerable to certain diseases which can attack the cork, such as cork weevil or acetate bacteria. The presence of these is encouraged by unclean conditions in the cellars. The cork weevil spoils wine by destroying the cork and letting in air. Bottled wine is well protected from the vinegar bacteria, but it remains an unwelcome inhabitant of any cellar. It is important, therefore, that wine kept in a cellar shall be free from the contamination that can come from vinegary half-emptied bottles or spilt wine. Strong smells or fustiness should also be avoided because these can attach themselves to the outside of the bottles and contaminate the wine when it is poured out. A wine stored in a flat, for example, near cosmetics or scent might well face an unnecessary hazard when it is released from its bottle. A cellar should not be hermetically sealed – there should be ventilation, but no draughts, at least no draught playing directly on the stored wine. A slight movement of air to keep the atmosphere fresh and prevent the growth of harmful bacteria is an asset.

BINNING

Wine must be stored lying down; spirits standing up. The reason is that in the case of wine the cork must be kept moist and swollen by contact with the liquid, whilst the effect of concentrated alcohol, such as whisky, gin or brandy, is to dehydrate and gradually shrivel the cork and so expose the liquid to the action of the air. There are various methods of binning in cellars, which most wine merchants will be glad to explain to their customers. They are all commonsense methods and can generally be evolved and adapted as required. The object should be to build a pile which is stable and from which a bottle can be removed without disturbing either the pile or other individual bottles. Each bottle should be perfectly horizontal so as to form a firm base for another row of bottles on top. In no event should the bottles slope towards the neck – this will place any eventual deposit in the least favourable position for decanting. In the old days laths were placed across every two or three rows, partly to spread the weight evenly and partly to maintain the structure in the event of a faulty bottle giving way under the weight. In certain forms of binning these are still necessary, as in the normal straight-sided bin where bottles are laid exactly on top of each other and not in the 'bed' formed between two adjacent bottles. For the normal household the question scarcely arises.

Wooden bins to hold any quantity can easily be erected, or modern steel Meccano-like bins, built up to whatever size is required, can be obtained from cellar equipment suppliers. There is generally no need for laths in bins holding up to ten tiers of bottles. For small houses and flats all sorts of dispersed cellars can easily be organized. Individual bottle bins which can be bought cut to any shape can be fitted into odd walls and corners. Wooden or cardboard partitioned cases, which wine merchants use to deliver wines in, can be laid on their sides, next to each other, and on top of each other, to build excellent single-bottle bins as required. With the aid of these dispersed bins, cellars can be organized in most homes. There is generally room for a case or two under the kitchen sink, under the stairs or in the box-room, at the bottom of wardrobes, or even on the top. Airing cupboards or places near hot-water pipes are not recommended.

Wines stored in direct cold draughts are apt to deposit tartrate crystals which look rather like the 'hypo' used by photographers. The crystals are solid and heavy and fall like stones through the brilliantly clear wine, which can be decanted off them with great ease. They in no way harm the wine. Indeed, to the extent that they reduce its acidity, they may even improve it. Yet great white wines which have matured for years to produce a delicate flavour and bouquet are continually having to be decanted and re-bottled, losing in the process the finesse of their bouquet, because of the ignorant prejudice against a harmless deposit in white wine. For some inexplicable reason, deposit in red wine is accepted whilst in white wine it is considered to be unacceptable.

Apart from this, draughts interfere with the development of wine and should be avoided.

Many wine merchants are ready to help customers with the storage of their wine by keeping it for them in their own cellars.

PART TWO

CHAPTER 8

VINEYARDS

VINEYARDS vary in size from an acre or two producing ten casks of wine to hundreds of acres producing large quantities of wine. Those producing wine other than the most ordinary are generally planted on gentle slopes or on the southern sides of precipitous hills and very often along the banks of a river, as in Bordeaux, Alsace, the Loire and the Rhine. Work in them continues all the year round, for unlike in many branches of agriculture not only does the soil need the usual ploughing and raking but the vine itself needs individual attention in the winter months to prepare it for its crop and to protect it from pests and sickness during the spring and summer. It very often takes more labour and much more money to produce a bad vintage than a good one. Theoretically, the wines from one vineyard should be the same – they have the same name on the label – but in fact there are many vineyards, particularly in Burgundy, that are divided up amongst different proprietors. This happens often in France, where rigid laws of succession make it difficult for one heir to inherit a whole vineyard if this happens to represent the major part of an estate. Apart, therefore, from the differences in wines bearing the name of one region there can be differences in wines bearing the name of one vineyard, as for example Clos de Vougeot, which has fifty-six proprietors all cultivating their own part and making their own wine. Quality and character will depend on the skill of the owner and the part of the vineyard in which his holding lies.

Because wine is so sensitive to any and every condition that is present during its production, from the elements in the soil to bad smells in the neighbourhood of the cellar, the authorities take as many precautions as possible to preserve the purity of the character of wines from the quality producing areas. Regulations define the area entitled to well-known names and eliminate from those areas any part where the soil is unsuitable. In Bordeaux, for example, that part of a vineyard situated in the rich alluvial soil near the river banks is not allowed to use the name of its district. Other regulations cover the type of the vines planted, the density at which they are planted and the manner in which they are pruned as well as the variety of vines allowed. These wine laws governing the names of vineyards vary from country to country. In France they are known as the law of Appellation d'Origine Contrôlée – A.O.C. for short – and have done a great deal to protect the public against the unscrupulous use of the names of famous districts on inferior wines. They are referred to more fully in the sections on French wines in Part Three.

The pruning of the vine, also controlled by the A.O.C. regulations in France, is of the greatest importance in the maintenance of quality. Each year this highly specialized activity goes on in the vineyards in various stages from November to March. It is carried out by vineyard labourers, often so experienced that they can tell you the number of bunches of grapes produced by an individual vine in past years and automatically adapt their pruning to its needs.

Immediately after the vintage in October the soil has to be hoed and before winter the earth banked well up the stems to protect them from frost. In the spring, in some vineyards, fruit-bearing branches are trained along string or wire to keep the fruit 18 ins. or 2 ft from the ground, where it can benefit from the warmth of the earth during the ripening months from June to September; in others the plant is allowed to grow higher, either because it is more natural to its growth or because its situation exposes it to strong ground frosts which retard the maturing of the grapes in late summer or early autumn. During the summer copper sulphate is sprayed on the leaves to counteract mildew, which warm damp weather can produce, and dry sulphur to protect the grapes against 'oïdium', another fungoid or cryptogamic disease brought on by the same condition.

A certain amount of fertilization of vineyards is generally practised, although with great circumspection and care because of the sensitivity of the grape to foreign smells and taste. In the spring replanting takes place of those parts of the vineyard where old, unproductive vines have already been pulled up. The ground is always allowed to lie fallow for some years, sometimes, as in the Rhône valley, for as much as twenty years. The young vines are planted either by grafting the *Vitis vinifera* (see p. 78) on to American roots planted the previous year, or in one operation by planting the whole graft prepared in the nurseries during the winter months. The economic life of the vine varies from twenty-five to fifty years in most French vineyards, depending on how it has been nourished, how much the yearly demands on it have been restricted by careful pruning, and on those mysteries that govern the life of all growing things. Most vineyards aim at an echelon of vines of different ages, both because it enables them to maintain a level of quality of wine which would vary too suddenly if a large proportion of old vines were replaced *en bloc* by young vines, and because it takes a newly planted vine five years to produce good-quality wine and a grower cannot afford periodic big gaps in his production.

CHAPTER 9

VINES, SOIL AND WEATHER

VINES

THE vine, the soil and the weather are the three influences which control the type and quality of wines. The wine-making grape is grown all round the world within latitudes 50° N and 40° S. In theory the grower can choose from something like five thousand varieties of vine which he can plant in his vineyard in whatever proportion seems good to him. In practice he may be limited by local regulations authorizing certain vines only or by the suitability of his soil and climate. He has sufficient choice of grapes alone to allow the production of an endless variety of wines, and when variations of soil, which is not identical in any two vineyards, and the differences in the weather from year to year are also taken into account, the possible permutation becomes limitless and the wine he produces will depend mostly on his own experience.

Wine-growing is an art based on a mass of empirical knowledge acquired by experience handed down from generation to generation. It is helped by science, which has made great progress in the treatment and prevention of diseases to which the vine is subject, but in its finer aspects depends on the experience and imagination of the grower. Imagination plays its part, for no one can know how good a wine can be or what form its quality may take. A grower of fine wines seeks perfection without any possibility of knowing how this will manifest itself. In the end Nature retains her secrets, and most growers, from the peasant to the proprietor of great vineyards, look upon themselves as trustees of the soil with a responsibility to posterity.

There are between thirty-five and forty different species of vine at least, each of which produces many varieties. There is only one species from which good wine can be made. It is known as *Vitis vinifera* and is indigenous to Europe. The other species are grouped as native to Asia or North America. Present-day so-called native American vines used for wine production are either European stock imported 150 to 200 years ago which have now acquired their different characteristics from the soil and climate of America, or European vines crossed with the American species, that is to say true hybrids which produce good wines under native American conditions. The word 'hybrid' is properly applied only to a crossing of species. The five thousand varieties of *Vitis vinifera* which exist in Europe are of unknown origin but as members of the same species are not hybrids in the true sense but varieties of one species. New varieties such as the Müller-Thurgau, a cross-breed of Sylvaner and Riesling, used in Germany, are not strictly speaking hybrids either although often referred to as such. They are cross-breeds within the same family.

American native vines have nevertheless played a decisive part in the survival of European vineyards. In the middle of the nineteenth century there arrived in France in a shipment of fruit from America a minute beetle-like creature known as 'Phylloxera vastatrix'. The insect, which nourished itself on the roots of the vines, completely destroyed the native *vinifera* plants. Within twenty years it had created havoc in the majority of European vineyards despite innumerable experiments to find a means of eradicating it. In the end it was found that American vines had acquired an immunity by developing the ability to heal the wounds inflicted on its roots. American vines, however, were not of the *vinifera* species and could not be planted in European vineyards with any hope of producing a drinkable wine. But there was no reason why American roots should not be grafted on to European plants which could then continue to produce their own fruit. In order that they should be able to do this uncontaminated by any foreign flavour it was necessary to select suitable root stocks from amongst the thousands of varieties available. There are about a hundred authorized in France today, enabling European vines to produce their traditional wine free from the threat of Phylloxera.

It is open to discussion whether the grafted vine produces a fruit of equal quality to the direct planted vine. Exact comparisons are difficult to make. There are vineyards in Europe in which the ungrafted vine is still grown, sometimes in sufficient quantities to make a separate wine. I have never tasted a wine from an ungrafted vine which has been inferior to the nearest grafted vine, but I have seen examples which are superior. How much this is due to the vine and how much to the soil I do not know.

By no means all the five thousand varieties of *vinifera* are used for wine-making; many are not cultivated at all and many produce only eating grapes. There remain enough to give the grower endless opportunities for continued experiment.

It is forbidden in most countries to use any but certain hybrids for the making of wine. In France the hybrids are divided into three groups: those forbidden, those tolerated and those recommended. The last two groups are allowed to make *vin ordinaire* but are not allowed to be used in the making of wine with any official claims to quality. Since the 1890s, when vineyards were being replanted after the Phylloxera, experiments in the use of hybrids for wine-making have been going on. Some promising results have been achieved, for the hybrid produces more grapes than *vinifera* and is resistant to many diseases that afflict the European vine. Today about 20 per cent of France's vine plantations consists of hybrid vines. The wine they produce is not exported.

Anyone wishing to study the highly technical subject of vines will find it complicated by the variety of names given to the same plant in different regions and countries. It is estimated that the five thousand varieties existing are known by 24,000 different names. For example, the Cabernet Sauvignon, the basic vine in the Bordeaux area, is known by no less than six different names in various districts.

In selecting his vines the grower is influenced first by the quality he hopes to achieve, but he is forced to take practical considerations into account as well. These resolve themselves mainly into resistance to disease and ability to mature under various climatic conditions. The Cabernet Sauvignon withstands well the effect of damp weather on its ripened grapes – they do not decay on the vine as easily as some other varieties. On the other hand it is subject to a fungus known as oïdium which is very prevalent in Bordeaux vineyards in certain weather conditions. The Merlot, a grape that gives a certain unctuous quality to the wine, is highly resistant to oïdium but very vulnerable to mildew, whilst the Malbec, a grape which has the advantage of maturing early, has had to be largely abandoned in Bordeaux because of its tendency to drop its fruit in the early stages – the sickness known as 'Coulure' in France.

These examples are taken from amongst grapes produced only in the Bordeaux vineyards, but they illustrate the problems that confront all vine-growers.

In addition to mildew, black rot and oïdium, which are the main cryptogamic diseases affecting the vine, there are certain animal parasites, such as Cochylis, which can destroy the fruit and to which all varieties of vine are equally subject. Treatments, both curative and preventative, are well known and universally practised, and it is seldom that any of these two types of disease cause large disasters in modern vineyards. Coulure, however, is less easy to deal with and was partly responsible for the very small size of the 1961 crop in Bordeaux. Violent climate explosions, like hail or severe frost, can still destroy whole crops in a few hours – and sometimes even the vines themselves, as did the early frost of 1956 in Bordeaux. There is not anything the grower can do about this except keep in mind the greater resistance to frost that some vines have compared with others.

SOIL

It is generally said that wine is produced on soil which could nourish nothing but the vine. This is partly true. There are vines grown on comparatively rich soils and in some parts of the world even amongst other crops – row for row. This indeed was the case in the twelfth century in Bordeaux. It is broadly fair to support that other facile statement that the best wines come from the poorest soil, although this is difficult to substantiate unless you are convinced that a fine Moselle is better than Château Yquem. In one sense the statement is true, since although the comparatively rich soils of the vast wine-producing areas, both in Europe and the American Continent, Africa and Australia, produce rich wines, satisfying, warming, full-bodied, soft and pleasantly flavoured, they cannot produce the wines with the aroma and bouquet, the facets and finesses of flavour which are generally considered to represent quality in wine. Even though they can produce wines which can live a long time in bottle, they remain stolid and unimaginative and can just as well be drunk young as old.

The delicacy of fine wine is not fostered by over-nourishment; like some poets it produces its best on a starvation diet. Good wine is nurtured on the purest of the salts of the earth unobscured by the richness of too fertile a soil. It is the variations in the chemistry of the soil that are the second great influence in the quality and character of wine. The wine made in Champagne from the Pinot grape is very different from that made in Alsace or Burgundy or Portugal from the same grape, and the white Sauvignon does not produce in Sauternes the same wine that it produces at Pouilly on the Loire.

What then are the qualities that good wine demands from the soil? The roots of the vine go deep so that it can draw from the earth all the nourishment that it contains. It needs a subsoil in which its roots can obtain moisture in the hottest August but in which they will not be drowned in wet seasons. For this reason a vineyard with a compact clay subsoil must be placed on a slope if excess water is to drain off, whilst one situated on a soil containing a good admixture of sand and silicate will drain easily. Vines planted on thick strata of gravelly and sandy soil get the advantage of this warmer, heat-reflecting medium in seasons lacking sufficient sun, but they suffer in hot years like 1945. Other types of soil such as light mould, stones, and above all limestone and chalk greatly influence the quality and flavour of wines, but as some of these retain moisture and others drain away quickly, the contours of the vineyard and the availability of a suitable subsoil to the searching roots remain of great importance. These considerations in their turn influence the choice of vine, the roots of which have different characteristics in differing varieties. As a general rule chalk and limestone can be considered essential for the production of good white wines. They are predominant in Champagne and Chablis, present in good quantity in many German vineyards and in the white areas of Burgundy and Bordeaux. Clay mixed with soil as subsoil makes for a higher alcoholic degree and deeper colours in red wines, as for example in Saint-Émilion and Burgundy, but rich alluvial soils with too much clay produce only deep-coloured red wines rich in alcohol and tannin but coarse in flavour. The stony soil of many vineyards is highly prized for two reasons. Not only is it good for the drainage of the vineyard and general aeration of the soil, but where it is present in substantial quantities on the surface, as in many white wine areas and that of Bordeaux and in the vineyards of the Côtes du Rhône, it acts as a source of heat that radiates warmth directly on to the ripening grapes unhindered by the leaves of the vine which protect only their top sides. This is particularly useful in the cool nights of late summer.

Wine grown on a Graves soil often has a taste of warm pebbles. Chalk and limestone sometimes give a slightly greenish tinge to white wines and a clear-cut impression to the flavour, giving a refreshing quality to the wine which is generally appreciated. Clay can give a kind of lazy luxurious taste to light red wines, whilst red wines grown on a stony soil have a more austere character and generally depend for their charm more on their bouquet and balance of flavour than on softness of texture.

CLIMATE

The grape takes about a hundred days to ripen from the end of the flowering, which is in May/June in middle European vineyards. It needs proper conditions if it is to attain perfect maturity. And it also needs perfect maturity if it is to make good wine. The climate from May to September – and in many white wine areas, in October – is of great importance. In the early stages when the new fruit has been formed, a good supply of moisture helps to consolidate it. Some gentle warm rains in May and June do more good than harm provided there are dry sunny periods that prevent the onset of crypto-gamic diseases induced by too much damp. The amount of rain required varies each year according to the amount of moisture retained by the soil after the autumn and winter. This varies from year to year and, of course, also from vineyard to vineyard according to its contours and the nature of its subsoil. The variation in vineyards is constant and is corrected by the careful selection of vines most suitable to its particular condition, but the variation due to weather conditions throughout the whole year is far from constant and must be accepted as one of the hazards of wine production. There is nothing the grower can do to counteract it. It is easy enough to imagine the effect of a sodden soil on a vine that has reached its flowering period – the dilution of the nourishing element of the earth in too much water, the consequent formation of strong vegetation and little fruit and the necessity of drier than usual conditions for the flowering periods. In general a certain amount of early morning mist followed by a temperately sunny day favours a successful flowering and fruiting. On the other hand if the previous autumn and winter have been abnormally dry so that the soil does not contain much moisture, a dampness in the flowering period is essential if much fruit is to form. Throughout the whole of the life of the grape this kind of deviation from perfect conditions goes on. It is not surprising, therefore, that no two vintages are ever quite the same. I have never yet heard anyone claim one vintage to be exactly similar in character to another and I doubt if such an exact repetition of all conditions affecting the quality and character of wine is ever likely to occur. Once the flowering is safely over and the fruit set, different conditions are needed. By July the weather should be getting hot and dry and by the end of the month the grape should have swollen to its full size, so that during the first week of August it begins to change its colour to a darker hue, be it either black, blue or yellow. This is the end of the growth period and the beginning of the ripening period. The vine has completed the first part of its job – has produced a strong and well-nourished fruit – and it now becomes a question of bringing it to maturity. The soil begins to play a minor part, and the sun and the light and heat become all-important. July and August should be hot, bright months during which the grape matures. Excessive heat and dryness is harmful. Occasional rain showers do no harm during this period. The important condition is a sufficiency of heat and sunlight during the day and warm nights.

If the weather has been very dry as September, the time of the vintage, approaches, a little rain or night mist is desirable, in order to allow the ferments to form on the grape skins. It is on the outside of the grape skins that the ferments form as a grey dust. Different varieties of ferments are produced in each district and they play an important, if mysterious, part in the eventual quality of the wine. They grow better with the help of some damp in the atmosphere and so a little rain followed by hot sun for the actual gathering are the ideal conditions for September. Rain during the picking has the effect both of washing the ferments from the skin of the grapes and of diluting the sugar content of the juice. The operation is, therefore, never undertaken in wet weather unless there is a danger of the grapes rotting on the vines and a whole crop being lost.

CHAPTER 10

VINIFICATION*

THE actual conversion of grape juice into wine is a natural process. If left to itself in a pail or a ditch the juice would ferment and become wine. But it would not necessarily become very palatable wine. Man's part in the vinification process is confined to protecting the fermenting juice from all sorts of hazards to which it is vulnerable, some of which would interfere with its taste and some with the completion of the fermenting process. In the case of fortified wines such as port and sherry, the natural process of fermentation may be deliberately interfered with or the finished product changed in order to make a wine different in character from that which Nature would otherwise have produced. Grape juice left to itself ferments naturally until it produces a liquid containing up to 14 per cent of alcohol. Then it stops fermentation and has generally consumed all its sugar. If it has not consumed all its sugar it still stops fermenting when it has produced 14 per cent of alcohol. For aperitif or dessert wines, a stronger degree of alcohol and of sweetness is necessary. The ways in which these are obtained vary with different wines and are described in Part Three.

Red wine: As the grapes are gathered by the vintagers into small baskets they are collected and tipped into small transport vats on carts or lorries and transported to the vat house. There the stalks are removed, either by mechanical means or by hand, by rubbing the bunches on a slotted table through the apertures of which everything falls except the stalks. The juice flows into a receptacle from which it is pumped into the vats, and the skins are also either pumped or shovelled into the vats. The stalks are discarded, later to be sold for distillation. Within forty-eight hours the 'must', consisting of juice, skins and pulp, will start to ferment. Though basically the fermentation is a matter of yeasts transforming sugar into alcohol, many other reactions are also necessary in order that grape juice can be turned into wine. As alcohol is formed it draws the colour from the skins and also tannin and other elements which will contribute to the style

* This chapter is an amplification of the description of the principles of wine-making giving in Chapter 1.

and developing qualities of the wine. The fermentation is usually completed within five days. Depending on the type of wine that is being made, the wine might then be run off immediately or left to macerate with the skins for a further period of up to three weeks. When it has been run off, the skins are also removed from the vat and pressed in hydraulic presses which squeeze out in two, or sometimes three, pressings a further quantity of wine which represents about 15 per cent of the production. This *vin de presse* is richer in tannin and acidity than the wine made from the free running juice. Depending on the characteristics of the vintage and the quality of the *vin de presse* a larger or smaller percentage may later be added to the main wine, and the remainder will be sold off as a secondary wine.

Rosé wine: As the colour of red wine is drawn from the skins by the alcohol during fermentation, it will be easily understood that rosé, or pink, wine can be made either by leaving only a small proportion of the skins in the fermentation vat, or by leaving the must in contact with the skins for only a short time. Most rosés are in fact made by separating the must from the skins after only about 24 hours. The must has then only had time to become slightly tinted. The skins are pressed immediately and the juice extracted from them is fermented separately.

White wine: When making white wine the grapes are immediately pressed as soon as they arrive in the vat house. The whole bunches, stalks and all, go straight into the press so that the juice is separated from the skins as well as the stalks before the fermentation begins. Up to six pressings may be made of white wine grapes, but the last two produce wine of inferior quality and it is important that they be separated from the main production and fermented separately. Temperature control is perhaps even more important in the making of white wine than in red. Ideally when making dry white wine the temperature should be kept at about 25° C. (77° F.). Hot fermentations tend to destroy the more delicate flavours of white wine.

FERMENTS

The actuating element in the process is a living self-reproducing organism, a yeast that turns grape sugar into alcohol. The most usual variety formed on grape skins is called *Saccharomyces ellipsoideus*, estimated by various authorities to provide between 70 and 90 per cent of the active ferments in the making of wine. But there are a great many types of *Saccharomyces* and many other alcohol-producing ferments besides *Saccharomyces*. Here, at the very beginning of the 'simple' fermentation of grape juice, or 'must' as it is called, lurk more dangers, for there are in the atmosphere ferments which produce vinegar from the newly formed alcohol, as well as the varieties of good ferments which offer a choice of methods to the wine-maker. Ferments can be controlled – they can be eliminated from musts or introduced into them. Different ferments have different effects: some waste sugar, some produce bouquet at cost of body, some produce body at risk of too high acidity. I have seen an ordinary white Mâcon in Burgundy fermented by yeasts gathered from grapes in the better area of Pouilly Fuissé and greatly improved thereby. Growers are apt to keep their secrets to themselves, and those who in any particular district have hit on a way to produce a better wine than their neighbours are not likely to reveal their methods, knowing that the odds are very much against any neighbour falling on exactly the same combination of soil, grapes and ferments, to say nothing of the many other variations of procedure during the process of vinification. Once again there is very little established knowledge to guide the grower. He relies on continual experiment in his search for quality.

TEMPERATURE

Temperature plays a dominant role during the period of fermentation. Yeast cells live at 1° C. but are inactive; they become normally active at about 15° C. and at 38° C. most of them die. Therefore, hot autumn days in wine-growing areas with air temperature sometimes of 30–33° C. don't leave much margin for the heat generated by the fermentation itself. As fermentation proceeds and becomes more violent the temperature of the liquid rises steadily and in hot weather there is a risk of a partially fermented vat stopping 'working' before all the sugar has been converted to alcohol. There is little prospect of restarting in such conditions. If this happens, the high temperature, the comparatively weak alcoholic degree, the presence of unconverted sugar, all render the wine vulnerable to all sorts of harmful bacteria which may in due course start a slow transformation into vinegar. Complete fermentation then is essential and in hot years can create a real problem for the cellar master. The year 1947 was a difficult year in this respect in France. I remember congratulating a Burgundian friend on the excellence of the wine he had made under these difficult conditions. He replied: 'I was lucky, I had a vineyard proprietor from Australia visiting at the time. He gave me a lot of good advice' – a nice return for the help Australian growers received in the past from the French.

All sorts of measures are used to prevent musts from becoming overheated. The liquid may simply be transferred to another vat, cooling in the process, or cold water may be circulated through pipes immersed in the fermenting vat or, more generally, the partially fermented liquid is circulated through lengths of water-cooled piping and back again into the same vat.

LENGTH OF VATTING

The length of time during which a newly fermented red wine is allowed to remain in contact with the skins and pulp greatly affects its character and quality. It has already been seen that accidents can be caused by climatic conditions if the cellar master is careless about his job and that quality can be affected by the deliberate policy of the vineyard owner. An owner who is more interested in quantity than quality may add all his *vin de presse* to his fine wines. He may even have to do this in order to add substance to a wine made from grapes he has gathered too early because of wet weather.

Sometimes the best-intentioned proprietors are forced by public demand to compromise between perfection and practical results. A proprietor cannot entirely ignore public taste even if he knows that his function is to lead it rather than to follow it. Today he is influenced by the modern idea that the public wants wine which can be drunk young. One cannot dispute that Nature provides many wines suitable for drinking young, but I doubt very much whether the best interests of anyone are served by denying to the great wines of the world the years they need in order to develop their full quality. Great wines, like great men, need time to develop. There are, of course, the exceptional geniuses that die young, but this is no excuse for inducing an early demise by starvation. Once the fermentation in the vat is completed, a red wine draws nourishment and colour from the skins, which sink to the bottom after the fermentation gases have dispersed. Until the late 1940s it was the general custom to leave the wine for some time on their mass of skin, pip and pulp, from which it acquired additional colour, a richer tannin content and nourishment of varying kinds. The presence of tannin, which gives a harsh quality to young wine, ensured that the wine would live a long life, and the extra nourishment gave it something to feed and develop on during that extra time. As a result, wines were not only bigger and stronger, but they developed all the qualities with which they had been endowed by the vine. They needed much longer in bottle before they were at all drinkable and by the time they had matured they had often thrown heavy deposits.

Today the newly fermented wine is often transferred from the fermenting vat as soon as the skins and pulp have fallen. It is not allowed to feed on them and is therefore lighter in colour and softer to the palate. It can be bottled after eighteen months instead of two and a half or three years and drunk after two or three years in bottle instead of perhaps ten to twenty years. It may have enough youthful charm to be pleasant and enough character to be recognizable, but it never fully develops quality and dies young and unfulfilled. These wines suit modern conditions when restricted storage space prevents wines being laid down and lack of time deprives them of proper care in decanting and serving. They also suit the wine trade, both grower and merchant, because they represent a much quicker turnover of precious capital. They suit in fact everybody except those wine-lovers who know how good they could have been if they had lived.

This is the last hazard of vinification, the temptation of the owner to be unfaithful to his trust and make a wine quicker than Nature meant it to be made.

CONSERVATION

Once the wine has been made the vinification proper can be said to have been completed. There follows a period of up to three years in cask for most table wines and an indefinite one for many fortified wines, when skilled care is necessary to its proper development and health. The dangers are now less numerous and less urgent. During its development young wine throws off various impurities which fall to the bottom of the cask and can give a bad taste if they are not regularly removed. The wine has to be racked, or poured, off its deposit periodically. This operation not only removes it from the deposit but renews its store of oxygen on which all wine is dependent for its development. Again, wine slowly evaporates through the wood of the cask and this must be kept filled. It easily acquires tastes and smells from outside, so the cellars must be kept clean. As the wine gets older after a few months in cask the impurities it throws off becomes less and are not heavy enough to fall through the wine and leave it clear. The wine has to be 'fined' (that is, cleared of floating impurities) with just the right amount of whatever medium is used, such as the whites of eggs or patent preparations, which, as they fall through the wine, take the impurities with them. It is then left 'on finings' for the right length of time, generally about four weeks. If it becomes infected with any stray ferments or bacteria or undergoes any unexpected chemical reaction it needs special treatment. These are part of the dangers which the cellar master must be prepared to face if he is to produce a wine in perfect health when it is ready for bottling.

Finally, the wine will often not be bottled in the cellar where it was made, but will be sent in bulk to merchants' cellars, either in the country of production or abroad. It is thus once again subjected to the hazards of rough movement, varying temperature and bacteria of different sorts. It then becomes the responsibility of the merchant to see that it is in perfect condition before he bottles it.

CHAPTER II

DEVELOPMENT IN BOTTLE

No one can explain exactly how wine develops in bottle. Pasteur spent many years trying to find out, and the reader who wants to dig further into the question will need a vast knowledge of chemistry and a lot of patience. The result of development, however, is easily recognized. The colour of red wine changes from purple when young to a brown-tinged brick when old, the bouquet develops and develops differently for every wine, the harshness of young wine disappears and is replaced by a softness, sometimes approaching the softness of velvet, and the flavour itself changes and intensifies. The process is inevitable, gradual and continuous as is the ageing process of any animal or vegetable matter, and like all such matter, it terminates in decay and disintegration.

The longest-lived of all wines are the Madeiras, which often live for more than a hundred years. At the other end of the scale, the cheapest light table wines may live little more than a year or so. Most wines that can be exported at all are robust enough to last at least two or three years in bottle before starting to deteriorate. The quickest change in wine takes place in cask by the natural action of oxygen already absorbed by the wine and continually breathed in through the wood. The acids, salts and minerals that wine contains play an important part, as does the action of organic components such as good and bad ferments. The oxygen of the air has much freer access to wine in a wooden cask than to wine in a glass bottle. Nevertheless after it is bottled changes of the same nature continue under the influence of oxygen absorbed by the wine during its time spent in cask and during the process of bottling. Experiments have shown that very little oxygen gets into the bottle after it has been corked. Ribereau-Gayon puts it at a few one-tenths of a cubic centimetre during the first three weeks – almost entirely from the oxygen already trapped in the cork – and only one hundredth of a cubic centimetre in the weeks that follow. This he maintains finds its way through the infinitesimal space between cork and bottle. Too much oxygen may have access to the wine in its later stages in bottles that have been stored upright in cellars (instead of lying down), thus allowing the cork to dry and shrink. The same thing may happen through ill-fitting or bad-quality corks.

Pasteur maintained that bottled wines needed a constant renewal of their oxygen content and that they obtained this by 'breathing' through the cork. Modern oenologists disagree with this. They maintain that the oxygen already absorbed by the wine at the time of bottling is sufficient for its development and that this takes place just as well in sealed tubes as in corked bottles. Whether this is true over the long periods needed by fine wines to mature or whether the finest wines would attain the same delicacy of flavour in sealed tubes is not yet known.

Spirits react differently on corks and are differently affected by oxygen. The high concentration of alcohol which they contain has a dehydrating effect on the cork, which dries up and shrinks, allowing air into the bottle and letting the contents out if the bottle is lying down. Spirits consequently should always be stored standing up. Spirits do not develop out of contact with the air but must mature in cask before they are bottled.

The length of time needed by wine to reach full maturity in bottle depends on the climatic conditions under which it was made, on the constitution it has received from the soil, on the type of grape from which it was made, in other words on the kind of wine it is. It also depends on the ideas of individual drinkers as to what constitutes maturity.

There are some who consider a wine is past its best when it has lost the freshness of its youth and others who do not consider it ready to drink until it has lost most of its vigour and become a kind of ghostly smell. Between these two extremes there is a time when a wine has lost its hardness, developed a distinct softness and acquired a bouquet and an attractive flavour. Whether the flavour is as attractive as it can ever be or the bouquet as intense is a matter of personal opinion, but for practical purposes a wine in this state can be considered mature and, on the principle that a satsifactory experience is better than the risk of a disappointment, should be drunk. Wines whose charms lie in the freshness of flavour, generally the wines served cool like Beaujolais and most white wines, can be drunk within a few weeks of bottling, as soon as they have recovered from the tiring effects of sudden change from cask to bottle. The lower-priced red wines from famous districts like Bordeaux and Burgundy generally need two or three years to overcome the awkwardness of their particular youth and can then be drunk with pleasure whilst they are still capable of living another ten years in bottle and gradually improving. They are unlikely ever to reach the great heights. Higher-calibre wines mostly justify their higher price because of the ability they have to improve in bottle, and they are wasted if they are drunk too young. Seven to ten years in bottle is a fair average to take for modern successful vintages, less for palatable but medium vintages such as Bordeaux 1956, 1958, 1960, whilst for vintages of exceptional quality like Bordeaux 1961, fifteen to twenty years may be necessary before they start to develop and another fifteen before they reach their peak. Table wines from the hotter countries, such as Spain, Portugal and Italy, as opposed to the fortified wines from these countries (that is wine made by the addition of alcohol), generally come to maturity quicker than those from more temperate climates. Most of them are intended for immediate drinking and are usually sold without any vintage on the label. Fortified wines, however, live and improve in bottle longer than any others. The classic example is port, for which twenty to thirty years is no exception in vintage years. Sherry will live long in bottle, but age is not considered to improve it much. The exceptions are the brown and dark sherries which, like Madeira, can attain unique distinction after a hundred years.

Guidance on the right moment to drink wines is best sought from a wine merchant who knows the history of his stock.

Once a wine has reached its peak it may well hold it for a few years. Lesser wines, including the lowest categories, may remain at their best for one or two years whilst great wines may easily remain static at the top of their form for five years. The rate of decline, once a wine starts to weaken, has a direct connexion with the rate of ascent; but the graph may not be symmetrical – the descent is generally quicker (though a great wine may well take an 'unconscionable time a-dying').

Whilst it is generally accepted that red wines improve with age, there are many who maintain that all white wines are better drunk young. Anyone who has tasted the great white wines of the Rhine or Moselle or Bordeaux after they have matured in bottle will know the undreamed-of flavours and aromas they reveal. Lesser white wines are capable of the same degree of improvement provided they are properly looked after in cask and bottled at the right time. Modern technique, however, is directed to the production of young fresh wines for early consumption and one of the pleasures that quite cheap wine can give may soon be lost for ever in consequence.

CHAPTER 12

GUIDE TO THE SELECTION OF WINE

THIS chapter is intended to give some guidance on the categories and types of wines suitable for various purposes and pockets. It refers to wines by groups, such as Red, Sweet White, Dry White, Rosé, etc., and contains a tabulated list of wines (p. 110) under these headings. The text should be read in conjunction with this list in order to establish the group of wines available for a special purpose and with Part Three in order to make selections of wines within those groups. A guide to the types of wine usually considered to suit various types of food is given in Chapter 5 and can be used in connexion with the table on p. 44 and the information on particular wines given in Part Three. Information is given below about the different purposes for which the reader may wish to purchase wine and the types and price groups to be considered. (With reference to prices in this reprint, see note on p. 14.)

VINTAGE CHARTS

Vintage charts can be useful in helping to select wine. There are several different charts published, some giving merely a list of years classified as 'Very Good', 'Good', 'Medium' or 'Bad', some attempting a more accurate classification by means of numbers or stars, some indicating the character of the vintage – full-bodied, light, quick-developing, etc. – and some, published every two or three years, adding to this information an indication of when the wines will be ready for drinking.

The chart giving comparative qualities of vintages for the last twenty years and nothing else is liable to be misleading. Some of the old vintages may be past their best and not worth drinking a few years after the chart is printed; some of the later ones may not be ready; and the best wines to drink may be those of a medium vintage which are at the height of their development. Furthermore, the experts nearly always disagree on the relative merits of vintages. It is also a well-known fact that poor vintages often produce some wines far above the average of the vintage in quality, and vice versa, so that a chart of this description can never act as more than a rough guide in selecting a wine from a restaurant list, or discussing a purchase with a wine merchant. It does, however, act as a reliable guide to price, since vintages with good reputations are more in demand and therefore more expensive than vintages with poor reputations. It follows that a good wine of a poor vintage, which may be better than a poor wine of a good vintage, may also be much cheaper. Such a wine will not be discovered by sticking too closely to the recommendations of any wine chart, but only by the advice of friends who have already discovered it, or by consultation with a wine merchant or a competent wine waiter.

Charts that give information about the state of maturity of vintages and the general character of the wines made in each recorded year can be of great assistance; wine merchants sometimes have these available. Wines bought for laying down cannot be selected from the same vintages as wines wanted for immediate drinking. Big, matured wines for serving late in the meal do not usually come from the same vintages as the light matured wines to be served at the beginning, although both years may have an equal quality-rating on the vintage chart.

Vintage charts are not to be despised as guides to the selection of wine, but their function and limitations should be understood, and their information used in conjunction with the advice of the wine merchant or wine waiter.

COOKING WINE

Very often light wines recommended for cooking will be available from the remnants of bottles that have been opened for previous meals, and will be perfectly suitable provided they have not been kept so long that they have become acid. Ideally, they should be corked up in a full bottle of some kind, but they will generally keep for a few days in partly filled bottles. The more subtle flavours and aromas of really fine wine, will, of course, be lost in the process of cooking, but may play a part when wine is merely added as a flavouring to hot soups or sauces. In general, only small quantities of wine are used in cooking, so that wine opened for drinking with the meal being prepared can often be used in the kitchen as well. If large quantities are needed, the wine merchant may have a special cheap wine to recommend for cooking, perhaps an oddment from stock, sound and healthy, but not in sufficient quantity to warrant putting on his price list.

EVERYDAY WINES AT 60–70p PER BOTTLE

There is a big selection of red and white table wines suitable for everyday drinking at 60–70p per bottle. Some of the less expensive Bordeaux wines come into into this category and, also from France, wines of Provence, Languedoc and the Rhône valley; also wines of the Loire: Anjou rosé and Muscadet are two examples. The latter is a particularly pleasant light, very dry, wine which goes particularly well with oysters.

From outside France there are good cheap, red and white, wines from Spain, Portugal and Italy, and attractive medium dry white wines from Yugoslavia. In addition there are tables wines from South Africa, Cyprus and Greece. There are also available at many wine merchants wines from Algeria, Morocco and Chile.

EVERYDAY WINES AT 70–90p PER BOTTLE

The quality of wine to be obtained between 70p and 90p per bottle rises out of all proportion to the modest increase in price. In the price of every bottle of table wine sold by a wine merchant, at least 35p is accounted for by the expense of shipping, duty and bottling, so that the 55p bottle provides 20p worth of wine and the 80p bottle provides 45p worth of wine. Or, put another way, the wine merchant will have paid something like £20 for a cask of the wine he sells at 55p and he will have paid about £50 for the wine he sells at 80p, so that the increase of 50 per cent in price to the consumer represents an increase of 150 per cent in price of the actual wine. This is reflected in the quality.

Broadly speaking, an 80p wine is more than twice as valuable as a 55p wine, and it is reasonable to expect that the consumer will profit by more than his pocket suffers.

This superior everyday-wine category overlaps the 'dinner-party' group. From this price-group upwards the choice is more and more limited to France for red and white wines and to Germany for white wines. Other countries producing table wines cannot often compete.

Fine wines from French regions other than Bordeaux will come into consideration in the higher price brackets, but here at the cheaper end of the quality categories Bordeaux is predominant. This is not surprising when it is remembered that Bordeaux produces 30 per cent of all the Appellation Contrôlée wines of France, that is, those French wines which, by their quality, have earned the recognition and special protection of the state. Most Bordeaux wines in this group belong to the categories known as Bourgeois or Bourgeois Supérieur. There are about two thousand of them and they rate just below the sixty-five best wines of Bordeaux, which are known as the classed growths. They come from the best wine-growing areas of the region.

These lesser château wines of Bordeaux will be more subtle in character and develop and improve more in bottle than wines from Burgundy at this price level. Some knowledge or guidance regarding vintage is necessary. Generally, they do not need more than four or five years in bottle to achieve their best, but this varies with the characteristics of the vintages. Their prices increase as they get older and if it is possible to negotiate with a wine merchant a special price for a dozen or two at the time of bottling, they can be laid down for three or four years and enjoyed as matured wine for a very small outlay.

Most other red wines in this 70p to 90p 'superior everyday wine' category are generally drunk young and do not need to be laid down; they can be bought in small quantities as wanted. Wines of this type come from the Mâcon and Beaujolais areas of Burgundy. They come also from the Côtes du Rhône – a large area with vineyards spreading into four counties, but with little variety in the character of its medium-priced wines. They are generally identified by the names of shippers or by brand names.

There are first-rate white wines to be had in this category, but tastes in white wines differ greatly and only the widest guidance is given here. Many wine-lovers maintain that medium-priced white wines do not improve in bottle. This is not my opinion. White Bordeaux (some first-class dry Graves come into this price group), Alsace and the cheaper hocks and Moselles are delightful when drunk very fresh, but they can benefit particularly from the added bouquet that age in bottle produces.

Dry Bordeaux wines often do not give the impression of dryness that the customer may be looking for. Although chemically dry, that is to say containing no sugar, they may have a softness that does not appeal to the buyer who is looking for a crispness and distinct fruit acidity when he asks for a dry wine. This quality, which so admirably presents the flavour and finesse of more expensive wines from Chablis and the Moselle and Loire, is not so easy to find in the 70p and 90p class. It should be looked for amongst the Rieslings from Alsace, white Mâcon and some white Bordeaux, and is now and again to be found in small wines from the Moselle of the type that should be drunk very young and very cold. To anyone who wants a dry white wine for normal drinking all the year round I strongly recommend a carefully selected Bordeaux Graves with three to ten years bottle age. The slight deposit which a white wine may throw off in bottle is no more harmful to it than the deposit generally expected to be found in old red wines and yet is accepted with difficulty by the public. Possibly this is because it can be seen floating in a newly unpacked bottle of white wine but remains hidden in the dark bottle of red wine. It can be dealt with in exactly the same way and with no more trouble than the deposit in a red wine.

The young white wines are usually well flavoured and robust and maintain their freshness easily for two or three days after being opened. Because of their invigorating qualities, they are becoming more and more popular as aperitifs and as an eleven o'clock pick-me-up. There is no doubt that some of the best value in wines is to be found amongst those in the 70-90p category. They generally have to depend for their popularity on their quality alone and without the support of well-known château names.

FORTIFIED WINES FOR ORDINARY USE

Fortified wines, that is port, sherry, Madeira and Marsala, pay a much higher duty than table wines. This, and other fixed charges like freight and bottling, represent something like 65p of the retail price of a bottle. In other words, a £1·55 port should be twice as good as a £1·10 port. Prices of sherry vary from £1 to £1·50 per bottle. Port is a little more expensive. Sherry is a blended wine produced in infinite variety to suit the taste of the public. It ranges from the pale straw-coloured dry wines to brown and golden-coloured rich wines and is divided into the types mentioned in Part Three of this book. The selection of sherry is entirely a matter of personal taste. It is bought for drinking at once, since its development in bottle is too slow to be of practical interest. It can be kept in bottle for years without deteriorating and an open bottle or decanter will retain its freshness for a fortnight or more. It is worth while taking a little trouble to taste a range of sherries at a wine merchants in order to select one suited to your taste. This is a straightforward exercise which anyone can undertake. Port is more difficult to taste. It is a wine of greater subtlety than sherry, which will live for a long time in bottle but deteriorate within a few days after it has been opened. Both tawny and ruby ports vary greatly in quality; all will remain drinkable for a week or more after opening, but the finer qualities will lose in a few days those characteristics that distinguish them from the rest. Whereas sherry is generally used as an aperitif, port is usually drunk at the end of a meal. There are exceptions in both cases and both wines are often drunk without any meal at all. Sherries and tawny port can be chilled or not according to taste. In general the type of wine selected as an aperitif can be chilled and that drunk with the end of a meal left at its normal temperature.

MEDIUM-PRICED TABLE WINES FOR LAYING DOWN

One of the most interesting aspects of wine is the opportunity it gives the drinker for exercising his own judgement. It is possible to collect wines that will improve so much if laid down that they reach a standard out of all proportion to the price that has been paid for them. Some categories – dealt with later – can even become profitable investments. A wine from an unknown vineyard, bought early at its opening price and kept for four or five years until it has matured and developed all its good qualities, is a good gastronomic investment.

The choice of a good wine that will improve in bottle needs all the accumulated experience of wine merchant and wine shipper, and the amateur will do well to start by taking trouble to select a good wine merchant as his adviser. Even with the best advice, there is no absolute guarantee of satisfactory development, but neither is there any risk of complete disaster. The expert may have to assess the likelihood and degree of development, but he will be in no doubt about the stability of the wine and its certainty of survival in bottle. Without doubt, it is the red wines of France that have the greatest possibilities of improvement in bottle in the medium price range so far as table wines are concerned. For all practical purposes these are limited to the wines of Bordeaux and Burgundy. For fortified wines, the great red wines of Portugal are supreme. They are also excellent from the point of view of monetary investment and are dealt with later, in the section dealing with the more expensive categories.

To consider, then, for the present, wines that can be an investment in pleasure rather than in money. Having selected one or more wine merchants as advisers, it is important for the customer to be able to explain the sort of wines he likes, if he is to get full advantage from his investment. The wine merchant will want to know a few details, such as the length of time the buyer is prepared to wait before enjoying his wine, and perhaps the amount of money he wants to spend and/or the quantity he has room to store. Many wine merchants will be prepared to store wine free of charge, or for a small fee, but they are becoming rarer in these days when so many of their customers have no storage place of their own and need the wine merchant's help. Once the wine merchant knows the preference of his customer, he will be able to suggest suitable wines.

An inquirer for red Bordeaux to lay down in 1970 would, other things such as price and type being equal, be recommended a 1961 if he was prepared to wait ten years or more for development, or a 1966 if he preferred something ready to drink in about five years. Similarly, according to his preference in type of wine, a selection would be made amongst the full-bodied Saint-Émilions, the aromatic Margaux wines, the strongly flavoured wines of Pauillac and Saint-Estèphe, or the suave Saint-Juliens. Possibly the wine merchant might consider that none of the recent Bordeaux vintages would suit the taste of his customer and recommend instead a Burgundy of recent vintage. No knowledge gained from books or articles on wine, or from vintage charts, can possibly be sufficiently detailed to ensure the satisfying of individual tastes. A wine merchant who knows his stock, and his customers, is indispensable.

Bought in this way, at the right time, twelve bottles of bourgeois clarets need cost no more than 75p per bottle, and according to quality could go up to £1, with a large selection in between. This bourgeois category excludes the cheaper wines, which do not develop sufficiently to warrant laying down, and it excludes also the best sixty-five wines of red Bordeaux known as the 'Classed Growths', which fetch relatively much higher prices because of their reputation, and are dealt with below. In Burgundy there is no viable classification; the nomenclature is complicated and prices much higher. Also the majority of Burgundies do not live so long or develop so well in bottle as the Bordeaux. Carefully selected Burgundies, however, will repay for laying down for shorter periods and the best, of which there are very few indeed, can live and improve for a long time in certain years – as, for example, the 1929s, 1937s, 1945s. Recent years have produced fewer examples of this type.

It is unlikely that Burgundies worth laying down can be found at under £1 per bottle, and they can easily cost as much as £1·75. The greatest of all are even more expensive.

It can cost as little as £20 a year to lay down a dozen or two bourgeois clarets and £60 invested in a good year can form the basis of a cellar worthy of the attention of any wine-lover. This does not mean laying out £60 every year, but only in good years. At the very most a decade will produce five vintages worth laying down, as did the 1950s (six if the 1957s are included, as they should be): the 1940s produced four, and the 1930s only three. The 1920s upset the balance by producing seven out of ten, but this compensated for the decade before, which produced only two. An expenditure of £60 per good vintage, invested exclusively in this most rewarding category, could produce two dozen bottles of three different wines per vintage, and a total stock of some thirty dozen bottles for an expenditure of not more than £330 in ten years, or £33 per annum.

For those who like the character which white wines develop with age in bottle, there is even more reason for buying early and laying down in the medium price range. Whilst wine merchants lay down the finest white Burgundies and hocks and Moselles, the medium categories are not generally obtainable with more than a year or two's bottle age. There is not such a wide choice as there is of red wines, and four or five years is long enough to enable the wine to develop. A study of Bordeaux Graves at about 75p per bottle, and white Burgundies up to £1 is worth while; so is the selection of a good Riesling from Alsace. Genuine Chablis, from Burgundy, comes into this category and should be available at under £1 per bottle if bought in case-lots of twelve bottles. Here a little extra care is needed in selection, because the word 'Chablis' is sometimes used in a generic sense to describe all white Burgundies, from the cheap, short-lived white Mâcons to the expensive, but very different, wines of Meursault and Chassagne-Montrachet. The cheap Mâcons are not worth laying down, the Meursaults are worth it, but have a character of their own and need careful selection. Therefore, it is important to make certain that the name Chablis refers to a genuine wine from that district, with its characteristic, incisive flavour and light colour.

FINE WINES TO LAY DOWN FOR INVESTMENT AND ENJOYMENT

This section covers not only the category of world-renowned wines which can be sold profitably merely by letting them take their chance in an auction sale, but also wines from smaller vineyards of such great quality that they always can find a market amongst the restricted group of true connoisseurs.

Initial prices for the young wines may range from £1 per bottle to £7 per bottle, and the eventual market price show an appreciation in value of 200 per cent and more after ten years or so. Before the post-war claret and Burgundy prices adjusted themselves to the increased demand for fine wine, the prices of growers and shippers were one third their present level. The fine vintages then shipped, such as 1945, 1947, 1949, 1952 and 1953, have not only increased in value by virtue of their development into great clarets and Burgundies, but they have benefited from the general rise in value which the increased demand has produced. The emphasis is especially on wines of the great vineyards, which are available in strictly limited quantities. Examples of these increased values can be seen from wine merchants' lists. The classified first-growth Château Latour of 1952, originally listed at about 23s. (£1·15) per bottle, is now sold at £4, and the third-growth 1955 Château Palmer, originally sold at about 15s. (75p) per bottle, is now quoted at £2·25 on some lists.

The value of wines depends on the degree of quality they reach and on supplies available, and so varies from wine to wine. There is, however, an additional rise in price common to all wine which is brought about by the fall in the value of currency. Wines for which a world demand exists maintain their real or 'gold' value.

Similar rapid price increases like these noted here cannot be expected in the future. Prices have adjusted themselves to demand, and young wines that opened at £1 in the early 1950s now start at £1·75. The opening price of the 1966 Château Palmer was, for example, about £1·50 per bottle, not 15s. (75p) as it was for the 1955. Investors, however, are always likely to be well rewarded by a steady increase in value as quality develops with age and irreplaceable stocks diminish.

Amongst table wines, the most remunerative red wines to lay down in the higher price bracket are the great clarets. They live longer and improve more than any others, their initial prices are rather less than comparable wines from Burgundy, and they come from large, well-defined estates with world-wide reputations. The section on Bordeaux in Part Three gives full particulars of these wines. Prices of the first growths (see p. 139) and Château Mouton-Rothschild, and of Cheval Blanc and Ausone in Saint-Émilion are generally out of proportion to the prices of the lesser growths, but they are, nevertheless, worthwhile investments. They are often superb and supreme in their quality. They probably do not make more than about a million bottles per annum between the seven of them on an average, which is not much for a world demand. There are many Champagne shippers who hold stocks of 2 million bottles. First growths of the 1949 vintage have recently fetched over £10 per bottle, and one magnum of 1864 Château Lafite fetched £82. This sort of wine buying is for rich men; for the majority it is better, when laying down fine wines, to concentrate on the lesser classified growths. They are likely to be easy to sell, though at less exaggerated prices than the first growths.

The wines best known in the U.K., and therefore those having the highest investment value, even though they may not offer the highest quality value, are specified in the section on Bordeaux wines. Reputations are, however, always changing, albeit slowly, and the true wine-lover will invest his money in the wines he likes best and back his own judgement rather than the reputation of past vintages.

The best *drinking* value in wines is often to be found amongst a score of top bourgeois clarets, which, being less known, do not attract speculators. Starting prices are about £1 per bottle. There are also half a dozen loosely defined 'crus exceptionnels', rated between the best bourgeois and the classed growths, such as Château Chasse Spleen, which start at about £1·25, and some wines from individual Burgundy vineyards, which can only be discovered with the help of wine merchants and which start at about the same price. In addition to these, there are expensive single-vineyard Burgundies, bottled on their respective estates, which apart from their drinking value rival the château-bottled classed-growth clarets as financial investments. Prices start at about the same level of £1·50 per bottle. Wines of this calibre, carefully selected from good vintages, can double in value between their youth and full maturity. This may mean something like twenty years for the Burgundies and longer for clarets. Those wines which can reach their highest point of development in under ten years are not likely to attain a quality that will earn a great reputation. Furthermore, care is necessary in these days of publicity and facile wine articles in newspapers when vintages sometimes acquire reputations before they are earned, and it is wise to get some professional advice before investing in fine wine.

White Wines

The higher price bracket covers many white wines of sufficient weight and quality to last a long time in bottle and to improve with age. The great Sauternes and Barsacs of Bordeaux are one example. There are many enthusiasts who seek them out, but their appeal is not as general as that made by old white Burgundies, hocks and Moselles. These, together with some of the Rhône wines, comprise the only group of white wines readily available to the public which are capable of great improvement with time in bottle. Almost all wine-producing areas have their exceptional examples of great wines, notably the very long-lived sweet wines of Hungary, which from time to time appear on the market at several pounds a bottle. Other countries, such as Spain and Italy, may possibly have treasures of this nature unknown to the author.

The smaller areas of France produce notable wines, rather special in character and flavour, and greatly appreciated by some enthusiasts. They are generally difficult to come by. The Jura (see p. 160) produces its *vin jaune* and *vin de paille*. Alsace occasionally rises to really magnificent white wines, comparable to fine hock in quality, and well below it in price. Fine Sauternes and Barsacs can be bought for financial investment, but they should be confined to the classed growths, bottled at their châteaux. Even so, the return is likely to be very much less than a similar investment in red wines. From a quality point of view there is no advantage in a château-bottling over a good London bottling by a responsible wine merchant, and there is a small disadvantage in price.

Hocks and some fine Moselles are in a different category from fine Sauternes and Barsac.

Great hocks can be as individual as great clarets. Modern technical methods make it essential that they are bottled in Germany. Hocks of great quality make their appearance on the British market frequently enough to make them of general interest. Their market value when old and fully developed depends, as in the case of red wines, on the reputation of the vintage, but since the vineyards are much smaller than in Bordeaux, and since the proprietor generally differentiates between the various qualities made at one vintage, be it from different grapes or combination of grapes, from different pickings, or even from different fermentations, and indicates all these differences on the label, there is seldom enough of any one individual wine to enable it to gain a wide reputation. The flavour and general quality of most of these wines is clear-cut and easily recognized, so that fine hocks and Moselles, because of their direct appeal, are more readily appreciated by the public than subtle red wines, and they command very high prices.

Of the four main areas in which Rhine wines (p. 184) are grown, the most likely to produce long-lived wines is the Rheingau, and then the Palatinate and a selected few from the Rheinhessen district. However, it should be remembered that it is far more difficult to select young white wines for future development than it is to select red wines. The palate is flattered by the freshness of young white wines, so that it is difficult to judge the general balance, so necessary to long life and graceful development. This obscuration is more apparent in the fine white wines of Bordeaux, where sweetness helps to hide defects.

Although the financial return may compare unfavourably with an investment in red wine, the fact that there is comparatively very little fine hock available makes its early acquisition almost essential for the collector. Prices for hocks worth laying down may start at about £1·50 per bottle and go up to almost any price; some are quoted at £7·50 per bottle today. Fine Moselles are in the same category. They are easier to select because their structure is not obscured by so much sugar, and is more easily assessed on the palate when young. Here again, the financial investment value is restricted because of the relatively small demand, but from the point of view of the amateur of fine wine, the rewards can be even greater than with Rhine wines, depending on individual tastes.

Fortified Wines

The most interesting fortified wines to lay down are again red wines. Amongst these the vintage ports are predominant. Opening prices for the 1966s vary from £1·25 to £1·50 per bottle for the same wine, depending to some extent on whether single bottles are ordered, or larger amounts in case lots. The 1950s are already quoted at £2·40, and older vintages are difficult to find. Port is an investment from all points of view: it is strictly limited in supply, its progress in bottle is generally steady and certain, and the fully matured result appeals strongly to a wider public than probably any other wine.

The large majority of shippers agree on which years are to be declared vintage years. Any exceptions, which have to justify by their quality their variance from the majority decision, are nearly always well worth consideration. The market value of any one vintage of port is well defined at any given period, with variations of the nature of 10 per cent in either direction, depending on the reputation of the individual shippers, or on the success or otherwise of particular bottlings. The time, place and efficiency of the actual bottling are important and influence the development of the wine to an extent easily recognizable to a normal palate. Wine merchants take a great pride in their bottling; it is an art for which British merchants are justly famous. A few vintage ports have always been bottled in Portugal and during the war more shippers were forced by circumstances to bottle their vintage wine there, particularly the 1945s. The practice has survived to a small extent, and the relative merits of Portuguese and British bottlings are still disputed. Vintage port is usually bottled in the second year after the vintage and on an average takes twenty years to reach its full maturity.

The longest-lived of all wines – Madeira – today never seems to be laid down as it once was. The demand for old Madeira is too restricted to make the operation of financial interest, and the stocks of old Madeira in wine merchants' cellars are sufficient to supply any enthusiast with his requirements. Madeira is, however, increasing in popularity, and the time may come again when it will be worth while laying down stocks for ageing. It improves greatly with age, and should a demand for old Madeira materialize, stocks of old-bottled wines, as opposed to old cask wines or soleras, may quickly disappear.

BUYING COGNAC

If fortified wines develop only slowly in bottle, Cognac and other brandies (indeed, all spirits) develop not at all. They mature only in cask and once bottled remain static until they evaporate after a few centuries. There is, therefore, no point in laying down Cognac (which in any case must be stored standing up and not 'laid down' at all) for development in bottle. A glance at the section on Cognac (p. 155) will convince the reader that there is an excellent case for grabbing any fine examples that he may come across of a good vintage, matured in cask, *under the right conditions*, and bottled at the right time. Such wines are found almost only in Great Britain; they represent a drop in the ocean of good and indifferent Cognacs marketed under brand names.

To acquire a few bottles of this naturally matured, pure distillation of the grape is not easy and is expensive. They need time, care and money to produce. About twenty years are needed for development in cask, during which time something like 30 per cent of the quantity is lost by evaporation. There is strong temptation to keep the cask refreshed with ever-younger wine instead of accepting the necessary shrinkage in quantity. After twenty years a 1940 Cognac that has been kept filled up may contain only 70 per cent of the original wine. British wine merchants resist this temptation and are helped in their resolution by the rules of H.M. Customs and Excise, which strictly forbid the filling up of casks in bond except with duty-paid stock. As the duty on a bottle of brandy – whether Cognac or not – is in the neighbourhood of £2·05 per bottle, depending on its strength, there is very little temptation to the wine merchant to fill up his bonded cask with duty-paid spirit on which he will have to pay duty again when he clears the cask from bond.

The demand for Cognac at £6 a bottle, without an advertised brand name behind it, is very limited, however good it may be, and the wine merchant is not encouraged to invest the necessary time and money in this particular search for perfection. There are a few importers who can still permit themselves this luxury and who ship into bond Cognacs one year old which they will not bottle for twenty years. The majority rely on French bottled spirits sold under shippers' brands for their supplies of expensive Cognacs.

WINES FOR DINNER PARTIES

A bottle of wine produces about six large glasses if filled three-quarters full, as they should be. All table wines are suitable for dinner parties, although some attention to the order of serving and the accompanying food is desirable. Guidance on both these points is given in Chapter 5 and a selection of wines of various types can be made by reference to the table included in this chapter. These indicate the traditional choice open for any occasion, but let me repeat once again that deviation from tradition in the marrying of wine and food is not a crime. The previous sections in this present chapter on wines for laying down will help in the selection of price categories, and finally – as usual – the wine merchant is ready to give advice.

Many of the groups of wine suggested in this chapter in the section 'Everyday Wines' (p. 97) are suitable for the less elaborate dinner party. Most of them can be served all through a meal. It is in fact easier to list those wines which cannot be served through a meal than the reverse. The only wines served with food are the so-called table wines – not the fortified wines. Of table wines, the only wines that cannot go all through the meal are the sweet white wines, since most people do not like them with meat or poultry or game, which generally form the main course of a dinner. Sweet white wines go well with a meal consisting of fish, sweet and/or fruit.

Dry white wines and red wines can go all through a meal, even though they may not taste at their best with the richer desserts. Any red wine is an excellent accompaniment to cheese. Highly flavoured wines, such as some from the Jura area of France, or the Rhône area, such as Hermitage or Château Grillet, must be used by the host in accordance with his own preferences and judgement. They have strong individual flavours which may or may not appeal. The one wine which can be served all through any dinner party without exception is, of course, Champagne.

If two or more wines are to be served with a carefully organized party, it is often a good thing to start with a well-chosen wine from the 70p to 90p category, which, besides being a pleasant accompaniment to the food, acts as a foil to the finer wines to follow. It may

TYPES OF TABLE WINE READILY AVAILABLE IN GREAT BRITAIN

	Red Wine	Dry White	Medium White	Sweet White	Rosé	Sparkling
France	Bordeaux Loire Burgundy Jura Rhône	Alsace Bordeaux Loire Burgundy Jura (strong flavour) Rhône	Alsace Bordeaux Loire Jura (strong flavour) Rhône	Bordeaux Loire Jura (strong flavour)	Bordeaux Loire Burgundy Jura Rhône	Bordeaux Loire Burgundy Champagne Jura
Germany		Moselle Hock	Hock	Hock (Auslese) and Trockenbeeren-auslese		Hock Moselle
Italy	Chianti Tuscan Barolo Valpolicella Bardolino	Orvieto Verdicchio Soave Frascati Lacrima Christi	Orvieto Tuscan Soave Frascati	Many Italian wines obtainable from specialists in Great Britain	Various	Asti spumante
Spain	Rioja	Rioja Spanish Various (low prices)	Various (low prices)			
Portugal	Dão Colares	Vinho Verde Bucelas	Dão	Granjo	Various	
Austria	Some	Various	Various			
Hungary	Bull's Blood	Various	Various	Tokay		
Switzerland	Dôle	Various	Various		Some	Perle
Yugoslavia		Various	Various	Tiger Milk		
Australia	Burgundy	Riesling Australian (only selected wines)	Various			
S. Africa	Various	Various	Various			

well be that for the moderate drinker this gradual encouragement to the palate at an early stage of the meal, leading up to the more subtle qualities of an older wine later on, will give better results than a direct plunge into the delicacies of fine wine. The change from the pre-dinner aperitif or cigarette, or the demand on a neglected palate, is eased in this way. It must be accepted that a little care is needed if wine is to show at its best, so that it is desirable for it to be delivered by or collected from the wine merchant a day or two before it is needed. Twenty-four – or better still – forty-eight hours' rest after delivery will make all the difference and give time for any deposit to settle so that the wine can be decanted and for the wine to acquire the right temperature. (See sections on temperature and decanting, pp. 46–51.) If even a modest cellar of a dozen or two bottles is maintained, this problem does not arise.

If very old wines, or other wines that have thrown a deposit, have to be bought especially for the occasion and it has not been possible to give them two days' rest, it is better to have them decanted by the wine merchant one or two hours before they are required, and transported thus to the dining-room. If none of these alternatives is possible and it is still desired to give outstanding wines, they must be chosen from amongst wines which have not thrown a deposit, and from wines that are not so delicate that they are demolished by the journey from wine merchant to home. Fine white wines, French or German, seem to be the natural choice under these circumstances.

APERITIFS

For all dinner parties where wine is to take its natural place as a pleasant accompaniment to the food, and not intended as a topic of analytical discussion throughout the meal, I believe that the choice of aperitif is relatively unimportant. It should depend on the company, rather than the food. Too much gin or whisky will certainly deaden the palate, but a glass or two may well help an 'evening' palate to revive from the effect of its daily dose of contaminated air and tobacco or from sheer weariness.

For the exhausted who are about to dine and have no time to relax, a quick pick-me-up is probably indicated rather than a slow-working reviver. Cognac and water is very effective. It is a drink that is gentle on the palate and leaves it clean and refreshed for whatever wines are to follow. A mild whisky is an excellent booster in the same category, but the flavour of whisky is foreign to wine and leaves the palate less ready for delicate flavours. In the circumstances where an hour or more is available for relaxation before dinner, there is room for the more gentle type of aperitif that leaves the head clear and calms the nerves. Sherry fills this role, as do the attractively flavoured manufactured aperitifs of France, Spain and Italy, some of them based on a concentrated wine.

For myself, I have found that a bottle of the sweet natural table wines of France, such as one of the classed growths of Sauternes, that can be bought for about £1 per bottle, makes a perfect aperitif for five or six people with time to spare before going in to dine. The cost of 20p per head must compare favourably with the cost of five or six people drinking gin before dinner.

For a conventional informal dinner party, the aperitif period is adequately covered by a medium-dry or dry sherry, with the alternative for non-sherry-drinkers of gin and vermouth, or orange juice. Dry sherry, like other aperitifs, is often served chilled. This is a matter of taste, and in the case of the more delicate sherries care must be taken not to kill the flavour.

Of all natural wine aperitifs, Champagne is the champion. Not only does it leave the palate clean, but it revives tired guests or hostess as quickly as any spirit, and by means of a far more gentle application of alcohol to the system. It is not the cheapest aperitif, but neither is it the most expensive, and sometimes, because of its stimulating qualities, it is indispensable to the success of a dinner party.

At certain times, such as hot summer evenings, or at dinner dances with a predominance of young people, tables wines appear to me to be preferable to any spirits as an aperitif. White wines, dry or sweet, well chilled, have obvious refreshing qualities. Rosé wines, chilled and drunk from large glasses, are excellent thirst-quenchers and revivers, and can be bought of excellent quality for about 65p per bottle. Alsace wines, particularly a good Traminer, make first-class aperitifs.

WINE AND CHEESE PARTIES

A variety of modern conditions and factors have made wine and cheese parties so popular a form of entertainment that it has seemed worth while giving them a little special attention here. The attraction of these functions to the guest seem to be mainly twofold. Unlike cocktail parties, they supply a whole evening's entertainment with food, and they provide an opportunity to taste and compare an unusual variety of wines in the company of friends. For the host and hostess, there is the added advantage that they are simple to organize and inexpensive.

Theoretically, all wines are equally suitable for showing at a wine and cheese party, but in practice the informal atmosphere, the amount of wine drunk, the accompanying noise and smoke make the inclusion of expensive wines or wines of great delicacy undesirable. Similarly, whilst distinct difference in type adds to the interest, if there is too great a difference in quality, demand will tend to concentrate on the best and supplies will be threatened to the detriment of the reputation of the commissariat. Expensive wines are best reserved for the more formal organized wine-tastings. For wine and cheese parties the choice can well be limited to those up to a maximum of 90p per bottle. There can be some connexion between the wines if it is desired to make the party an informal tasting. This aspect is elaborated in the next section. A wine and cheese party can, however, equally well be just a pleasant social occasion in which wine to suit the taste of everybody plays its part.

In general, the wines should be quite distinctive from each other and not separated merely by shades of flavour. The character should be distinctive so that guests may choose and declare, if they so wish, their preferences quickly and certainly, and thenceforth enjoy the wine of their choice for the rest of the evening. All wine and cheese parties should include both red and white wines, to cater for varying tastes. The average consumption at these parties varies greatly with the type of guest and length of party. As a minimum appropriate to a gathering of ordinary sober citizens with a sufficient leavening of ladies, I would suggest half a bottle per head; there is no known limit to the maximum. The duration of the party needs only a casual thought in determining the amount of wine, since the amount of wine generally effectively determines the duration of the party.

WINE TASTINGS

Tastings are another manifestation of the modern interest in wine. They are generally arranged by clubs specially formed for this purpose, and are an altogether more formal and disciplined affair than the social wine and cheese party.

Clubs are founded on the principle that one bottle is sufficient for about twenty people when the object is careful tasting, and not drinking. Six to eight wines are about sufficient for the average palate if critical tasting is to be carried out. At an average price of £1·25 to £1·50 a bottle for fine matured wines that induce prolonged discussion, a tasting for a club of twenty members can be organized easily at the cost of 50p to 65p per head, and affords the soundest way I know of for learning about wine and developing a palate. Ten tastings a year for the expenditure of £5 per member, and including the willing attendance of a specialist in the wines to be tasted to point out traditional characteristics and occasional deviations, are a very useful exercise to wine enthusiasts.

All that is needed is a table long enough to carry six or eight bottles spaced out in a row, preferably placed in the middle of the room so that members can approach it from two sides; two tasting-glasses per member, so that comparisons can more easily be made between two wines if desired; a few strategically placed boxes of sawdust or pails of water for spitting wine into and – if the strictest economy is to be observed – a few small glass funnels for pouring back into the bottle any wine from the taster's glass that may be superfluous to his needs. If members are not squeamish and are prepared to taste out of the same glass, only two glasses per bottle and not per member are required, to be filled before the tasting to the regular level and, placed strictly in front of their respective bottles where, for purposes of identification, they must also be equally strictly replaced by each member after tasting. This eliminates any waste and also the need for the funnels. It is the method used in professional tastings.

The variations of comparison on which wine-tastings can be based are almost unlimited. All the areas producing fine wines provide, each vintage year, a series of wines that can be usefully compared. Bordeaux, for example, produced at least some sixty classified wines in 1959 which can be compared. In groups of eight, one vintage alone provides a programme for half a year on the basis of ten tastings per annum. Bordeaux alone produced the same quantity in 1950, 1952, 1953, 1955, 1957, 1961 and 1962 – not, of course, all now easily procurable from wine merchants. Instead of comparing different wines of one vintage, it is also possible to compare one wine through different vintages. As an absolute safeguard of the basis of comparison, it is best that all should have been bottled by the same bottler and it is therefore wise to select only château-bottled wines.

Burgundies can be tasted, the selection being based on different shippers' wines from one district or one area of different vintages, or a price range of different areas from one merchant. Hocks and Moselles and ports can be arranged on the same basis of different shippers of one vintage, or different vintages of one shipper. Sherry and Madeira, sold always without vintage, can be compared shipper against shipper, or the whole range of one shipper compared wine against wine, with an eye on the price of each wine. Types of wines can be compared, such as dry white wines at comparable prices from different countries, or the same can be done with red wines. There should be no difficulty in the selection of wines for tasting, as members of tasting clubs may be presumed to have already acquired an overall knowledge of the varieties and variations possible.

CHAPTER 13

GROWER, SHIPPER AND MERCHANT

THE responsible originator of good wine is the grower. In the majority of cases the man who owns the vineyard and cultivates the vine is also the maker of the wine. In some cases he may sell his grapes to wine shippers who have their own presses or to the cooperative wine-making society to which he, in company with the other local growers, belongs, but generally he grows the grape, presses it and makes the wine, and it is a full-time job. He has no time to study home or foreign markets, control sales organizations or deal with the many detailed activities involved in selling fine wine to the consumer. He looks upon himself as a trustee of the soil that he has inherited, to help it to produce the highest quality that it is capable of producing. He needs faith, courage and money. Faith to believe that there exists somewhere in the world people capable of recognizing the existence of the most refined subtleties of flavour that he is able to produce; courage to take the risks that have to be taken if the second best is to be rejected and only perfection accepted; money because without it he is at the mercy of a commerce that is always looking for bargains to be had from growers who lack it and because he may have to survive years when his wines cannot be sold. His year is a succession of anxieties, starting with the fear of late frosts in the spring after the sap has started rising, bad weather to interfere with the vital flowering period, storms, hail, insect and cryptogamic invasions, lack or excess of sun or rain. Not until the grapes are gathered in the autumn and the first pressings have finished fermenting in his vats will the intelligent grower predict what sort of wine he is going to produce. Even then, as often as not, after tasting his wine he will admit his inability to judge it objectively. He will recognize it as his own child, different from and incomparable with any other and so impossible to judge as better or worse. He has made the best quality he can with the resources that Nature has entrusted to his care, he must rely on the wine trade to assess its value, to find a market and to encourage him to go on striving.

The grower's contact with the consuming world is the shipper, who, if he does not often grow his own grapes, always matures and cares for the young wine, which he keeps in his cellars until it is ready to be bottled either in its own country or abroad. The shipper needs the same assets as the grower – faith, courage and money. He also needs a discerning palate, a knowledge to interpret what his palate discovers, because the taste of young wines often has little relation to the taste of the matured wine ready to be sold. He must have also a sympathetic understanding of the home or foreign wine merchant who has the responsibility of bringing good wine to the notice of those who can pay for it and appreciate it. The somewhat confusing term 'shipper' presumably comes from the days when English merchant fleets sailed annually to Bordeaux to collect the new wines from the King of England's French domaine. He still remains the explorer who searches for something to satisfy a particular market. Whatever the origin, the term today describes the first selective outpost in the line connecting the vineyard with the wine-drinker. The importance of the shipper's function varies with the kind of wine he deals in. If the variety of wine available in any area makes his skill as a selector important, his name on the label is important; if the wine has a reputation of its own and an assured authenticity, the name of the shipper is of no interest and often will not appear on the label at all. The name of a shipper on a château-bottled claret of an accepted vintage is of no interest, but on a bottle of wine from a primary or large secondary wine-growing area such as Médoc or Saint-Julien, in each of which many hundreds of different wines are produced each year all bearing the same description, the name of the shipper or wine merchant is the only practical guarantee of quality.

A shipper has a positive objective, both as concerns the grower and the wine merchant. With each he strives to establish a reputation for knowledge and quality – with the grower in order to ensure that the best wines are offered to him each year in the knowledge that he is capable of appreciating quality and ready to pay for it, and with the wine merchant in the hope that the latter will consider it worth while examining the shipper's selection of wines when they are ready for bottling. Sometimes the importance of his name on the label is paramount as being the only means of distinguishing between wines of the very highest quality. Bordeaux has its individual châteaux to identify its finest wines, Burgundy its domaines or clos or named vineyards such as Beaune-Grèves. Germany has its carefully indicated individual vineyard names, Schloss Johannisberg, Piesporter-Goldtröpfchen, but its sparkling wines have to be defined by the name of the shipper who has made them. The finest of all sparkling wines come from Champagne, in France, a primary producing area with no practical subdivision to indicate quality or character, so that a shipper's name on Champagne is essential as the only means of identifying one wine from another. Champagne is nearly always a blended wine, so that even if there did exist named individual vineyards, as in Bordeaux, the wine, blended from the produce of different vineyards, would not have the right to the name of any one of them. The same applies to port and sherry. Both these fortified wines are blended and are identified only by the shipper's name, or by a made-up brand name belonging to the shipper – or by a combination of both. Since it is possible to produce a large variety of types of these blended fortified wines from full-bodied to light, from sweet to dry, most shippers produce a whole range under their labels. To differentiate between them sherry shippers add a brand name to their label, whilst port shippers often rely on their own name with an additional description such as vintage, tawny, crusted, vintage character, ruby, etc.

Brand names are used also by Bordeaux and Burgundy shippers, by German wine shippers and to a lesser degree by others who want to establish wine blended from various vineyards in a primary or secondary wine-growing area that will not vary in character or price from year to year. In these cases, however, brand names used by shippers are mostly confined to wines in the lower or medium priced categories.

The shipper does not sell his wine to the public, at least not in Great Britain or in the U.S.A., where the demand is not big enough to enable him to sell his wine in shipping quantities to individual consumers. He sells to the importing wine merchant, with whom he cooperates in every way and to whom he remains loyal as a specialist in those areas from which he ships his wines. The merchant is the specialist in the tastes of his customers. He covers the whole field of wine and, whilst often an accomplished wine-taster and extremely knowledgeable about wine-growing areas and their products, cannot keep abreast of the continually changing qualities of new vintages. Just as the shippper relies for his success on his reputation with wine merchants, so the wine merchant attracts to himself numbers of the public who have faith in his integrity and judgement.

Most wine merchants, whether they admit it or not, are dedicated to good wine and most have to compromise from time to time with their own judgement in order to satisfy a demand created by advertisers instead of by selection and experience. They are ready to consult with potential customers in order to find for them wines which suit their palates and their pockets and they are anxious always for an opportunity to recommend to the initiated new wines which they have discovered in the course of their visits to shippers' tasting rooms or cellars. They are ready to help anyone who wants to take an intelligent interest in wine by selling to them single bottles or half-bottles for tasting purposes. Not unreasonably, too, they are more delighted to sell a wine of their own individual selection that finds favour than a popular brand whose price may be inflated by the cost of advertising. Many independent wine merchants in their efforts to serve the public with the best quality available at different price levels will have sherries and ports blended for them by shippers. To these they often give brand names just as shippers do to their own wines, so that wine merchants' brands are freely to be found on the market as well as shippers' brands. To a smaller extent this applies also to Champagne and to light table wines – particularly the Graves and Sauternes from Bordeaux.

Although 4½ bottles per head of the population per annum are consumed in Great Britain, we are still a long way from becoming a wine-drinking nation. Sufficient progress has been made since 1945 in the consumption of lower-priced table wines to justify the creation of enormous distributing organizations able to bring to the public this category of wine efficiently and at attractive prices. The creation of these organizations has involved the buying-up of smaller independent wine merchants, some of whom, although by no means all, prided themselves in the past on their role as selectors of fine wine. Many traditional wine merchants have, therefore, disappeared into the larger organizations, where some of them have lost both their identity and their role as selectors. Others in these groups have retained a large degree of independence so far as fine wine is concerned, whilst still others have formed themselves into consortiums allowing full independence to all their members. The picture of the chain of distribution is changing, but its final form will be determined by the attitude of the public to the standards of quality and service which the new régime can offer.

PART THREE

EUROPEAN WINES

Austria

THE vineyards along the bank of the Danube are one of the original natural wine-growing areas of Europe. The soil is particularly suitable to the production of the light white wines which form the majority of Austrian production. Altogether the vineyards cover an area of about 135 square miles and produce on an average 30 million gallons of wine per year. At an estimate, about 25 per cent of this can rank as superior wine of a character similar to the wines of Alsace, whilst the remainder is *vin ordinaire*. A substantial quantity is exported to West Germany and also to Czechoslovakia. Until recently little had been imported into Britain, but Austria is now being used by at least one large importer as the source of supply for one of the several inexpensive branded wines that have recently been launched. It seems likely that these pleasant wines will grow in popularity on export markets during the coming years. The Austrians themselves drink about thirty bottles per head of the population per annum – they drink four times that amount of beer – which, with exports, accounts comfortably for the yearly crop.

The wine industry is traditional and well organized, and it is un-hampered by complicated nomenclature laws, although there is legislation to control description and vinification. As nearly all the wine made is naturally fermented table wine and very little is turned into fortified or any form of exotic wine, as it so often is in countries which over-produce, the laws are sensible and respected and the reputation of well-known areas safely left to growers and merchants. There are a few but not many large wine-growing estates, over 50 per cent of the vineyards belong to growers owning no more than ten or twelve acres and another 45 per cent to growers owning between twelve and fifty acres. The industry is organized very much on the lines of the German vineyards and the wines are made by experts and distributed through traditional and responsible channels. The names too are reminiscent of German wine names. They are not much known in Britain, but the following list of vineyards and villages may serve as some guide to the student who stumbles upon an opportunity to taste any, either at home or abroad.

The following are the main wine producing areas with notes on some of those wines more readily available in Britain.

From the Vienna Province: Grinzing, Nussberg.

From Lower Austria:
> Wachauer Schluck: Generally without a vintage, made from the Sylvaner grape. The word *Schluck* means a drop of wine and has no other connotation.
> Gumpoldskirchen: highly rated. Many grape varieties used.
> Durnstein: a dry refreshing wine, made from the Grüner Veltiner, the sample tasted was very soft and medium dry.
> Loibner: made from the Riesling grape, though the sample tasted was medium dry and more reminiscent of Traminer.

From the Burgenland Province: Retz, Oggau, Marbirch, Gols, Weiden-am-See, Pottendorf, Eisberg an der Pinka, Sandweine.

The reader will possibly agree that it is a pity that not more of these evocative names decorate British wine lists. Those that are available cost from 75p to £1·10 per bottle retail.

The suffixes *Spâtlese, Auslese, Beerenauslese* seem to be used more freely than in Germany and the difference in quality they imply is not always recognizable.

Steiner Hund Rheinriesling is an individual wine whose quality and the legend attached to its name makes it worthy of a special mention. It is said that a vintner in a time of famine exchanged one of his vineyards for a dog in order to satisfy the hunger of his family. It was of course his best vineyard. It now belongs to the Stein monastery in the Warban district; the wine has great finesse, is more sweet than dry and has a clear-cut, clean flavour.

All the wines mentioned above are white, and anyone who is interested in finding really dry natural white wines, clean in flavour and with the refreshing qualities that such wines should have, will do well to explore them.

But the red wines also are well worth attention. As already mentioned they are being imported to be sold under the importers' brand label and it can be assumed that, with all the world's wines to choose from, if an Austrian wine has been selected for this purpose it is because they offer outstanding value. They are soft, straightforward and uncomplicated though sometimes with a pleasing individual flavour.

Attractive *Perle* wines are also made. This indicates that they are slightly sparkling, and they represent excellent value for festive occasions.

Bulgaria

Like Rumania, another Balkan country, Bulgaria is increasing its wine production. The vine covers about 700 square miles and accounts for nearly 4 per cent of the arable land available. The total production of wine in 1960 amounted to 42 million gallons, most of it red. Only a small proportion is officially considered at present to attain the quality of good table wine. In 1958 1¾ million gallons only was so classified, the rest being described as *vin ordinaire*. It may well be that a high standard is set. It is likely that with time more good wines will be made. Those that I have been able to taste are well-made, clean-tasting wines that compare favourably with wines from other countries sold at similar prices. In addition to light table wines, a substantial quantity of sweet fortified wine is made, mostly for export to the U.S.S.R. Small quantities of table wines are also exported to the U.S.S.R., Czechoslovakia and Germany.

The vineyards are scattered over the whole country. In the east, the provinces of Tarnovo, Bourgas, Rousse, Kolavograd and Varna grow the vine, in the west, Vratsa, Vidin and Michailovgrad, in the north, Pleven, in the south, Stara Zagora, and in the centres the largest producing area of all, Plovdiv and Pazardzhik. The grapes grown are mostly old traditional national varieties, with some classic European varieties, such as Riesling for white wines and Cabernet for red. The whole wine industry is in fact being modernized under the guidance of West European experts and a great deal of progress is being made, both in viticulture and in vinification. The soil is particularly well adapted to making fine wine, being rich in mineral salts and light and friable in character. The climate also is favourable to the production of well-balanced wines; the long hours of sunshine, without the exaggerated heat that some southern European vineyards have to suffer, not only nourish the grape but permit an unhurried and steady ripening. Wines are named by their grape or by regional names, and sometimes by a combination of both.

Although they are sold at the modest price of 60–65p per bottle, it has been my experience that they are capable of developing finesse and delicacy in bottle The following are listed on some British wine merchants' lists:

Trakia: A Bordeaux-type wine, a little light in colour, gentle, with a good clean soft flavour. The word 'Trakia' means Thrace. The wine is made from Pamid and Maverud grapes.

Grozden: A white, medium-full, soft, clean-tasting wine, medium dry. Made from the Misket grape.

Bulgarian Riesling: Crisp, good bouquet, dry, very clean, and a distinct flavour of the Riesling grape. Very pleasant white wine.

Bulgarian Gamza: Well-made red wine. Clean, very well-balanced, strong, clear-cut classic flavour of good grapes. Resembles Bordeaux in character. Gamza is a grape variety.

Bulgarian Kadarka: Soft, sweet, light-coloured red wine, almost a rosé. Very pleasant to drink cooled. Kadarka is a grape variety.

All the above retail at 65p a bottle, comparing in quality with many popular wines sold at higher prices.

Cyprus

Cyprus, like Greece, is the cradle of wine in Europe. Today, the island is the third most important source of supply of wine to the United Kingdom, which bought 3·5 million gallons from Cyprus in 1969. Total wine production is now approaching 9 million gallons a year, and 5·3 million gallons were exported to a variety of markets in 1969. Although, in Britain, the bulk of Cyprus wine brought in has been Cyprus sherry up to now, great progress is beginning to be made in promoting the table wine; the great Cyprus speciality, Commandaria, has been known in export markets since the Crusades. The British Government appointed a Commission to examine the possibilities of putting the Cyprus vineyards in order and of producing wines in a sound commercial way. The Commission's Report was received in 1956, and was a notable example of international cooperation, for the late Fred Rossi, an English wine shipper of Italian origin who was in charge of the Commission, enlisted the help of Professor Branas of the oenological department of Montpellier University in France, and also received advice from Roseworthy College in Australia. The Commission's findings resulted in the augmentation of the native grapes (black Mavron, white Xynisteri) by other European varieties which had proved successful after experimental planting; the wineries in and near Limassol were either modernized or built, employing the most up-to-date skills, and the overseas marketing of Cyprus wines was primarily planned as a corporate exercise, before success enabled firms to promote their own wines and brands competitively. At least one-fifth of the population of Cyprus is engaged in the making of wine in one way or another. The vineyards are mostly situated on the slopes of the Troodos Mountains and most of the wine is made at the Limassol wineries of the three firms KEO, SODAP and ETKO. The Vine Products Commission, established in 1964, deals with the administration and control of the wine industry, advises the government on measures for protection and promotion, and also supervises table grapes, dried grapes, concentrated must, and Cyprus brandy.

The wines are officially divided into seven main groups, each recognized and controlled by legislation:

1. Dry red and white table wines with a *maximum* alcoholic content of 17 per cent – generally in fact not exceeding 13 per cent.
2. Sweeter dessert wines with a minimum alcoholic content of 15 per cent.
3. Fortified wines, which can be very sweet and have a maximum alcoholic content of 23 per cent.
4. Commandaria.
5. Special wines made from the Muscat grape which can be dry or sweet.
6. Sherry type – officially called 'Cyprus sherry'.
7. Concentrated musts, that is, unfermented grape juice dehydrated as far as possible, without spoiling its essential character. It is exported to countries that like to make their own wine, but cannot grow the grapes from which to make it.

Cyprus sherry. Wines in this category represent about 80 per cent of the total production. They have become popular in the U.K. because, at the time of writing, Cyprus still enjoys a preferential duty on imports to Great Britain, so that merchants are enabled to import a reasonably strong wine of this type at a very low duty indeed, since the preference applies both to the rate of duty and to the alcoholic strength. The bulk of Cyprus sherry imports are of the 'cream' or sweet types, but there are other drier wines some of which, a blend of high and low strength, are made up in the U.K., others of which, in the higher price ranges, are shipped straight. Even so they all enjoy the preferential rate of duty, which accounts for the comparatively low prices.

By law, Cyprus sherry must be matured at least two years in cask before being bottled, and the fortifying of the wine must be done with grape brandy. In fact the vitality of the local yeasts is such that unusually high degrees of alcohol can be obtained by straightforward fermentation. The sweeter wines are very 'raisiny' and full of flavour; the 'medium' wines and the 'dry' wines may be compared with those of similar style from South Africa, and appraised in their own right. The superior dry sherries of Cyprus, however made with 'flor' are clean, elegant wines likely to interest even the most conservative and classic of wine drinkers. The progress that has been made in their evolution in the past five years is as remarkable as the advancements in the equipment and atmospheric control of the bodegas, in which they are made according to the solera system. Prices range from about 70p to £1·10, according to quality as well as style.

Commandaria. The name comes from the headquarters of the Knights Templars and Knights of St John, formerly established on the island and known as the Grande Commanderie. It is a sweet red dessert wine, with a strong brownish tinge which it can acquire naturally with age, made from red and some white grapes in the mountain villages. The grapes, after picking, are spread on the roofs of the buildings to dry in the sun for about three weeks and are then pressed and the juice runs off into stone jars where it is left to ferment and clarify for twelve months or more. Various processes of blending and ageing are generally carried out by the merchants of Limassol, the wine centre of the island, to whom the village wines are delivered after their preliminary maturing period. There is a considerable difference between various Commandaria wines, which are usually sold with some identifying brand name, the qualities being influenced not only by the farmer, who makes a single wine, but also by the merchants who treat and blend them. They are sold at about 75p per bottle.

Table wines. Each of the great wineries produces a range of red, rosé and dry, medium dry and sweet white wines. The rosé wines tend to be darker in colour than most rosés made elsewhere, but are dryish and not sweet. The red wines, which are full-bodied, usually with a robust bouquet, are usually better after being allowed to gain a little bottle age, and it should be interesting to see whether it is ever going to be possible to make a long-matured red wine of significance; experiments indicate possibilities. As yet, only KEO's single vineyard Domaine d'Ahera, a wine of definite refinement, is the sort of wine that will arouse the serious speculation of the wine drinker experienced in other good red wines, but others make pleasant drinking with foods of Mediterranean character.

The dry white wines represent a considerable achievement on the part of those who make them in this hot climate. Several of them are very fresh, crisp and clean, enjoyable for everyday drinking and at low prices. Recently a new one, slightly *pétillant*, called Bellapais has been introduced but demand in Cyprus itself still exceeds supply, so that it is not available elsewhere. Prices of the still table wines are about 70p upwards on merchants' lists.

Names: In the U.K., the wines, both table and fortified, may be marketed under the brand name of the shipper or merchant, although some are sold under the same names as those they bear in Cyprus.

The Cypriots themselves consume about twelve bottles per head of the population per annum.

Czechoslovakia

Czechoslovakia produces 7½ million gallons of wine from eighty square miles of vineyards spread throughout the three provinces and in the Carpathian Hills. The majority of wine made is white and for early consumption – there appears to be no movement to restore the vineyards to the relatively greater importance they enjoyed before the Phylloxera disaster in the latter half of the last century. Home needs are augmented by the importation of some 5 million gallons annually.

France

France runs neck and neck with Italy as the biggest wine producer in the world. Together they are responsible for about 48 per cent of world production, with a yield each one of about 1,300 million gallons a year. This impressive figure is produced from $3\frac{1}{4}$ million acres of French vineyards, about 5,000 square miles planted with vines. Only a very small proportion produces wines of a quality generally defined as fine – roughly this means wine that is matured in cask for bottling and further improvement, instead of going into consumption direct from the cask. This *vin de consommation* category, as it is called, or sometimes *vin ordinaire*, is often stored in cask in private houses, or restaurants and cafés, and drawn off into carafes as wanted each day as part of the staple diet of the majority of French families. An average of 180 bottles of wine were drunk in 1960 by the men, women and children of France; adjusted for non-drinkers and young children, this probably means a bottle a day at least for the ordinary French man in the street. It compares with under five bottles per head per annum of the population in Britain. The production of fine wine amounts to about 190 million gallons a year, and of this almost a third, some 60 million gallons, is exported.

French law controls the production and protects the reputation of its fine wines by a series of regulations known as the *Code du Vin* and administered by an independent body known as the Institut National des Appellations d'Origine Contrôlées or I.N.A.O. for short – and generally referred to phonetically as Inao. The regulations cover two groups of wines, each amounting to between 10 and 15 per cent of the total annual production of the country. The superior group known as Vins d'Appellation d'Origine Contrôlée (A.O.C.) consists of the wine-growing areas in which vineyards for one reason or another have over the years evolved traditional or unusual methods of production, or whose soil is capable of producing wine of great quality and individuality provided that certain disciplined traditional methods of production are followed. The laws are comprehensive and control the number of vines that may be planted per acre and the way in which they must be pruned in order to discourage over-production and a consequent sacrifice of quality to quantity. They also control very exactly the kind of vine that may be planted in order to maintain the quality on which the reputation of the area is founded. They prevent as far as possible the name of the area being given to a poor quality wine which may result from a poor vintage year. There are regulations about the minimum degree of alcohol a wine must contain to qualify for the area name, and in some districts there is also a tasting test. In this way the quality and characteristics of the wines from Bordeaux, Burgundy, Champagne, the Loire, the Côtes du Rhône and Alsace are protected by law, as well as those from some less well-known districts such as Jurançon (seldom seen in export markets), Bergerac, Gaillac and Côtes du Jura. In many of these areas there are sub-areas which have their own appellations, particularly in Bordeaux, Burgundy and the Loire. These are indicated in the sections dealing with individual areas in the pages following.

The secondary group of controlled wines consists of areas which have earned a reputation for their general quality whilst not producing wines of such individual characteristics as the A.O.C. The law is designed mainly to protect them against infringement of their area name by growers in other districts who may produce wines of a similar type, and they concentrate on strictly defining the area entitled to a specific name and less stringently, although still effectively, on the method of production. This group is known as Vins Délimités de Qualité Supérieure – referred to as V.D.Q.S. – and vineyards in the group are scattered over the whole wine-growing area of France. It should be noted that the A.O.C. is accorded to a region, such as Bordeaux, to a secondary area within that region, such as Médoc, or to a village within the secondary area, such as Saint-Julien; it is not given to the vineyard itself, the reputation of which can be adequately assured by its proprietor. The proprietor, however, is bound by the regulations applicable to the region if he wishes to use the name of the region on his label.

The wine-producing area of France covers the whole country, except roughly that part north of a line drawn from Nantes on the west coast, through Paris, to the eastern frontier with Luxembourg. The various areas are listed in the pages that follow, either under the group names by which they are best known, or under the Appellation Contrôlée name of their primary areas. Thus there is a Loire group, although the Loire is not an Appellation Contrôlée, but is divided into a number of sub-areas which have an appellation, whilst other well-defined areas, such as Bordeaux, Burgundy and Champagne, which are themselves Appellation Contrôlée names, serve as a logical heading under which to group their numerous A.O.C. sub-areas. Individual sub-areas will be easily found by reference to the index at the end of the book and the text will reveal the groups to which they belong.

ALSACE

The Alsatian vineyards are probably the most picturesque of all French vineyards. They are situated on the slopes of the Vosges hills, which rise from 600 to 1,500 ft, a little distance from the western banks of the Rhine in an area about forty miles long and three miles wide in the two *départements* of France known as the Haut-Rhin and Bas-Rhin. From 1870 to 1914 Alsace was part of Germany, and her vineyards concentrated on the production of cheap white wine, which did not compete with the high-class wines of famous German vineyards on the lower Rhine or on the Moselle. It was not until after their liberation by the victory of the Allies in the 1914–18 war against Germany that the Alsatians were free to resume their efforts to improve the quality of their wines and earn for themselves the reputation which the excellent position and soil of their vineyards made possible. By the time the Hitler war broke out in 1939 the quality of Alsatian wines had improved so much that they were well able to compete with their ancient rivals in all except the very finest categories. Today they are very popular throughout France and have established themselves in many export markets as reasonably priced, well-made, dry white wines of consistent quality, which are capable of improvement in bottle. In 1962 they were promoted to A.O.C. status.

They grow on a limestone and granite soil – perfect for the production of fine white wines. The 30,000 acres of vines are divided up amongst 50,000 peasant proprietors and in a good year can produce as much as 17 million gallons of wine, 75 per cent of which qualifies as A.O.C. The small peasant proprietors who form a large percentage of Alsatian owners seldom press their own grapes; they generally belong to growers' cooperative societies, or sell them to bigger estates or shipper-merchants who have their own press houses.

There are about eighty villages authorized to give their names to wines, but up to the present time only very few of these are ever used and then most sparingly. The general custom is to name Alsatian wines by the grape from which they are made and only very seldom to add to it the name of the village or district. Still rarer is the name of a particular vineyard, although one or two famous names such as Kaefferkopf at Ammerschwihr, Zahnacker at Ribeauvillé, Sporen at Riquewihr, and Mamburg at Sigolsheim are generally added to the name of the grape on the label.

The fact that Alsatian wines are usually made from one only of the various kinds of grape authorized adds both to their charm and to the attraction they have for students of wine. The differences in taste and character due to variation in the soil of different areas are easily discernible. It is possible that the granting of A.O.C. status to the region may bring about some alteration in the traditional method of naming the wines, as local communities, encouraged by their right to an A.O.C. name, develop a pride in the produce of their own vineyards; but for the present all wines of Alsace are known and identified by their grapes only. In a few cases growers or shippers have registered brand names to identify their wines amongst the mass of wines bearing the same grape name on the label, but for the most part they rely upon the name of the firm on the label as sufficient identification.

The authorized grapes are divided into two groups: the *'cépages nobles'*, which make the fine wines for bottling, conservation and export, and *'cépages courants'*, which make carafe wines for local consumption (*cépage* = vine). The *cépages nobles* number six in all; their names are seen on all wine labels except those relying on a brand name alone, generally blended wines of standard quality. They are:

Riesling. Considered the king of Alsace grapes and producing a dry, crisp and aromatic wine of great breeding, which develops very well in bottle. 95p to £1·20.

Gewürztraminer (Savagnin Rosé). A more immediately appealing wine of very distinctive flavour, which is gradually becoming the typical representative of Alsace wines. It is quite different from any other wine and has a strong, musky perfume. It has some aristocratic qualities and great charm; it also develops well in bottle. £1·05 to £1·30.

Traminer (Savagnin Blanc). Very similar to the Gewürztraminer, but on a lesser scale. The above distinctions between Gewürztraminer and Traminer plants are not universally recognized and are not accepted by the majority of Alsatian growers. They are given on the authority of Yves Renouil's *Dictionnaire du Vin*, but are not confirmed by that other authority, P. Galet, in his *Cépages et Vignobles de France*. M. Galet supports the Alsatian growers in maintaining that the Traminer is very similar to the Savagnin Blanc but has completely degenerated in Alsace and that the description Traminer is properly used to designate a lesser-quality Gewürztraminer wine. From the point of view of the drinker this is all that matters. £1 to £1·20.

Muscat resembles in its aromatic flavour the intensity of the Traminer, but has the well-known taste of Muscat grapes. Like all Alsatian wines it is a dry wine. £1·05 to £1·20.

Pinot Blanc and Pinot Gris. The latter, known often as Tokay d'Alsace, has nothing at all in common with the famous Tokays of Hungary. The wines earn their place among the *noble* class, but are less definite in character than the four first-mentioned. They are soft wines, giving a less dry impression than the Riesling. 80p to 90p.

Sylvaner is partially admitted amongst the *cépages nobles* and flourishes particularly in the northern or Bas-Rhin end of the region. It produces a soft, well-constituted wine, dry but of less distinction than the others of its class. 75p to 85p.

The following less specific descriptions are also widely used:

Edelzwicker, literally 'noble mixture', is the name given to wines made from a mixture of the *cépages nobles*.

Zwicker, meaning 'mixture', is a name authorized for a wine of *cépages courants* grapes or containing any *cépages courants*. Blends of both qualities are sold in the U.K., generally under a brand name and without any indication of grapes. 70p to 80p.

Grand Cru or *Grand Vin*. Any wine bearing this description on the label must contain at least 11° of alcohol from the natural sugar of the grapes before the addition of extra sugar at the time of fermentation.

Alsace wines are bottled in the familiar long-necked, sloping-shouldered bottles used for German wines. The wines resemble the German hocks in character and flavour. The Riesling grape is common to both districts and in each makes wines unblended with other grapes – the Traminer and Sylvaner are also widely used in Germany. There is some difference in the way the wines are made and in general the Alsace wines are lighter and drier than similar-priced hocks. They do not compete with the finest wines of Germany, although some growers are increasing the production of very fine quality wines which sell at £1·25 to £1·75 a bottle and are particularly appreciated in Paris.

ARMAGNAC

Armagnac lies in the ancient province of Gascony, about half-way between Bordeaux and the Spanish frontier. It is a small area of about 75,000 acres of vines, grown with a view to producing a wine that can be distilled. The wine itself is of poor quality, but the spirit that it produces under the A.O.C. Armagnac is comparable to Cognac. The grapes authorized in its production are several in number and very much the same as those authorized in Charente for Cognac. The chief variety used is the Picpoul, a local name for the Folle Blanche, the main grape in Cognac. Control of production, including methods of distillation, is strict, complicated and highly technical and a strict examination of all spirit sold does much to assure a high standard of quality. No spirit sold for consumption is allowed to leave the district at a strength less than 40 per cent of alcohol, that is to say 70° proof in British measurement (80° American), the same strength as a bottle of whisky. Like all spirit, Armagnac is matured in cask and not in bottle. It is, however, seldom, if ever, shipped by British merchants for maturing in bond and is for the most part imported fully matured in bottle. Like all spirits, Armagnac is colourless when distilled and gets its colour, as well as a particular characteristic flavour, from the cask of local oak in which it matures for several years. The United Kingdom is, however, one of the smallest export markets for Armagnac, which might be said to have a rarity status with us. It costs about £4 a bottle, about the same price as Three Star quality Cognacs.

BORDEAUX

Bordeaux has sent wines to Britain regularly since the twelfth century, when Gascony, the south-western province of France, belonged to the English. English merchants sent their ships to buy and bring back the local wines and became the first shippers – a description still applied to Bordeaux firms who are responsible for shipping wines to Britain, even though they no longer own ships.

Bordeaux has always been one of France's greatest ports and as such in the Middle Ages was the centre of an export trade which included Britain. Its wines have always been renowned for their lightness and delicacy in comparison with the heavier and cheaper wines from the South of France, which used to pass through the port and of which stocks were held for local consumption by tavern-keepers. Because of their lighter colour the Gascons called them 'clairet' wines and they became known in England as 'claret', as they are today. Because of special laws favouring the exporters of local wines to their countrymen in England, the wines of Bordeaux got a three-hundred-year start over wines from the rest of France and established a popularity for themselves in this country which they have never lost. The city today has about 260,000 inhabitants and is the centre of the *département* of the Gironde, about 5,000 square miles in area and containing 500 square miles of planted vineyards. The River Garonne, flowing from the Pyrenees, runs through the city and fifteen miles to the north joins the River Dordogne, flowing from the Massif Central, to form the River Gironde, with its estuary in the Bay of Biscay. Most of the vineyards producing fine wines are along the banks of these rivers.

In an average year about 88 million gallons of wine are produced, sometimes rising, as in 1962, to 110 million gallons or about 10 per cent of all the wines of France. It is not this large amount of wine for which Bordeaux is famous, but for the fact that it is responsible for between 33 per cent and 40 per cent of all the A.O.C. wines of France. On an average, over two-thirds of all the wine made in Bordeaux is of good enough quality to earn the status of an A.O.C. The proportion between red and white production varies quite widely; on average it is about equal, with a tendency in favour of white wine.

With the rapid growth in the popularity of red wines this is likely to
change in the next decade, as vineyards in those areas which are able
to produce both red or white satisfactorily are gradually replanted.
Individual holdings are substantial in size compared with other
French vineyards; the great clarets and medium-priced château wines
come from estates averaging probably 25 acres of vines and producing
200 casks of wine a year. The bigger estates may be twice this size;
anything large is exceptional. Statistics for 1960 show the average
holding, including small peasant holdings and large estates, to be 6
acres per proprietor.

There are something of the order of 2,000 individual and substantial properties making wine worth keeping in bottle – what the
French call '*vin de garde*' – amongst the red wines of Bordeaux alone.
They all merit attention, but very few of them are known by name
in Great Britain or the United States. See later reference to bourgeois
wines.

Classed Growths

The sixty-two best red wines were classified in 1855 by an official
committee into five 'growths' or '*crus*', known collectively as the
Classed Growths, or *Crus Classés*.

Premiers Crus

Ch. Lafite	Pauillac
Ch. Margaux	Margaux
Ch. Latour	Pauillac
Ch. Haut Brion	Pessac (Graves)

Deuxièmes Crus

Ch. Mouton-Rothschild	Pauillac
Ch. Rausan-Ségla	Margaux
Ch. Rauzan-Gassies	Margaux
Ch. Léoville-Lascases	Saint-Julien
Ch. Léoville-Poyferré	Saint-Julien
Ch. Léoville-Barton	Saint-Julien
Ch. Durfort-Vivens	Margaux
Ch. Lascombes	Margaux
Ch. Gruaud-Larose	Saint-Julien

Deuxiemes Crus (continued)

Ch. Brane-Cantenac	Cantenac
Ch. Pichon-Longueville	Pauillac
Ch. Pichon-Longueville-Lalande	Pauillac
Ch. Ducru-Beaucaillou	Saint-Julien
Ch. Cos d'Estournel	Saint-Estèphe
Ch. Montrose	Saint-Estèphe

Troisièmes Crus

Ch. Kirwan	Cantenac
Ch. Issan	Cantenac
Ch. Lagrange	Saint-Julien
Ch. Langoa	Saint-Julien
Ch. Giscours	Labarde
Ch. Malescot-Saint-Exupéry	Margaux
Ch. Cantenac-Brown	Cantenac
Ch. Palmer	Cantenac
Ch. Grand la Lagune	Ludon
Ch. Desmirail	Margaux
Ch. Calon-Ségur	Saint-Estèphe
Ch. Ferrière	Margaux
Ch. Marquis d'Alesme-Becker	Margaux
Ch. Boyd-Cantenac	Margaux

Quatrièmes Crus

Ch. Saint-Pierre-Sevaistre	Saint-Julien
Ch. Saint-Pierre-Bontemps	Saint-Julien
Ch. Branaire-Ducru	Saint-Julien
Ch. Talbot	Saint-Julien
Ch. Duhart-Milon	Pauillac
Ch. Poujet	Cantenac
Ch. La Tour-Carnet	Saint-Laurent
Ch. Rochet	Saint-Estèphe
Ch. Beychevelle	Saint-Julien
Ch. Le Prieuré	Cantenac
Ch. Marquis de Terme	Margaux

Cinquièmes Crus

Ch. Pontet-Canet	Pauillac
Ch. Batailley	Pauillac
Ch. Haut-Batailley	Pauillac
Ch. Grand-Puy-Lacoste	Pauillac
Ch. Grand-Puy-Ducasse	Pauillac

Ch. Lynch-Bages	Pauillac
Ch. Lynch-Moussas	Pauillac
Ch. Dauzac	Labarde
Ch. Mouton-d'Armailhacq (now Baron Philippe)	Pauillac
Ch. Le Tertre	Arsac
Ch. Haut-Bages-Libéral	Pauillac
Ch. Pédesclaux	Pauillac
Ch. Belgrave	Saint-Laurent
Ch. Camensac	Saint-Laurent
Ch. Cos-Labory	Saint-Estèphe
Ch. Clerc-Milon	Pauillac
Ch. Croizet-Bages	Pauillac
Ch. Cantemerle	Macau

Their names are world-famous and the demand for them widespread. They attract the wine-lovers of England, Holland, Belgium, Germany, Scandinavia, U.S.A. and Switzerland, apart from the biggest demand of all in France itself. Their authenticity is guaranteed in the majority of cases by château-bottling and in good years they represent a safe and remunerative investment for capital. For this reason and because their fame and quality earn for them a demand amongst the rich and prestige-conscious, the prices of the first classed growths are very high in comparison with those of the second, third, fourth and fifth. Prices of first-growth clarets of good vintages go as high as £3 to £4·50 per bottle, while even less good vintages fetch £2·50. The best of lesser growths can be bought for £1·25 and are often far superior in quality to lesser vintages of first growths at 50 per cent higher prices.

The classed growths cover a large price area, from £1·35 per bottle upwards. At the lower level they overlap with the best of the 'bourgeois' growths, which is the 2,000-strong group outside the classed growths.

Bourgeois Growths

It is this bourgeois group which forms the backbone of the claret output and draws to itself the attention of all claret lovers. The names of the châteaux are often unknown, but their labels inform buyers of their vintage and the district from which they come. Since they are all wines of the A.O.C. class and improve greatly in bottle, and since they vary in price from 80p to £1·50 a bottle, they offer an interesting field of exploration for rich and poor alike. A guide is easily found amongst the wine merchants of this country. Below the bourgeois wines in price and quality the district wines, entitled to the A.O.C. of their district, supply a large variety of everyday wines that can be drunk young. They come from the Médoc – in which are included well-known villages like Saint-Julien, Margaux, Saint-Estèphe – from Saint-Émilion, Côtes de Fronsac, Pomerol and Bourg, and may be either blends or vintage wines. Their qualities will depend on the wine merchant and shipper who have selected them. The name of one or both of these should be on the label. They cost 75p to £1 per bottle.

White Wines

The finest white wines of Bordeaux – those from the Sauternes area – are made from grapes that have been attacked by a fungus known as *Botrytis cinerea* and referred to as the '*pourriture noble*', or 'noble decay'. The fungus has the property of converting part of the sugar into a less fermentable form of glycerine and is responsible for the unctuous flavour of Sauternes. Its appearance in the vineyard is haphazard, but it occurs in varying degrees in all but bad years.

The white wines are classified in very much the same way as the red wines. The 1855 Classification selected twenty-two wines from Barsac and Sauternes and grouped them into two classes of growths:

Grand Premier Cru		
Ch. Yquem		Sauternes
Premiers Crus		
Ch. La Tour-Blanche		Bommes
Ch. Peyraguey	Clos Haut-Peyraguey	Bommes
	Lafaurie-Peyraguey	Bommes
Ch. Rayne-Vigneau		Bommes
Ch. de Suduiraut		Preignac
Ch. Coutet		Barsac
Ch. Climens		Barsac
Ch. Guiraud		Sauternes
Ch. Rieussec		Fargues
Ch. Rabaud	Rabaud-Promis	Bommes
	Sigalas-Rabaud	Bommes

Deuxièmes Crus

Ch. de Myrat		Barsac
Ch. Doisy	Doisy-Dubroca	Barsac
	Doisy-Daëne	Barsac
	Doisy-Védrines	Barsac
Ch. Peixotto		Bommes
Ch. d'Arche (and d'Arche-Lafaurie)		Sauternes
Ch. Filhot		Sauternes
Ch. Broustet		Barsac
Ch. Nairac		Barsac
Ch. Caillou		Barsac
Ch. Suau		Barsac
Ch. de Malle		Preignac
Ch. Raymond-Lafon		Fargues
Ch. Lamothe	Lamothe-Bergey	Sauternes
	Lamothe-Espagnet	Sauternes

Some of the original properties have since been split among two or more owners as indicated.

Château Yquem – labelled Château d'Yquem – is in a class by itself as incomparably the finest wine amongst the white wines of Bordeaux. It sells at £3 to £3·50 per bottle, compared to £1·25 to £1·75 per bottle for other classed-growth Sauternes. It will be seen from the table that the description Sauternes is given to the whole primary area in which the village of Sauternes is situated. It is the A.O.C. for the whole area. Within the area there are, as always, a number of villages. One of these, the village of Barsac, produces a wine of so distinctive a character that it has been accorded an A.O.C. of its own. A wine from Barsac is therefore also a Sauternes known under its distinctive name.

Most of the white Bordeaux wine sold in the U.K. and for export in general is known under the name of its primary area: Graves, Sauternes, Entre-Deux-Mers; or its village: Barsac, Loupiac, Sainte-Croix-du-Mont, and few single vineyard wines outside the classed growths are ever seen. The reason probably is that white wines are generally drunk young and seldom get the chance to develop their full qualities in bottle. This is a pity, because there are very many fine white wines grown in the Graves and Premières Côtes areas which can be sold at 70p to 90p per bottle and compare very favourably in quality with wines at £1 and more from other countries, or from other parts of France. In 1959 eight wines were classified amongst the white wines of Graves. They are known as '*Crus Classés de Graves*':

Ch. Bouscaut	Cadaujac
Ch. la Tour Martillac	Martillac
Ch. Laville-Haut Brion	Talence
Ch. Couhins	Villenave-d'Ornon
Ch. Carbonnieux	Léognan
Ch. Olivier	Léognan
Domaine de Chevalier	Léognan
Ch. Malartic-la-Gravière	Léognan

Nomenclature

Bordeaux wines, both red and white, vary infinitely in character. Without doubt this is mostly due to the differences in the soil in different districts. It is logical therefore that they should be known by the district from which they come. A wine from the Médoc may be expected to have a different character from the wine of Saint-Émilion. Within the Saint-Émilion area there are no sub-areas of distinctive character, but within the 240 square miles of the Médoc, largely planted in vines, there are several sub-areas in which the soil is different. These areas enjoy their own A.O.C. – usually that of the village itself, such as Saint-Julien – and being a limited area it is therefore a more valuable name than Médoc. Within each sub-area are the individual vineyards – Château Beychevelle and Château Langoa Barton, and many others in the Saint-Julien sub-area. These single vineyards again make wines quite distinctive from each other, although all within the same sub-area. The reason may again be slight or considerable differences in soil over a small part of the vineyard, but they are also due to the grapes used. There are six varieties of grape authorized by I.N.A.O. for red Bordeaux wines, of which four are currently used: Cabernet Franc, Cabernet Sauvignon, Merlot and Petit Verdot; the Malbec and Carmenère are falling out of use. The vineyard proprietor has a degree of latitude in deciding the proportion of each of these grapes he wishes to use, but the I.N.A.O. control this also, and will not allow the proportion of Merlot and Petit Verdot to become too high. The variation of the proportion of the different,

PRICES AND TYPES OF BORDEAUX WINES

Price	Red	Dry White	Medium White	Sweet White
65p to 75½p	District wines from Primary and most Secondary Areas. Also Rosé		Graves Entre-Deux-Mers	Loupiac
80p to £1	Lesser bourgeois vintages	Graves Supérieur	Graves Supérieur	Sauternes Barsac Sainte-Croix-du-Mont
£1·05 to £1·50	Finer bourgeois of good vintages	Fine château Graves	Fine château Graves	Château-bottled Sauternes
£1·75 to £2·50	Classed growths of good vintages	Fine old bottled Graves and Sauternes, château-bottled, and London-bottled		
Up to £4·50	First-growth clarets, château-bottled of best vintages			Château Yquem

grapes is another reason why the wines of one vineyard can be different from its neighbour. The château name of a wine is therefore also important, even though, as already mentioned, it is not protected by A.O.C. laws. For these reasons Bordeaux wines are known by the place from which they come and not, as in Alsace, by the grape from which they are made, or, as in Champagne, by the name of the shipper who has selected them. The system is exactly the same for white wines and red wines. The authorized grapes for white wines are the Sauvignon, Sémillon and Muscadelle.

The Primary Area A.O.C. for Bordeaux wines is Bordeaux or Bordeaux Supérieur, according to the degree of alcohol. It covers both red and white wines grown within the Bordeaux A.O.C. area.

The Secondary Areas (all of course situated within the Primary Area) for *red* wines are mainly: Médoc, Haut Médoc, Saint-Émilion, Pomerol, Côtes de Fronsac, Bourg, Blaye, Graves, Lussac-Saint-Émilion, Montagne-Saint-Émilion, Parsac-Saint-Émilion, Puisseguin-Saint-Émilion, Saint-Georges-Saint-Émilion and Sables-Saint-Émilion, Bordeaux Côtes de Castillon, Lalande de Pomerol.

The Secondary Areas for *white* wines are: Graves, Sauternes, Entre-Deux-Mers, Premières Côtes de Bordeaux, Sainte-Croix-du-Mont, Loupiac, Saint-Foy Bordeaux, Graves de Vayres, Côtes de Bordeaux, Saint-Macaire.

Villages with independent A.O.C. situated within the above Secondary Areas:
In Haut Médoc: Saint-Estèphe, Pauillac, Saint-Julien, Margaux, Moulis, Listrac.
In Graves: Cérons.
In Sauternes: Barsac.

Saint-Émilion is a large area containing some ten square miles of vines. There are no superior sub-areas within its boundaries, the hyphenated Saint-Émilion districts listed above being outside the Saint-Émilion area and of a lesser standing. In 1954 the best vineyards of Saint-Émilion were classified by the I.N.A.O. and divided into two groups. This classification, unlike the Médoc 1855, has the authority of an A.O.C.

SAINT-ÉMILION

Premier Grand Cru Classé

Ch. Ausone
Ch. Cheval Blanc
Ch. Canon
Ch. la Gaffelière-Naudes
Ch. Pavie
Clos Fourtet

Ch. Beauséjour
Ch. Belair
Ch. Figeac
Ch. Magdelaine
Ch. Trottevieille

Grand Cru Classé

Ch. l'Arrosée
Ch. Balestard-la-Tonnelle
Ch. Bergat
Ch. Cadet-Bon
Ch. Cap-de-Mourlin
Ch. Chauvin
Ch. Coutet
Ch. Curé-Bon
Ch. Fonroque
Ch. Grand Barrail
Ch. Grand-Corbin-Pécresse
Ch. Grand-Pontet
Ch. Guadet-Saint-Julien
Ch. la Carte
Ch. la Clusière
Ch. la Dominique
Ch. Lamarzelle
Ch. Larmande
Ch. Lasserre
Ch. La Tour-Figeac
Ch. le Couvent
Ch. Mauvezin
Ch. Pavie-Décesse
Ch. Pavillon-Cadet
Ch. Faurie de Soutard
Ch. Sansonnet
Ch. Soutard
Ch. Trimoulet
Ch. Troplong-Mondot
Ch. Yon Figeac
Clos la Madeleine

Ch. l'Angélus
Ch. Bellevue
Ch. Cadet-Piola
Ch. Canon-la-Gaffelière
Ch. Chapelle-Madeleine
Ch. Corbin
Ch. Croque-Michotte
Ch. Fonplégade
Ch. Franc-Mayne
Ch. Grand-Corbin-Despagne
Ch. Grand-Mayne
Ch. Grandes-Murailles
Ch. Jean-Faure
Ch. la Clotte
Ch. la Couspaude
Ch. Larcis-Ducasse
Ch. Lamarzelle-Figeac
Ch. Laroze
Ch. La Tour-de-Pin-Figeac
Ch. le Châtelet
Ch. le Prieuré
Ch. Moulin du Cadet
Ch. Pavie-Macquin
Ch. Petit-Faurie de Souchard
Ch. Ripeau
Ch. Saint-Georges-Côte-Pavie
Ch. Tertre-Daugay
Ch. Trois-Moulins
Ch. Villemaurine
Clos des Jacobins
Clos Saint-Martin

Vin Rosé is also made in Bordeaux with an A.O.C. Bordeaux Rosé or Bordeaux Clairet.

Vintages

The character and state of readiness of recent vintages are given on p. 271. The quality of the last forty-five vintages is given here.

Poor: 1927, 1930, 1931, 1932, 1935, 1936, 1939, 1941, 1963, 1965, 1968.

Moderate: 1925, 1933, 1938, 1940, 1942, 1944, 1946, 1951, 1954, 1956, 1958, 1960, 1969.

Good: 1926, 1928, 1934, 1937, 1943, 1948, 1950, 1952, 1955, 1957, 1964, 1967.

Very good: 1929, 1945, 1947, 1949, 1953, 1959, 1961, 1962, 1966.

BURGUNDY

The vineyards of Burgundy were cultivated by the Romans; their origin is unknown, but they are said to have existed in 600 B.C. The area known as Burgundy today stretches some 120 miles from Chablis in the north to Villefranche-sur-Saône in the south; the bulk of the vineyards are concentrated in the middle part known as the Côte d'Or and at the southern end where the wines of Mâcon and Beaujolais are grown. Altogether the area covered by vines amounts to about 200 square miles. They produce on an average 20 million gallons of wine per annum. but the quantity varies greatly from year to year. By far the largest production is from the Beaujolais area, where red wines form 99 per cent of the crop. The overall proportion for red and white in the whole Burgundy area is on an average about five of red to one of white.

The properties are much smaller than in Bordeaux. The average in the best area – that of the Côte d'Or – works out at $1\frac{1}{2}$ acres per proprietor. There are very few big estates and the majority of the vineyards belong to peasant proprietors who look after their vineyards themselves with the help of family and friends at vintage time. There are few château names in Burgundy, or names of individual properties. Those that do exist are generally entitled 'Clos' or 'Domaine'. Some of the most famous vineyards are divided amongst many different proprietors, each of whom makes his own wine and produces a quality different from his neighbours. Clos de Vougeot has around sixty different owners, each producing part of the total of some 20,000 gallons. At the other end of the scale are vineyards like Romanée Saint Vivant with several owners to share the 700 or 800 gallons that it produces. There are several hundred vineyards producing so little wine that their names seldom become known. They are generally sold under the name of their village, with the addition of the words '*premier cru*', which are officially recognized as part of their A.O.C. Because of this division of famous vineyards amongst several proprietors there is no longer one owner who is responsible for the reputation of his wine, as there is in Bordeaux. The State has stepped in to protect the quality of wines that are rightly considered to be part of the glory of France and the A.O.C. laws are extended to include the most renowned of individual Burgundy vineyards.

Part of the confusion that exists about Burgundy names stems from this multiplicity of fine wines from one vineyard bearing the same name but varying in quality. Clos de Vougeot is an example. Further confusion arises from the habit of not naming very small vineyards individually, but using instead the words '*premier cru*'. It is highly probable that a dozen wines labelled Gevrey-Chambertin *premier cru*, offered by twelve different wine merchants, come in fact from twelve different vineyards and consequently vary considerably in quality and character. Even this is not the end of the confusion caused by Burgundy names, because it has become the custom, blessed by the A.O.C. laws, to add to the name of the village the name of the most famous vineyard within its boundaries. Thus the village of Aloxe has become Aloxe-Corton, Chambolle becomes Chambolle-Musigny, Vosne is Vosne-Romanée, Nuits is Nuits-Saint-Georges and Gevrey is Gevrey-Chambertin. Chambertin, which is a vineyard, and the best in the district, is therefore a better wine than Gevrey-Chambertin, which is a village. In the same way, Corton is better than Aloxe-Corton, Musigny than Chambolle-Musigny, etc. The student who hopes to clarify the situation by remembering that a hyphenated name in Burgundy is never as good as a simple name is making progress in the right direction, but must confine his definition to hyphenated *village* names. It is not too difficult to memorize the village names, as will be seen from the table following. He must do this because there are fine vineyards, ranking just below the supreme Chambertin, which have the right, again authenticated by an A.O.C., to add the name Chambertin to their own, Ruchottes-Chambertin,

Mazis-Chambertin and three more tabulated below are, at least theoretically, less fine than Chambertin, but they are far better than Gevrey-Chambertin because both hyphenated names are the names of vineyards and neither of them a village name. Possibly the best way to master this complication is to learn the village names and so discover vineyard names by a process of elimination. This particular complication is limited, since it only arises with Chambertin and Romanée in red wines, and Corton and Montrachet in white wines. Unfortunately the position is in fact reversed at Corton, where the white Corton-Charlemagne ranks above the white Corton. As Corton is, however, mainly a red wine and makes only about 140 gallons of white, the deviation from the principle is not of much consequence.

Vines

Red wines must be made from the Pinot grape in the finer districts, or the Gamay in Beaujolais. The two may be mixed at the cost of abandoning the description 'Bourgogne Rouge' and substituting for it 'Bourgogne Passe-Tout-Grains'. In the fine white wine areas the grape is the Chardonnay and Pinot Blanc, two very similar varieties, and in the cheaper areas the Aligoté. If the Aligoté grape is used, the fact is indicated in the name. It is a less fine grape than the Pinot Chardonnay and wines made from it are unlikely to develop much in bottle.

Names

In the following table the Primary Areas are given and also the Secondary Areas in the few places in which they exist. All village names are given which are in general use on wine labels and all individual vineyards which have the protection of an A.O.C. It will be remembered that there are a great many fine vineyards that have not applied for A.O.C. protection but are identified only by the addition of the words '*premier cru*' to the village name. Only the best known of these are listed here.

PRIMARY AREAS

Chablis, producing about 400,000 gallons of white wine A.O.C.

Côte d'Or, producing about 3,300,000 gallons of red and white wine with a 90 per cent preponderance of red.

Côte Chalonnais, producing about 250,000 gallons of which a quarter is white.

Côte Mâconnais, producing about 3,750,000 gallons, with a slight preponderance of white.

The Beaujolais, producing about 14,000,000 gallons of red wine, with only an insignificant production of white.

SECONDARY AREAS

In Chablis: Chablis, Petit-Chablis.

In Côte d'Or: Côte de Nuits, Côte de Beaune.

VILLAGES

In the Côte de Nuits: Gevrey-Chambertin, Morey Saint Denis, Vougeot, Flagey-Echézeaux, Nuits Saint Georges, Fixin, Chambolle-Musigny, Vosne-Romanée.

In the Côte de Beaune: Aloxe-Corton, Savigny, Beaune, Volnay, Auxey-Duresses, Blagny, Puligny-Montrachet, Santenay, Pernand-Vergelesses, Chorey-les-Beaune, Pommard, Monthélie, Meursault, Saint-Aubin, Chassagne-Montrachet, Dezize-les-Maranges.

In the Chalonnais: Mercurey, Givry, Rully, Montagny.

In the Côte Mâconnais: Pouilly-Fuissé, Pouilly-Vinzelles, Pouilly-Loché.

In the Beaujolais: Saint Amour, Juliénas, Morgon, Chénas, Fleurie, Brouilly, Moulin-à-Vent, Chiroubles.

VINEYARDS

At Fixin: Clos de la Perrière.

At Gevrey-Chambertin: Chambertin, Chambertin Clos de Bèze (ranks equally with Chambertin), Ruchottes-Chambertin, Chapelle-Chambertin, Mazoyères-Chambertin, Griotte-Chambertin, Mazis-Chambertin, Latricière-Chambertin, Charmes-Chambertin, Clos Saint Jacques, Véroilles, Fouchère, Éstournelles, Cazetiers.

At Morey Saint Denis: Clos Saint Denis, Bonnes Mares (part), Clos de Tart, Clos de la Roche, Clos des Lambrays.

At Chambolle-Musigny: Le Musigny, Bonnes Mares (part).

At Vougeot: Clos de Vougeot.

At Flagey-Echézeaux: Les Grands-Echézeaux, Les Echézeaux du Dessus.

At Vosne-Romanée: La Romanée, Romanée-Conti, Les Richebourg, La Tâche, Les Verroilles.

At Nuits Saint Georges: Les Saint-Georges, Les Boudots, Les Cailles, Les Cras, Les Murgers, Les Porrets, Les Pruliers, Les Thorey, Les Vaucrains.

At Aloxe-Corton: Le Corton, Le Clos du Roi, Les Renardes, Les Chaumes, Le Charlemagne.

At Pernand-Vergelesses: Ile-des-Vergelesses.

At Savigny: Les Vergelesses, Les Marconnets, Les Jarrons.

At Beaune: Les Fèves, Les Grèves, Les Cras, Les Champimonts, Les
  Marconnets, Les Bressandes, Clos de la Mousse, Clos des Mouches.
At Pommard: Les Épenots, Les Rugiens-Bas, Le Clos Blanc.
At Volnay: Les Caillerets, Les Champans, Les Fremiets, Les Angles.
At Meursault: Les Santenots-du-Milieu (red), Les Perrières (white).
At Puligny-Montrachet: Le Montrachet (part).
At Chassagne-Montrachet: Le Montrachet (part).
At Santenay: Les Gravières.

The above listed vineyards are all *têtes de cuvées*, that is the highest
class in their village area. There exists no coordinated classification
and since the wines of some villages are better than others, it must
not be assumed that the *têtes de cuvées* of different villages are equal
in quality. Many names of the next category – the *premier cru* or
cuvée, which are too numerous to list here – may be well known to
readers and may be better than some of the *têtes de cuvées* listed.

There is in Burgundy no official classification as there is, for example, in Bordeaux. There is, however, one isolated group of wine
greatly sought after because of its quality. These are the wines of the
Hospices de Beaune, a hospital and home for old people, whose fine
buildings dominate the town of Beaune. The Hospices wines are the
products of vineyards which have been bequeathed to the charity

PRICES AND TYPES

Prices	Red	White (all dry)
75p to 90p	Mâcon Beaujolais	Mâcon. Also Rosé Wines
90p to £1·10	Village wines from Beaujolais	Pouilly-Fuissé Petit-Chablis
£1·10 to £1·30	Younger vintages from Côte d'Or villages of good quality	Chablis. Fine quality white wines from Meursault and Chassagne
£1·30 to £1·50	Matured Côte d'Or village wines and single vineyard wines of good vintages	Chablis *1er cru*. Single vineyard wines from Meursault and Chas- sagne
£1·30		Sparkling wines
£1·50 to £3	Old vintages of best growths of Côte d'Or	

during the centuries which have passed since its foundation in the middle of the fifteenth century by Nicholas Rolin and his wife Guigonne de Salins. Nowadays they are sold by public auction in the Market Hall of Beaune on the third Sunday in November, after the vintage, to anyone who cares to bid. It is a picturesque and festive occasion conducted according to ancient traditions and enlivened by banquets and wine-tastings during the week-end. The vineyards belonging to the Hospices are amongst the finest in the region and wines bearing their label are always worth tasting even though their prices may sometimes be exaggerated.

True Burgundy, the Burgundy of France, has very little in common with so-called Commonwealth Burgundies which have borrowed its name. The latter, often excellent in themselves, are heavier, darker, richer wines and are justly popular. They are sold at much lower prices then genuine French Burgundy. They are probably partly responsible for the widespread belief that Burgundy is a 'big' wine. Wines like the Mâcons and Beaujolais are often lighter in alcohol than claret and are excellent 'quaffing' wines, often treated with far less respect by their supporters than are the wines of the Côte d'Or by their local population. These are often a degree stronger in alcohol than many clarets, but since the habit of producing wines that will mature quickly has taken hold, they are no darker in colour or stronger in substance than the wines of Bordeaux. They owe their high reputation to their quality of flavour and not to their weight. The difficulty in classifying a group of wines, many of which bear the same name whilst varying widely in quality, make it difficult for the student to get a clear picture of the wines of the district. Burgundy is capable of the same improvement in bottle as claret and it can often attain the same degree of finesse of flavour and bouquet. The student has a right to set his standards high. It will cost more to make the acquaintance of good Burgundy, because there is so little of it made, but under the guidance of a competent wine merchant the effort and expense will prove rewarding.

Vintages

The character and quality of recent vintages is given on p. 271. The following is a classification of the last forty-five years, irrespective of whether they are available for drinking now.

Very good: 1926, 1928, 1929, 1945, 1947, 1949, 1953, 1959, 1961, 1964, 1966.

Good: 1934, 1937, 1948, 1952, 1955, 1957, 1962, 1967.

Medium: 1942, 1943, 1946, 1950, 1969.

CHAMPAGNE

The Champagne vineyards are the most northerly of France. They lie east and north-east of Paris and cover an area of some 27,000 acres, or 40 square miles, mostly in the *département* of Marne. The making of Champagne is a highly skilled art, more complicated by far than the making of still wine. There are various ways of making a sparkling wine, but the *Méthode Champenoise* is more costly and takes longer than the others. It is protected by the A.O.C. laws. That is to say that all Champagne must be made by the *Méthode Champenoise*. The main difference between this and other methods is that the sparkle must derive from the gas generated by natural fermentation and that this fermentation must take place in bottle. This involves a long process, first for the fermentation to complete itself in a cold cellar, and secondly for the deposit which the process forms to collect in the neck of the bottle so that it can be removed before the wine is dispatched.

To begin with the wine is made in the same way as any other white wine is made, with the unusual difference that it is made from both black and white grapes: the Pinot Noir – the grape that makes red Burgundy – and the Pinot Blanc or Chardonnay, which makes white Burgundy. To make an untinted white wine from black grapes is in itself a delicate operation, which involves the careful elimination of any unsound grapes from the presses and great care in the pressing itself. Nearly all Champagne is made from a blend of black and white grapes, but a small quantity is made each year from white grapes only. The resulting wine is lighter and finer in texture than the wine from blended grapes and is preferred by some connoisseurs in spite of its higher price. It is described on the label as 'Blanc de Blancs'. Within five or six months of the vintage the wine, until then in cask, is blended by the shipper with other wines of the same vintage from various districts within the Champagne area. Sometimes a still Champagne from the year before, specially kept in cask for the purpose, is blended in at the same time in order to enable the shipper to maintain the particular character of his wine. At the same time a solution of pure cane sugar dissolved in the wine of the year is added to the cask with ferments and clearing solution or 'finings'. The strength of the sugar solution, which is destined to ferment entirely into alcohol and carbonic acid gas and *not* to sweeten the wine, depends on the amount of sparkle that is required. It is in most cases a standardized amount. Immediately this solution has been added, that is to say about six months after the vintage, the wine is bottled, and the whole of the development of the wine takes place in bottle. It takes some months for the whole of the added sugar to be transformed into alcohol and CO_2 gas and during that period the bottles are stacked horizontally in great piles across the floor of the cellar, often to some 10 ft in height. Cellars, which are generally dug out of the limestone rock, vary in size, but the floors are often 16 ft or so in width and in some cases can total a length of 10 miles. The stacks of bottles having been left undisturbed for one or two years are then transferred to wooden frames in which each bottle lies in a cage of its own, with the cork pointing downwards, at a slight angle, to enable the deposit which the fermentation has left on the side of the bottle to start sliding down towards the cork. Every two or three days the bottle is given a slight twist and the angle of the slant is increased. After about six months the bottle is almost standing on its head and the deposit is lying on the cork. Thereafter the bottle is left upside down in a vertical position until the time comes for disgorging and liqueuring. This takes place as soon as convenient after the deposit has settled. It entails two operations. One, to remove cork and deposit together from the bottle, the other to replace the small amount of wine lost by the *liqueur d'expédition*, or dosage, which determines the sweetness of the final wine. Different markets demand different degrees of sweetness and so at the time of the disgorging, or removal of deposit, the shipper likes to know the probable ultimate destination of the wine in order to be able to give the right amount of dosage and to avoid having to repeat the lengthy and expensive operation of uncorking and re-corking a second time. The *liqueur d'expédition* is therefore often added two or three years before the wine is sold or shipped. It consists of pure cane sugar dissolved in old Champagne and stabilized, to prevent it from fermenting, by the addition of high-class grape brandy. For the best Champagne, young spirit from the best district of Cognac is used.

The operation of disgorging is a highly delicate one and fascinating to watch. There are different methods possible, but the most usual is to retain the bottle in its inverted position, remove the temporary wire which has been holding the cork into position, allow the gas in the wine to blow out cork and deposit, quickly restore the bottle to an upright position, add the right amount of 'dosage' (*liqueur d'expédition*), recork with a permanent cork and lay the bottle back in a horizontal pile of its fellows to mature for a year or two. The whole operation is carried out at as cold a temperature as possible, so as to avoid an excessive loss of wine owing to an over-activated sparkle at the moment when the cork is withdrawn. Some shippers, in fact, freeze the neck of the bottle whilst it is stored in the upside down position. When the wine in the neck is turned to ice, the deposit on the cork is automatically trapped and the bottle can be returned at leisure to its upright position and the whole disgorging operation carried on from there. The degree of sweetness of a Champagne is indicated on the label, according to a formula respected by the whole trade. The words 'Brut' or 'Extra Dry' or 'Extra Sec' represent the driest of all – a dosage of 1 per cent or 2 per cent of liqueur: 'Sec' or 'Dry' is slightly sweeter, 'Demi-Sec' begins to taste distinctly sweet, 'Demi-Doux' leaves no doubt that it is a sweet wine, and finally 'Doux' caters for a special taste that likes anything from 12 per cent to 20 per cent of liqueur added to the wine. 'Goût Américain' depends on individual shippers' estimates of this elusive quality.

In addition to the shippers, all of whom carry out this highly skilled manipulative part of the production of Champagne as well as the pressing of the grapes in their own cellars, there are a small number of growers who do the same thing and market their wines either direct to wholesalers under a brand name, or to shipping houses that need emergency stocks. Since shippers generally own some vineyards themselves as well as buying grapes from others, the difference between these two groups of Champagne producers is fundamentally one of capital resources. Some shippers hold stocks of several million bottles in order to be able to supply their market with matured wines; the cellars in which they lie are enormous and costly and the staff employed for the production of each vintage and its subsequent expert treatment is highly skilled and much in demand.

Champagne is sold either as a vintage wine or non-vintage. The conditions under which a wine is entitled to a vintage are laid down and strictly controlled by I.N.A.O. Provided that these regulations are followed, a shipper may sell any wine which he considers good enough to represent his house as a vintage. In general, there is a high degree of unanimity amongst shippers in their estimates of wines good enough to be sold as of vintage quality. Whereas the character of vintage wines must of necessity vary from year to year, the non-vintage wines are generally blended by each shipper to maintain a particular type and character which becomes associated with his house. Their price is considerably lower than the price of vintage wines.

The calcareous, chalky soil of Champagne is the main reason for the unique quality of its wines. Very little still Champagne is made, but a small quantity of both red and white is produced. It has not the right to the appellation 'Champagne', but must be described as 'Vin Nature de la Champagne' – the feminine 'La' indicating the district, whilst the wine itself is masculine – in the same way that La Bourgogne is the Burgundy country and Le Bourgogne refers to the wine. Still Champagnes sometimes appear on the list of French restaurants under the heading 'Vin Nature de Champagne', together with the name of the area from which they come, such as Bouzy or Sillery.

Champagne produces about 90 million bottles of wine per year. Seventy-five per cent of this is consumed in France. Britain is still the largest importer – about 6½ million bottles per year – followed by the United States which imports some 4¾ million bottles.

Buyers' brands, that is the wine merchants' own brands, can generally be bought at £1·75 to £1·90. Shippers' vintage wines can be as high as £2·50 per bottle. The cheaper brands are by no means to be despised.

COGNAC

Any spirit distilled from wine is brandy and every wine-growing country distils part of its production into brandy, sometimes only for local consumption. But only the spirit distilled in the registered Cognac area of France has the right to the name Cognac. Since its quality is due to a highly skilled and very strictly controlled method of distillation, as well as to the particularly chalky soil on which its best vineyards are planted, this protection of the name Cognac is in the interests of everybody. The delicacy of flavour and bouquet which good Cognac, when properly matured, can achieve give it an unchallenged position as the finest brandy produced anywhere in the world.

The area is situated north of Bordeaux and south of La Rochelle, on the west coast of France, and stretches inwards to Angoulême. The River Charente runs through the district and gives its name to the two *départements* in which the large majority of the vineyards are planted: the Charente and Charente-Maritime. The vineyards cover about 160,000 acres (250 square miles) and produce anything from 2 million to 4 million gallons of pure spirit. Owing to the great variations in the soil and the consequent quality of the spirit produced, the area is divided into five A.O.C. controlled sub-areas. In the centre, around the town of Cognac, lie the two best areas:

> *Grande Champagne*
> *Petite Champagne*

so called because the chalky limestone soil is very similar to that of the Champagne country. Together they are responsible for 21 per cent of all Cognac distilled. They can be sold under their own names or blended together and sold as 'Fine Champagne' provided that the blend contains not less than 50 per cent of Grande Champagne. Merchants and restaurateurs often label their Cognac 'Fine Maison' and a glass of Cognac is sometimes referred to in France as '*une fine*' but these descriptions are illegal in France and do not necessarily indicate a spirit from Cognac at all. Legally they must be followed by the name of a district, i.e. Cognac, Languedoc, etc. The Fine Champagne areas are surrounded by the next in order of merit, known as:

> *Les Borderies*

This is a border area between the chalky soil of the central part and the more clay-rich soil of the outer areas. It makes only about 4 per cent of the total. The brandy distilled from its wine does not reach the same standard of delicacy as Fine Champagne, neither does it live as long in cask. It is, however, very fine Cognac and in isolated places produces a spirit almost indistinguishable from the best. Around this area again are two separate areas called:

> *Fins Bois*
> *Bons Bois*

They are areas formerly covered by primeval forests and are responsible together for over 60 per cent of the production of the area. The soil is largely clay and marl, with very little of the highly desirable chalk. Brandy from these areas is more common in taste and smell and matures much more quickly.

The outermost areas of the district are called:

Bois Ordinaires
Bois Communs

They are not controlled appellations in themselves but come under the general A.O.C. Cognac or Eau-de-Vie de Cognac. They cannot be used in any spirit described as Grande or Fine Champagne, or any of the other three A.O.C. names mentioned above. They cover roughly 13 per cent of the vineyard area of Cognac.

The wine from which Cognac is distilled is of very poor quality. It is a white wine, made mostly from a grape known locally as the Saint-Émilion (in no way at all connected with the claret area of Saint-Émilion) and the Folle Blanche. The latter, since it was grafted on to American wine stock after the Phylloxera scourge of the 1880s, has weakened in character and its one-time supreme position in the vineyards of Cognac is now largely filled by the Saint-Émilion. A third variety – the Colombard – is gradually falling out of use. One or two other varieties authorized are of very little importance to the total production.

The distillation which produces such a superb spirit from a poor wine is strictly controlled, as is everything that appertains to it. Cognac is double-distilled in order to obtain the required purity. It is matured for anything from three to fifty years in cask and under the best conditions can live for a hundred years in wooden casks. It cannot mature in bottle, since like all spirits the concentration of alcohol is too strong to be affected by the small amount of oxygen that is present in a sealed bottle. Again like all spirits, it is a colourless liquid when newly distilled, but takes on colour from the wood of the cask in which it is stored. Great importance is attached to the quality of the cask, which should be of Limousin oak and of properly matured wood. A good deal of American oak is now used to supplement the diminishing supply of Limousin. Immature wood will at once spoil the taste of the brandy as well as giving it too dark a colour during the years in which the spirit must remain in the cask in order to achieve its full development. The cellar in which the cask lies is also important to development. An average matured Cognac needs from twenty to thirty years in the cask. During this time the alcohol gradually evaporates, and the drier the cellar the more it evaporates, so that after twenty years as much as half of the contents may have been lost. In a damp cellar the alcohol that evaporates is replaced in the cask by water extracted from the atmosphere by the brandy remaining in the cask, for alcohol is a powerful dehydrant or drying medium. In this case the contents of the cask will disappear much less quickly, but its alcoholic degree will fall, owing to the absorption of moisture. Since the strength of newly distilled Cognac may be as much as 70 per cent pure alcohol, far too strong to be drunk, it has in any case to be diluted with distilled water before it is bottled and ready for sale. If this dilution can take place gradually over a period of twenty years or more, instead of quickly in the space of a few weeks, the quality benefits. Producers or wine merchants who hold stocks of Cognac for maturing therefore pay great attention to the atmospheric conditions of the cellars in which they store it. Only a small proportion of the Cognac distilled each year is kept separate for maturing into vintage Cognac by this long and expensive process. The greater part is destined for shippers' blends, to be sold under their names or brands as a Cognac of standard quality and character. The blends are made up of brandies of varying ages, from a few years old to a comparatively small proportion of very old spirit. This is the main use to which a shipper must put his fine old stocks, since the demand for fine Cognac at £3·79 to £7·55 per bottle is infinitely greater than the demand for vintage Cognacs at £6 to £9 per bottle. Most of the great shipping houses own vineyards themselves and press their own grapes and distil their own brandy, but nearly all need more stock than they can produce from their own vineyards. This is supplied by smaller proprietors of vineyards who produce their own brandy without having the financial reserves to permit them to mature it, or by peasant cooperative distilleries who produce brandy on behalf of their members who supply the grapes.

A small quantity of Cognac is triple-distilled to produce a 100 per cent pure spirit, for the '*liqueur d'expédition*', or dosage, of Champagne (p. 154). This is generally sold direct by small independent proprietors to the Champagne houses, or produced from the first or last part of the final Cognac distillate, which is eliminated from the main production.

Great Britain is the biggest export market for Cognac, using about

33 per cent more than the U.S.A. Other countries are a very long way behind. It is sold mostly under conventional signs which have been adopted by the trade in general and indicate roughly the age of the spirit. V.V.S.O.P. – reputed to stand for Very Very Superior Old Pale, although one authority maintains that the P. stands for product – is the highest grade of this group, claimed to represent over thirty-five years in age; V.S.O.P. is claimed by various authorities to represent anything from seventeen to thirty-five years, V.S.O. according to the same authorities twelve to twenty-five years. Other descriptions, such as V.O.P. and V.O., are sometimes used and these are followed in descending order by the three, two and one star system. None of these, however, are in any way controlled and initials and stars should be considered only in relation to the shipper who uses them as a means of identifying a particular type and quality. Where district names are used they may be taken as authentic products of the area they claim. Grande Champagne, Petite Champagne or Fine Champagne can be relied on as can the other A.O.C. district names. Vintages on Cognac labels have in the past been very misleading. In the first place, since Cognac only improves in cask and not in bottle, the important thing to know is how long it was in cask before being bottled. Secondly, since Cognac is a blended spirit, or at least nearly always a blended spirit, it is important to know if the vintage applies to all the components of the blend, or only to the oldest part of it, which could be anything from 1 per cent upwards. Finally, if the brandy is a single unblended product or a blend of one vintage only, has the yearly loss by evaporation been made good by a younger wine each year? Up to the present there has been only one guarantee of the authentic age of Cognac and it is provided by the fact that wines kept in U.K. bonds are not allowed, under Customs regulations, to be filled up except with duty-paid stocks. Many British wine merchants are in the habit of shipping new Cognacs when one year old, placing them in bond to avoid laying out the crippling import duty, and leaving them to mature for the necessary twenty to thirty years. Such Cognacs are obviously genuine when they are eventually cleared from bond for bottling in duty-paid cellars. They often bear their history on their labels with date of shipment, date of bottling and vintage and can be bought with confidence and a good deal of money.

New French regulations governing vintages, however, came into force in 1963. The authenticity of the age is now controlled by the

French authorities from the time of distillation to the moment of shipping and a certificate is issued by them to the British importer. There will be far fewer vintage Cognacs in future, but they will be genuine.

Prices today vary from £3·50 to £10 per bottle in wine merchants' lists, according to age and quality.

As in all products of the grape, purity, delicacy of flavour and lack of strong foreign odours like vanilla are the mark of authenticity of quality throughout the whole price range.

An aperitif known as Pineau des Charentes is made from the unfermented grape juice, stabilized by the addition of Cognac.

JURA

This small district, about eleven square miles in area of vines, lies at the foot of the Jura Mountains, about eighty miles east of the Burgundy area. It makes some of the most strikingly unusual wines of France and it makes them in an unusual manner, largely from grapes grown in no other area. Pasteur lived in the district for some years and it was on the wines of the Jura that his experiments that led to the explanation of the process of fermentation were carried out. The vineyards are mostly divided into small holdings and produce anything from 700,000 to 2 million gallons per annum. About a quarter of the total production is good enough to merit an Appellation Contrôlée and of this about 60 per cent is white, the remainder being red or rosé. Some sparkling wine is also produced by the Champagne method (see pp. 152–4). It is the white wines that are the most remarkable and different from any other French wines.

The soil is mostly a mixture of calcareous nature and clay, perfect for the production of full-bodied yet subtle white wines, which the specialized vinification methods of the area are designed to produce. Besides the normally made wines, there are two special groups known as the *vins jaunes* (yellow wines) and the *vins de paille* (straw wines). *Vins jaunes* are made entirely from the Savagnin grape, the Traminer of Alsace, and they are made in very much the same way as the sherries of Jerez, except that they are not fortified. The fermentation takes place slowly at low temperature and takes several weeks; as soon as it is over the wine is transferred to small casks, kept in a very cool cellar, and stays there, by law, for a period of not less than six years. During this time the volume gradually sinks by evaporation and is never replaced, again by the regulation of the A.O.C., whilst there forms, on the surface of the wine, a grey dust, known in Spain as the '*flor*', and consisting of a particular form of ferment which gradually oxidizes the alcohol and eventually gives the wine the taste best known in the U.K. in sherry. This '*flor*', which has no special name in the Jura, but is referred to as '*le voile*' (the veil) or '*mycoderma vini*', is a shy and uncertain starter; it may in fact not appear at all and in any case takes a long time to form, depending as it does on the amount of air in the cask, and wine surface made available by gradual evaporation. During all this time, six years in all be it remembered, the wine is vulnerable to all kinds of other less beneficent and actively harmful bacteria, for no sort of treatment is allowed during the six-year period. There are many casualties and these, added to the great expense involved by the time necessary for full development in casks, make *vin jaune* very expensive.

The greatest of all the *vins jaunes* of the Jura are those from a small area known as Château-Chalon, not a simple property, be it noted, but a name borne by a group of vineyards within a specified area. It must have a minimum degree of 12 per cent of alcohol, as opposed to the 11 per cent for other *vins jaunes*, and is an A.O.C. on its own. It is quoted on a few lists at about £3·25 per bottle.

The description '*jaune*' given to this group of wines is due to the distinct yellow colour which they achieve through their long stay in cask. They taste very much as light sherry might taste, although since they are not fortified they may be drunk with a meal, their strong flavour standing up well to spiced dishes.

Vins de paille, the second of the unusual white wines of the Jura, get their name from the straw mats on which the black Poulsard and Trousseau grapes are dried for several weeks before being pressed. Other methods of drying are also used, legitimately, but whatever the method the juice from the pressed grapes is very rich in sugar and cannot all be fermented into alcohol. Since the grapes are gathered late, and laid out to dry for two or three months, they are not pressed until January or February, when the weather is cold. The fermentation is a long and slow process because of this and because of the great richness of the juice in sugar. Being white wines, the skins of the grapes are kept out of the fermenting vats. The wine must ferment out to 15 per cent alcohol if it is to be entitled to its A.O.C. – and incidentally overshoot the alcoholic limit set for duty on table wines by British Customs regulations. Since at this strength of alcohol the ferments become inactive, especially at low temperatures, and give up trying to turn any more sugar into alcohol, the wine retains a certain amount of sugar. It is therefore a dessert wine and although a very pleasant one, of great breed and finesse, it is by British standards a light dessert wine, since it only contains 15 per cent of alcohol compared with over 20 per cent of port or sherry.

The other wines of the Jura, red, white and rosé, as well as sparkling, are made in the normal manner, largely from the same two grape varieties seldom seen in other parts of France – the Poulsard, making very light coloured red wine, and the Trousseau, which on the contrary produces a particularly dark red colour, and also the ubiquitous Pinot. The white are made from a grape known as the Melon, which is in fact the Chardonnay of Burgundy. They have a strong characteristic taste of their own, but like the red do not pretend to any great qualities and are sold by a few wine merchants at 70p to 90p per bottle.

Jura wines with any pretension to quality are entitled to one at least of the following Appellations Contrôlées:

Côtes de Jura, covering all types: red, white, rosé, *jaune* and *vins de paille*.

Arbois, covering the same types as above.

L'Étoile, white, *jaune* and *vin de paille* – producing only about 35,000 gallons.

Château-Chalon, covering *vin jaune* only, making under 10,000 gallons. It is bottled in special dumpy bottles, holding less than a full bottle, known as the '*clavelin*'.

Red wines made from the Poulsard grape, also locally called the Plant d'Arbois, and used by itself in the best Arbois vineyards, makes the best red wine of the Jura. It is light in colour and is often referred to as '*pelure d'oignon*' – onion skin. Its colour belies the fullness of its flavour.

THE LOIRE

The Loire, the longest river in France, is not in any sense a compact viticultural area. Along the six hundred miles of its banks and those of its many tributaries, starting from the centre of France where it rises, up to its estuary at Nantes, there grow a variable collection of vines. Some belong to the aristocratic Appellation Contrôlée group, but the majority are only entitled to be graded as V.D.Q.S. (Vins Délimités de Qualité Supérieure).

The year 1955 produced about 16 million gallons of Appellation Contrôlée wine, of which two-thirds was white, the remainder red or rosé. It also produced 120 million gallons of V.D.Q.S., of which only one-fifth was white. There are about 420,000 proprietors of this group of Appellation Contrôlée, which works out at an average of not more than 324 gallons per owner – a very small figure compared with the big estates of Bordeaux. The group is classified below under the regional group names to which each is entitled. Each regional group is further subdivided into the appellations applying to the region.

Vines

Most of the white wines are made from the Chénin grape, also known as Pinot de la Loire, and most of the red wines from one of the two varieties of Cabernet, and also sometimes from the Pinot Aunis.

Anjou Wines (A.O.C. Anjou)

The ancient province of Anjou gives its name officially to those wines grown in the *départements* of Maine-et-Loire, Deux Sèvres, la Vienne and, since 1950, the Loire Atlantique, which conform to the standards of quality and restrictions on production imposed by the I.N.A.O. Little red wine is made, the soil being best adapted for the production of white wines and rosé. The whites in particular vary greatly in taste and sweetness. They are fairly well known in Great Britain and are obtainable without much difficulty. The reputation of Anjou rests mainly on its rosé wine. The table on page 164 gives the main areas and descriptions under which they are known.

Prices in the U.K. vary from 70p for the lighter wines to £1·25 for selected wines from the best vineyards, such as Quart de Chaume. There are occasionally to be found a few more expensive wines from small areas like Savennières; these are generally bottled in France. The rosé wines of Anjou and the whites of Saumur are the most likely to be of interest; they are firm, fresh and pleasant in character, refreshing in hot weather and good at any time with buffet or snack meals. They are difficult to match from any other part of France. The finer

Name	Quantity (gallons)	Type	Description
Bonnezeaux	14,000	White	Sweet
Coteaux de l'Aubance	150,000	White	Medium dry
Coteaux du Layon	750,000	White	Sweet
Quart de Chaume	10,000	White	Sweet
Saumur	} 300,000	Red and rosé	} Light wines, drunk young. Vary from dry to medium sweet
Coteaux de Saumur		White	
Saumur-Champigny		Red and rosé	
Saumur Pétillant		Slightly sparkling white	
Saumur Mousseux		Sparkling white	
Savennières	6,000	White	Dry
Anjou	} 2,800,000	Rosé and red	} Light wines to be drunk very young
Anjou Pétillant		Slightly sparkling white	
Anjou Mousseux		Sparkling white	

qualities of white wine made in Anjou are available in small quantities and have a flavour so distinct from other areas of France that their price is influenced more by the demand from their particular admirers in France itself than by the demands of the export market.

MUSCADET (A.O.C.)

The Muscadet is not a region but a grape. It is the name used by the appellation authorities for wines made from the Muscadet grape, grown in the *départements* of the Loire Atlantique, in accordance with the rules and regulations of the Institute. It includes also small quantities made in the adjoining *départements*, but only because the character of the wine is the same. The official names are:

Name (A.O.C.)	Quantity (gallons)	Type and Description
Muscadet de Sèvre et Maine	3,000,000	Dry white
Muscadet du Coteaux de la Loire	180,000	Dry white
Muscadet	1,200,000	Dry white

These wines are sold in Great Britain at about 80p a bottle. Slightly chilled, they are excellent accompaniments to oysters and all shellfish. They can well be drunk throughout any meal and, whilst blending particularly well with shellfish, will taste well with any food. Their robust character is accompanied by such a delicate flavour that they would not spoil the taste of any dish; they are generally considered wines to be drunk within five years of their vintage.

TOURAINE (A.O.C.)

Another ancient province, like Anjou, which has been adopted as the official description of wine grown in the area. It is represented today by three *départements*: Indre-et-Loire, Loire-et-Cher and l'Indre. The main vineyards are sometimes known as those of the Val de Loire, referring to vineyards on both banks of the River Loire. Lesser areas are spoken of as belonging to the Vallée du Cher, de l'Indre, de la Vienne, or de la Claise, all tributaries of the Loire. The official controlled appellation for all of them is 'Touraine' and they are subdivided into the officially recognized sub-areas and descriptions listed below. There are many more red wines made here than in Anjou, some of them worth serious consideration to anybody looking for a change from the more ubiquitous Beaujolais, Burgundy and claret. They are distinctive in flavour, strong, soft wines, some of which are capable of great development in bottle. See table, p. 166.

There are a few other isolated vineyards on the banks of the Loire and its tributaries, bearing a controlled appellation and sufficiently robust to be exported. They are available in Great Britain. The complete list is as follows:

Jasnières (A.O.C.). 2,000 gallons only are made. It is a light, medium-dry white wine, resembling in character the Vouvray, and, though rarely available in Great Britain, would cost about 90p.

Quincy (A.O.C.). 80,000 gallons of dry white wine are made, this time from the Sauvignon grape, which produces great white wines in many parts of France, including Bordeaux. A wine to drink young, firm in texture, dry and distinctive in bouquet, excellent with shellfish, available in Great Britain at £1.

Sancerre (A.O.C.). Produces about 120,000 gallons of dry white wine. Like the wines of Quincy, this is made from the Sauvignon grape and

Name (A.O.C.)	Quantity (gallons)	Type	Description
Bourgueil	360,000	Red	Strong flavour, perfumed red wines, quite light in alcohol, made from a classic Cabernet grape, soft in texture, develop well in bottle. Available in London at 60p per bottle.
Chinon	200,000	Red	
Saint Nicolas de Bourgueil	160,000	Red and rosé	
Montlouis	200,000	White, dry	Light, soft white wines, develop quickly, drink young.
Montlouis Pétillant		Slightly sparkling	
Montlouis Mousseux		Sparkling	
Vouvray	400,000	White, dry and sweet	Best known as a sparkling wine. Still wines develop very well in bottle. Sparkling wines obtainable in London at 82½p, still wines at 60p.
Vouvray Pétillant		Slightly sparkling	
Vouvray Mousseux		Sparkling	
Touraine-Amboise	480,000	Red and rosé	These are mostly light wines of no great quality, generally drunk young.
Touraine-Azay-le-Rideau			
Touraine-Mesland	480,000	White, dry and medium dry	
Touraine			
Touraine Pétillant		Slightly sparkling	
Touraine Mousseux		Sparkling	

not the more usual Chénin. It is crisp, definite and lively and should be drunk within five years of its vintage. Available in Great Britain from £1 a bottle.

Pouilly-sur-Loire (*A.O.C.*). 20,000 gallons of dry white wine made from the big producing and less fine Chasselas grape. It does not keep long and is best drunk young and cold in its country of origin.

Pouilly Fumé (A.O.C.) – or *Blanc Fumé de Pouilly* – not to be confused with Pouilly Fuissé, which is a white Mâcon from the Burgundy area. Pouilly Fumé produces about 60,000 gallons of wine, fine, long-living dry white wine, with a distinctive and attractive bouquet, made from the Sauvignon grape. It is this grape which is locally known as the Blanc Fumé. It is a dry wine of real quality. Available in Great Britain from £1·50 a bottle. A wine that can well go all the way through a meal.

There is one wine amongst the lesser group of wines with no Appellation Contrôlée, but graded as a V.D.Q.S. (Vins Délimités de Qualité Supérieure) which is worth mentioning here:

Saint-Pourçain-sur-Sioule. This is a light, dry white wine, that varies a lot in quality because of the variety of grapes that are used to make it, and the choice amongst those grapes made by the growers. It is sometimes available in Great Britain and is worth trying.

Bottles

Most of the red and white wines of the Loire are bottled in Burgundy-shaped bottles, the reds in dark glass, the whites in clear glass. The rosés, however, are sometimes in hock-shaped bottles, made of clear glass.

RHÔNE

The Rhône is a vast river flowing south from the Swiss border through the south-eastern portion of France and joining the sea in a large estuary near Marseilles. The country through which it flows is largely planted in vines and produces some of the most full-flavoured red wines of France, as well as unusual white wines and a lot of rosé. On the whole, the Rhône wines can be described as similar in type to Burgundies, both red and white, with more body and rather less finesse, due allowance being made for a few wines of special quality. As usual the general name 'Rhône wines' can be misleading, since some, grown in the *département* of the Rhône, belong to other appellations, and some wines with the appellation 'Rhône' come from the valley of the Rhône in other *départements*. To avoid as much confusion as possible, the names of *départements* have been avoided in this chapter, as well as throughout the rest of the book, except when they are in current use as descriptions of wine. In some cases the wine area names coincide with the name of the *département*. The whole area is large and rambling and the boundaries between areas sometimes ill-defined. There is no tidy system of naming as in other large areas; there are thousands of acres producing no wine at all and minute areas of a few acres producing famous wines interspersed among more ordinary vineyards. There are sub-areas with official A.O.C., well defined and controlled, and there are others with no official appellation, which have submitted themselves to the discipline of local regulations and take a pride in differentiating their wines from those of neighbouring districts. Because of this rather loose organization, the wines described below are limited to those available in the U.K., or worthy of notice for some other special reason. They are arranged in groups based on their geographical position, starting from the most northerly of the Rhône area.

It seems likely that the modern trend, both in Great Britain and the U.S.A., to accept wine as a normal accompaniment to a meal is going to bring the wines of the Rhône into more and more prominence. Already the strain on supplies in Burgundy, both Côte d'Or and Beaujolais, is reflected in prices that increase steadily year by year. Burgundy has very little room left in which to plant new vines and production per acre cannot be increased without damage to a jealously guarded reputation for quality. In the Rhône area there are thousands of acres of authorized vine land still unplanted. The soil is unusually productive and the vines, different varieties from those in Burgundy, bear generously. Two thousand two hundred vines per hectare of ground produce more wine than 10,000 vines per hectare planted in Bordeaux and Burgundy. There are about 89,000 hectares – nearly 350 square miles of vines in the area, producing on an average 66 million gallons of wine per annum, of which about 20 per cent are entitled to an A.O.C.

The vineyards are in some cases on hills so steep that they have to be worked entirely by manual labour and in some cases on the plateaux bordering the river. There is much more red wine produced than white, there is more rosé produced than white, but it will be seen that some of the most famous wines of the area are white. As further evidence of the confusion that Rhône wines cause the student, it will be noticed that there are very few individual vineyards with château names and that those which do exist are seldom seen on merchants' lists. Some of the château names that are known refer not to individual properties but to districts, such as Châteauneuf-du-Pape.

Many varieties of grape are authorized and used, particularly in the fine red wine area of Châteauneuf-du-Pape, where there are at least a dozen. The foundation of nearly all the Côtes du Rhône red wine areas is a grape called the Syrah, which has a very distinctive pleasant warm flavour, but tends to make a hard wine. For this reason, in areas where it is the only red grape authorized, it is often fermented in the same vat as a small percentage of Viognier, the white grape which makes the fine white wine of Château Grillet. The Syrah is not the only highly individual strong grape of the area. The Grenache is predominant amongst all grapes used in Châteauneuf-du-Pape and is becoming more and more a rival to the Syrah in the cheaper areas of the Côte du Rhône. Its wine, however, is apt to age quickly, probably the reason for its increased popularity amongst growers, and it needs to be blended with grapes like the Syrah to make the big, dark-coloured, long-living Châteauneuf and Rhône wines that many people still like.

The soil is in general a well-balanced marl, with a good proportion of calcareous elements and silicates. The Hermitage red and white areas and that of the Côte Rôtie are granite, whilst the Châteauneuf area is covered in large flat stones, which make the vines appear to be growing out of a stone terrace and help greatly in maturing and softening the stubborn Syrah.

For the record, and for the sake of students whose researches may bring them into contact with the appellation structure of the area, it will be necessary to make one mention of *départements*. The A.O.C. Côtes du Rhône covers wines grown in altogether six *départements*, or counties. They are the *départements* of Rhône, Loire, Drôme, Ardèche, Vaucluse and Gard. Over 90 per cent of the A.O.C. come from the last two *départements* and the lowest A.O.C. they can bear is that of Côtes du Rhône if they are not entitled to one of the superior appellations mentioned below. The wines of the first four *départements* sometimes do not come up to the standard required for the Côtes du Rhône A.O.C. and are then permitted to add the name of the *département* to the words Côtes du Rhône. Thus the lowest appellations of all in the Côtes du Rhône are:

Côtes du Rhône – Rhône
Côtes du Rhône – Loire

Côtes du Rhône – Drôme
Côtes du Rhône – Ardèche

I have never seen them quoted on British or U.S.A. wine lists. The lowest-priced wines likely to be encountered will bear the description:

Côtes du Rhône – with possibly a vineyard name or a brand name on the label. They are dark or medium-dark red wines, soft on the palate, full in flavour, medium in alcoholic degree. They can be drunk young, but can also improve with age. In this respect they vary greatly according to the grapes from which they have been made. In general character they resemble the lighter Burgundies, such as Beaujolais, but with a different flavour of their own. 70p to 80p.

Côte Rôtie. Makes only about 20,000 gallons of red wine. This is the wine which is made chiefly from the Syrah grape, with up to 20 per cent of the white Viognier added. In character, something between Burgundy and claret, with distinctive flavour of Syrah grape. 90p to £1·20.

Condrieu. Only about 2,500 gallons of white wine. Often slightly sparkling, light and refreshing. Available occasionally in the U.K. at £2·25.

Château Grillet. Only about 350 gallons – or seven casks of white wine – made from the Viognier grape. The vineyard is owned by one family. It has its own appellation. It is known for its sweet, rich wine, often made from grapes that have benefited from the *pourriture noble* (see p. 140). I have also tasted a dry wine made in 1959 from a different variety of the Viognier, known as Viognier d'Oré, and the Serine grape – the local name for the Syrah. Until recently it was available at £2 but the proprietor has now increased his price so drastically that it would have to retail at about £6 per bottle. It is not therefore at present available in the U.K., and the previous importer is directing consumers' attention to Condrieu instead.

Hermitage (or Ermitage), Crozes-Hermitage and Tain-Hermitage. About 120,000 gallons of red and 40,000 gallons of white wine, between them, mostly at Crozes. The most famous is a white wine called **Chante-Alouette**, which is supposed to resemble the Château Grillet, but which I find lighter, more refreshing and easier to drink. The red wines of this area are grown on a granite soil and the white on suitable chalky earth. £1·20 to £1·50.

Clairette de Die. A few miles south east of Hermitage is the village of Die, where the Clairette grape produces excellent white and rosé sparkling wines. It is a very pleasant wine, with a gentle sparkle which tends to disappear after some years in bottle. About 120,000 gallons. About £1·20, when available.

Cornas. About 20,000 gallons of a wine similar to Hermitage.

Châteauneuf-du-Pape. This is the best known of the high quality red wines of the Côtes du Rhône. It makes around 1,250,000 gallons of red wine and about 10,000 gallons of less interesting white. Although there are over twelve varieties of grapes used or authorized for the making of the wine, the two predominant varieties are the Grenache and the Syrah. Both are strong-flavoured grapes and have a great influence on the wine made. The flavour of each, whilst strong, is different and there is in consequence considerable variety in the character of Châteauneuf-du-Pape. The growers of the area maintain that the best wines are made by the use of all the authorized grapes. Since the proportions used may be expected to vary from grower to grower, this adds a considerable unknown factor to the label Châteauneuf-du-Pape and increases the possibility of finding one suitable to individual tastes. In general the wines are like the bigger Burgundies from the Côte d'Or (see p. 151) but with a stronger flavour and a softer impact. They however lack the breed of fine Burgundies and although they improve for many years in bottle do not acquire either the subtlety of flavour or aromatic bouquet of fine Burgundy. There are a few large properties making fine wine, but they are seldom seen quoted on merchants' lists. Château Fortia and Château Vaudieu both are offered in the U.K.; Château de la Nerthe and Château des Fines Roches are of the same standard. Prices of these top qualities are about £1·37 per bottle and those of slightly less quality from 95p to £1. The demand for these full-flavoured warming wines is beginning to strain the supply, which is strictly limited. The area is more favoured than most in the regularity of its quality, but one poor vintage can have an immediate effect on the price of good wines, because they are for the most part sold and consumed within four or five years of the vintage and neither growers nor shippers are able to hold large stocks to even out the supply. Their fullness and intensity of flavour makes them particularly suitable for drinking with highly flavoured dishes, such as game.

Côtes du Rhône Villages is a courtesy title accorded to certain villages that have submitted themselves to local restrictive regulations in addition to those imposed by the A.O.C. Villages such as Chusclan, Gigondas, Laudon and Cairanne permit their growers to accept the appellation Côtes du Rhône only if they submit to these regulations designed to make a better wine than the average. They are grouped under the unofficial title Côtes du Rhône Villages.

Lirac and Tavel make about 250,000 gallons of vin rosé between them, two-thirds of it at Tavel. Tavel Rosé is probably the best known of all the rosé wines of France. Unlike the general run of rosé wines, both Tavel and Lirac is made from a mixture of red and white grapes, fermented together. The poorness of the soil on which the vines grow assures the finesse of flavour so necessary for quality in white or rosé wines; they age well in bottle, particularly Tavel. £1 to £1·20.

OTHER WINES OF FRANCE

There are vineyards scattered over the whole of France whose names are not well known outside that country, either because the quality of their wines is not good enough to interest export markets, or because they have to be drunk very young to be enjoyed and would deteriorate whilst waiting for customers in those countries where wine is not a national drink, or because the quantity produced is too small to be spread about. The best of them are briefly mentioned here for the benefit of readers travelling in France and as a guide to students who would like to explore for themselves. Most of them will not be found on British or U.S.A. wine lists. For the sake of convenience they have here been divided into three groups: the West, the South and the East; each group covers several Appellations Contrôlées and in each the most interesting of the Vins Délimités de Qualité Supérieure have been mentioned.

Western Section

This covers areas contiguous with or near to the Bordeaux area.

Bergerac starts at the eastern border of the Bordeaux country. It is an A.O.C. primary area with several secondary areas within its borders with their own A.O.C. The best known are:

Monbazillac: 1,500,000 gallons of excellent sweet and rich white wines, like Sauternes.

Montravel: 2,500,000 gallons of dry white wine.

Rosette: 120,000 gallons of similar wine.

Pécharment: 1,200 gallons of very pleasant red wine.

The remaining Bergerac area makes about 3,500,000 gallons of less interesting red and white wines.

Côte de Duras A.O.C., in the southern corner of the Bergerac area, makes 500,000 gallons of mostly white wine, all rather mediocre.

Gaillac A.O.C. This is a large area roughly north-east of Toulouse and making 7,500,000 gallons of white wine. Many of them are very pleasant and refreshing when drunk young. They make both medium sweet and sweet wines. The latter often improve a lot with bottle age.

Jurançon A.O.C. Lies south of Armagnac near the Spanish border. It makes about 250,000 gallons of rather unusual white wine from five varieties of unusual grapes. A taste for the wines of the Jurançon has to be acquired if their natural finesse is to be enjoyed.

There are a lot of V.D.Q.S. wines belonging to this western section, most of which can adequately refresh the traveller but would themselves suffer by journeying. It is worth while mentioning the wines from *Cahors*: powerful red wines, made from the Malbec grape – one of the traditional Bordeaux grapes – and with an amazing ability to withstand the action of oxygen. They develop for many years in cask and then for many more in bottle, and although they never attain the finesse of the wines of Bordeaux, they live much longer and appear to have unusual therapeutic qualities. There are not more than about 600 acres altogether authorized to use the name and of these only some 125 acres produce the true, traditional wine. I recommend any reader travelling in the area to seek out M. Jouffreau, who is a producer of the old school and proud of his inheritance. Finally, the small district of the *Béarn*, between Armagnac and Jurançon, makes some rosé wines which are beginning to increase their reputation.

Southern Section

This covers the Mediterranean coast from the Spanish frontier to
Italy. It is a fertile area for the vine and is responsible for a large part
of the *vin ordinaire* used in France. Here and there in this area of big
production there exist small areas where, because of the suitability of
the soil, wines with a greater claim to distinction are produced. They
are listed here from west to east, with one or two diversions to the
north away from the coast to include areas that have not fitted in
anywhere else.

Grand Roussillon. This is an omnibus A.O.C. given to the wines
grown in various parts of the Plaine de Roussillon, just north of the
eastern end of the Pyrenees and stretching up to Perpignan. There are
within the boundaries four areas producing A.O.C. wines – Maury,
Côtes d'Agly, Rivesaltes and Banyuls. These four separate A.O.C.
wines are collectively known as Grands Roussillons. It is not quite
the same as the primary and secondary areas encountered hitherto,
because there is no limited area designated as producing Grand
Roussillon, only authority given for the four separate areas of A.O.C.
wines mentioned above to have the sole right to be known by that
name. It is an important area and makes about 8 million gallons of
wine in a good year. They are all *vins doux naturels* – that is to say
wines in which some of the natural sugar of the grape must has been
prevented from fermenting – in other words fortified wines like port.
Some of them are turned into *vins de liqueur*, which involves the same
process, but is permitted with less good wines containing more
fortifying alcohol than is allowed for the *vins doux naturels*. These
natural sweet wines can improve very much with age in cask and
bottle. When they achieve the taste and colour of old wines by
maturing in cask, they have the right to add the word 'Rancio' to
their descriptions. Used in connection with these four wines, the word
'Rancio' is roughly equivalent to our 'Tawny' when applied to port.
As a description of other wines in the southern area it takes on only
its basic meaning of 'old developed' – it does not in those cases mean
that the wine has been matured in wood. There are some V.D.Q.S.
wines made in the Roussillon area known as Corbières de Roussillon;
they are red, rosé and white and are appreciated for their light and
refreshing qualities when drunk young. There are Corbières wines
made also in the Languedoc.

The Languedoc A.O.C. area is north and east of the Grand Roussillon, still along the Mediterranean coast. The appellation belongs only to fortified *vins doux naturels* made in the area, the best known of which are the Muscat de Frontignan and the Muscat de Minervois. There are light white wines made also; they are graded as V.D.Q.S. and known as Côtes de Languedoc, Minervois and Costières du Gard. None of these or of several other names belonging to the area are seen very much in the United Kingdom, although they are well worth searching out in France.

Blanquette de Limoux is a small A.O.C. area lying west of the Langue-doc about twelve miles south of Carcassonne. It produces about 160,000 gallons of sparkling wine by the *Méthode Champenoise* (see p. 152). The name 'Blanquette' comes from the white underside of the leaves of the Mauzac grape from which the wine is made. There is a still wine made also, called Limoux Nature (A.O.C.) – a very light, dry wine.

Fitou. Another small isolated A.O.C. area in the midst of the Corbi-ères V.D.Q.S. vineyards, on the Mediterranean coast due east of Limoux. It makes a soft, refined, agreeable red wine from a rather hard Spanish grape called Carignan, fermented, as in some Rhône wines, together with a small percentage of white grapes. Seldom seen on British wine lists.

Clairette du Languedoc is a full-bodied white wine, made from the Clairette grape, with a powerful flavour. It is an Appellation Con-trôlée and is used frequently as a basis for vermouths. It makes about 600,000 gallons a year. The description 'Rancio' (see under Grand Roussillon above) may be added under certain conditions of age. The word 'Clairette' – which is the name of a white grape – should not be confused with 'Clairet', which signifies a clear-coloured red wine. Except for the rare 'Rancio' wines, the Clairette du Languedoc is best drunk young.

Clairette de Bellegarde. A small area in the Rhône district, not far from Châteauneuf-du-Pape, making about 80,000 gallons of a rather clumsy white wine which should be drunk young.

Cassis. Between Marseilles and Toulon; makes about 60,000 gallons of white and rosé wines. They are of no great interest and should not be confused with the word, spelt in the same way, which means blackcurrant. A popular liqueur is made from blackcurrants in other parts of France and is known as Cassis. Mixed with white wine, it is often used as an aperitif drink in France, called 'Vin Blanc Cassis'. This term has nothing to do with the white wines made at Cassis.

Bandol. About fifteen miles east of Cassis, also on the coast. It produces about 60,000 gallons, mostly of a full-bodied strong red wine, which can live a long time in bottle. The few white wines made resemble those of Cassis.

Eastern Section

There are few vineyards in the eastern area of France other than Alsace and the Jura, which are dealt with separately.

Crépy. A small area on the borders of Lake Léman on the Swiss border; makes about 24,000 gallons of light white wines, very dry, with a pleasant flavour. They are made from the Chasselas grape which is responsible for some of the cheap wines of Alsace.

Seyssel. Between Annecy and Aix-les-Bains; makes about 20,000 gallons of wines similar to those of Vouvray on the Loire. They are dry or half dry, delicate, full-flavoured white wines, many of which are made into sparkling wine.

General. The traveller in France will find a great many wines not mentioned here. They will be wines that are not exported because there is not enough made or because their quality does not justify it. Nevertheless, many of them can be drunk with pleasure in their own locality and forgotten as individuals, for indeed they have not sufficient character to be remembered. Their destiny is fulfilled when they have been drunk and enjoyed.

Germany

Germany is not one of the large wine-producing countries of the world. It comes about seventh on the list and in 1960 produced about the same quantity as the U.S.S.R. – about 3 per cent of world production. Germany, however, is supreme as the producer of fine white wines; not only are her finest Rhine and Moselle wines unbeaten, if not unchallenged, by those of any other country, but the general level of her more ordinary wines is consistently higher than that of other countries. The year 1960 was an unusually prolific one; in an average year Germany accounts for under 2 per cent of world production and comes about eleventh on the production list. In 1959 she produced about 90 million gallons of wine – about the same as the Bordeaux area of France. There were about 250 square miles of vines planted in the whole country in 1960, but the yield per acre is over twice that of Bordeaux, with which the wines can be compared for quality, and 50 per cent greater than the average for the whole of France with her enormous production of *vin ordinaire*. The area under vines is increasing steadily and so, during the last seven years, is the export trade in wine, which amounted to about two million gallons in 1958. Great Britain and the U.S.A. are the biggest customers, taking over 50 per cent of the total exports between them, and in about equal quantities. The Germans themselves drink an average of twelve bottles per head of the population per annum, mostly their own wines, supplemented by some 18 million gallons imported mainly from France, Italy, Spain and Portugal, not counting a much larger quantity destined for the production of German brandy, vermouth and sparkling wines.

VINEYARDS

Most of the vineyards are planted on steep hills on the banks of the rivers Rhine and Moselle. They are two very different rivers and very different types of country: the Rhine, a swift-flowing, majestic and busy commercial highway from Switzerland to Rotterdam, with vineyards lining its banks from Worms to Koblenz and the craggy summits of the hills often crowned by castle ruins; and the Moselle, which ambles and twists its way through green-covered hills and orchards to join the Rhine at Koblenz. In spite of the amiable nature of the countryside, nothing could be more austere than the soil of vineyards of the Moselle or the labour necessary to cultivate them. The steep hills are composed of slaty rock and continual back-breaking labour is required to maintain a sufficient topsoil of broken-up slate to provide a terrain in which the vines can grow. The Rhine and the Moselle dominate the main wine-producing areas of Germany and each are served by important tributaries, giving their own names to extensive vine areas; these are tabulated below. In addition to these two main areas, wines are made in the more southern part of Germany down to the Swiss border, in the provinces of Württemberg and Baden – on a level with the vineyards of Alsace on the other side of the Rhine, and also, rather more successfully, in Franconia, on the east side of the Rhine on a level with the best west-bank vineyards of the Rheinhessen and Rheingau. These also are listed later. They are responsible between them for under 20 per cent of the small German wine production.

WINE LAWS

German laws controlling the production and distribution of wine are designed to protect quality and to facilitate the spreading of the general reputation of her wines without pandering to vested interests in either whole parishes or individual vineyards. In the main they are concerned with the various treatments to which new wines may be submitted in order to counteract any weakness brought about by unsuitable vintage conditions. On the whole they work on the principle that man has the right to try to produce the best quality of which his vineyard is capable, and to do his best to put right damage done by the vagaries of the weather in particular years. For example, vineyards which can normally produce in their must a sugar concentration capable of producing 13° of alcohol in the finished wine are allowed to add sufficient sugar to bring a weak must up to this density; districts less favoured by nature are allowed to add correspondingly less sugar so that man's interference is limited to repairing the damage done by an occasional failure of natural conditions – too little sun, too much rain, etc. In no case may a must (unfermented grape juice) be enriched in sugar beyond the average that might be expected in a normal year. No wine which is the product of a '*verbessent*' – i.e. 'improved' – must can be described as anything but the ordinary product of the vineyards. Superior qualities, such as *Spätlese*, *Auslese*, etc., can only be produced from natural, non-sugared musts.

The amount of sugaring permitted is mainly controlled by regulations covering specified districts. A certain amount of latitude is allowed to individual vineyards normally producing richer musts than the average in the district. Not all wines bearing the name of a district or vineyard only are wines made from sugared musts; they may simply not have been made under the conditions which would entitle them to the descriptions of higher quality, such as *Spätlese* or *Auslese*. Such lesser wines sometimes add to the label the qualification '*Natur-Wein*' or '*Naturrein*'. For example, a Niersteiner Domthal Spätlese or Auslese must be a wine from natural must; Niersteiner Domthal alone might be from an enriched must, or equally well from a natural must. In the latter case it would be entitled to proclaim this by the word '*Naturrein*', '*Natur*' or '*Natur-Wein*' on the label, but is not under any obligation to do so and often, in practice, does not.

NOMENCLATURE

The principles governing the naming of German wines have been dealt with in the chapter on wine nomenclature and illustrated in a separate chart. They cause a good deal of quite unnecessary confusion to the layman, and are summarized again here. They are in essence simple and logical. The relevant factors affecting the character and quality of a wine are, in order of importance:

(1) The vintage year.
(2) The soil on which it is grown (district and vineyard).
(3) The vine variety (Sylvaner, Riesling, etc.).
(4) The degree of maturity when it was picked (late, selected berries, etc.).

The Germans indicate these factors on their labels in the logical order of merit. The grape is seldom mentioned unless it is the Riesling – the king of all German wine grapes, which nowhere else in the world produces wines of the quality it produces in Germany. On the Rhine and Moselle it reigns supreme despite the fact that it ripens late and needs fine weather in the early autumn to produce its best wines.

To read a German wine label it is only necessary to know whether the first word indicates a district or a vineyard, e.g.:

> *Nierstein* (district)
> *Domthal* (vineyard)

to recognize a grape variety, e.g. Riesling, and finally to have a knowledge of the descriptions used to qualify the dates of picking i.e. degree of maturity of the grape. This requires only the following vocabulary in German:

Lese	picked
Spät	late
Auslese	selected (referring to bunches)
Beeren	berries (grapes)
Trocken	dried (i.e. overripe and raisin-like)
Feinste or *Feine*	finest or fine

and as a consequence the following terms are easily understood:

Spätlese	late picked
Auslese	selected bunches (ranks higher than Spätlese)
Beerenauslese	selected berries
Trockenbeeren-auslese	selected overripe grapes

These descriptions are freely used by growers and by tradition have come to indicate quality in the ascending order in which they are given here. In fact, the significance of each description, if strictly used, would depend on the conditions in individual vineyards in different years. A gathering postponed in the hope of sustained fine weather might produce a *Spätlese* of a higher quality than an *Auslese* which had been undertaken to preserve just-ripe bunches from a possible deterioration in the weather feared before the whole vineyard had ripened. The wine trade and the layman are saved this confusion by the general adoption of the above convention.

Descriptions such as *feine* or *feinste*, *Cabinet* (*Kabinett*), are used by growers to indicate the comparative quality of different casks of their own wine. Sometimes cask numbers are given on the labels of great wines and in some cases *Cabinet* wines are further classified by individual owners by the use of different-coloured seals or capsules, to indicate their relative quality.

THE NEW GERMAN WINE LAW (1971)

Readers who have been able to absorb the complexities of the German labelling and wine laws will be delighted to learn that the system is in the process of being changed. A new Law has been published during 1970, and is due to come into operation during 1971. At the time of writing full details are not available but the main points of the new law are as follows:

In future all German wines will be divided into three categories:

(a) Tischwein (Table wine)
(b) Qualitätswein (Quality wine)
(c) Qualitätswein mit Predikat (Quality wine with qualifications)

The category into which a particular wine falls will depend on its natural sugar content. Any wine aspiring to category (b) or (c) will have to be submitted to the authorities, analysed and tasted, before it can be marketed as such. The only wines that will be entitled to the top, category (c), rating will be those which at present are entitled, by their degree of natural sugar, and the method in which the grapes have been harvested, to such descriptions as *Spätlese, Auslese*, etc.

Various qualifications and descriptions such as *Natur* and *Original-abfüllung* will no longer be used. These new laws will of course only apply to future vintages and older vintages will still be found on the market labelled according to the old law.

QUALITY PRODUCTION

The tradition of keeping individual casks of the finest pressings separate from the main wine, instead of allowing it to be blended with it and so contribute to an increased all-round quality, is tending to change. The ever-growing demand for wines in the middle price ranges from the increasingly affluent middle classes of all nations, combined with improved techniques which enable wine to be satisfactorily stored in large vats, tend to encourage the grower to increase both the quality and quantity of his medium price category easily sold wine at the expense of small quantities of superb wines, and at the same time to eliminate the risks and considerable expense entailed in maturing fine wine in small casks of 130 or 260 gallons. The difference in the quality of various casks stems from two main factors: firstly, the variation of soil in even a single vineyard and the fact that one part of a vineyard may receive more hours of sunshine per day than another, and secondly, the unevenness in the maturity or condition of grapes due to variations in the weather during the weeks it takes to gather a harvest, or simply to the natural development of the state of maturity during those weeks. The reader who by now has appreciated that the finest qualities of great wines are dependent on factors outside the control or knowledge of the grower will equally appreciate the possibilities of great variations in the quality of wine made from grapes picked on different days from different parts of a vineyard. It will be a pity if the facilities made available by the progress of science are once again to deflect the wine maker from his efforts to achieve perfection. The principle of 'apartheid' for casks practised by German wine growers has produced in the past wines that set a standard and challenge to all wine growers, whilst still leaving the rest of their wines sufficiently sturdy in character to exist on their own. It is not much practised in other countries for a variety of practical reasons. Sometimes, the greater part of the product of a vineyard may be undrinkable if deprived of its best casks, sometimes several grape varieties are planted in a vineyard and fermenting vats will consist of an uneven proportion of different varieties, depending on the day's picking. Very often a vineyard proprietor, for practical commercial reasons, prefers to have one wine only to represent his vineyard and is in fact left with very little choice in the matter in countries where the market price of wines is based on the integrated wines of each property and no demand exists for varied qualities, all bearing the same vineyard name. There is no doubt that, whereas the German wine laws do a great deal to avoid the confusion caused by a plethora of names, the single-cask system, by producing greatly varying qualities of wine under one label, complicates the identification of some of Germany's finest wines. I must add that I believe the difficulties caused by this complication are justified and well worth while.

GRAPE VARIETIES

There are not a great many varieties of grape used in German wine-making – the Sylvaner and the Riesling are the two main varieties. The Sylvaner is used mainly for cheaper wines, although it also produces fine wines in Rheinhessen and the Palatinate. Its wines are softer and quicker to mature than the Rieslings. The Riesling is responsible for all fine Moselles, with the exception of a very few, and for most of the fine Rheingaus which, as will be seen from the list below, include most of the renowned vineyards of Germany. The Traminer or Gewürztraminer is partly responsible for the distinctive bouquet and aromatic flavour of the wines grown in the richer soil of the Palatinate or Pfalz area, but is less used now than it was, possibly on account of its need of perfect weather to mature properly. A distinct change in the nature of these attractive Palatinate wines is noticeable in consequence of this. This is the same grape which, a little further south, produces the highly distinctive Traminer and Gewürztraminer of Alsace in the French Rhineland. In Germany it is used mostly in conjunction with the Sylvaner and the Riesling. There is a fourth grape, known as the Müller-Thurgau after the name of its perpetrator, which is being more and more used in the Rheinhessen. It is a cross between the Sylvaner and the Riesling which, it is hoped, will give some of the stamina of the Riesling to the more easily produced and softer Sylvaner. Its qualities are not yet fully proved, although it has its enthusiastic supporters. Its wines at present seem to lack character and definition, as blended wines do before they have had a chance to 'marry'. It may well be that when the Müller-Thurgau has come to terms with the soil in which it is planted, it will become a valuable addition to German wine varieties. It was first produced in 1872 and is now increasingly planted in Rheinhessen and the Palatinate. Another grape, the Scheurebe, also produced from Sylvaner and Riesling, and at present in an experimental stage, is also sometimes mentioned on wine lists.

RED WINE

About 16 per cent of the wine made in Germany is red, but it cannot compare in distinction with either the white wines of the country or the red wines of France. Various varieties of red grapes are used, mostly in vineyards around Assmannshausen and Ober-Ingelheim and the Ahr Valley, but the wines from this and other red wine areas of Germany are seldom seen in Great Britain.

LIEBFRAUMILCH

Although German vineyards are often split up amongst several proprietors and there are comparatively few large estates in the hands of single owners, the confusion that this might be expected to cause is greatly lessened by the wisdom of the nomenclature laws and the fact that very often only one vine variety is planted in the whole area. A further simplification is obtained by the official recognition of a 'type' name, which enjoys the same protection of its quality as do the wines of specified districts. The name 'Liebfraumilch', without doubt the best-known German wine name, has become an officially recognized national brand name and does not refer to any particular vineyard or even district. It had held this special position since a few years after 1909, when the present German wine laws became effective. The origin of the name is connected with the Liebfrauenstift Wein, the wine made from vineyards belonging to the Church of Our Lady (*Liebfrauenkirche*) at Worms in the Rheinhessen. Liebfraumilch was almost certainly originally used to describe the wines from this vineyard.

As the law stands today, it may be used to describe wine from any district whatsoever, provided that it is a pleasant wine of the traditional quality – two conditions which it might perhaps be difficult to define in a court of law. Some attempts have been made to confine the use of this name to wines from the Rheinhessen, so far without success. Liebfraumilch is therefore the description of a type of wine, an agreeable, medium-dry to medium-sweet, soft, pleasantly flavoured wine, well constituted and therefore capable of conservation and development in bottle for at least three or four years. Its degree of sweetness may vary and so may its flavour, so that in fact there may be – and are – many varieties of this national type of wine. There is no means of distinguishing one variety from another, except the name of the blender or shipper, and it has become the custom for shippers who want to make it easy for the public to remember and recognize the wines they like to design special labels and relate them to a brand name for the particular quality and variety of Liebfraumilch which they produce.

DISTRICTS

The main German wine districts are given here with the occasional names of vineyards, so that the student may get the 'feel' of the German nomenclature system. The better-known parishes or villages are all named.

The Rheingau. This consists of about eight square miles of vineyards

on the nothern bank of the Rhine (which here flows from east to west)
lying between the towns of Mainz and Lorch. It is the home of great
estates, the Riesling grape and wines which can vary from 95p to
£5 per bottle in price and live from five years to fifty years in bottle.
It is here that the most widely-known of the great wines of Germany
are grown: Steinberg, Schloss Johannisberg and Schloss Vollrads –
all, as it happens, vineyards with single owners. The Marcobrunnen
vineyard, shared by six owners, is another of the famous wines grown
in the Rheingau.

Here, then, is a list of the wine-growing parishes in the Rheingau
with the names of two vineyards within each parish taken at random:

Eltville:	Sandgrube, Sonnenberg
Erbach:	Honigberg, Marcobrunn
Geisenheim:	Klauserweg, Rosengarten
Hallgarten:	Deutelsberg, Sandgrub
Hattenheim:	Klosterberg, Wisselbrunn
Hochheim:	Kirchenstück, Neuberg
Johannisberg:	Schloss Johannisberg, Schlossberg
Kiedrich:	Sandgrube, Wasserose
Östrich:	Doosberg, Leuchen
Rauenthal:	Burggraben, Geierstein
Rüdesheim:	Hinterhaus, Schlossberg
Winkel:	Schloss Vollrads, Hasensprung
Kloster Eberbach:	Steinberg

There are, of course, a great many more vineyards, many of them
well known in Great Britain and the U.S.A., within each of the
parishes mentioned. The above will help to clarify the German
method of naming wines. An Eltviller Sandgrube is accurately placed
as a different wine from a Hallgartener Sandgrub or a Kiedricher Sandgrube, being separate vineyards in separate parishes that happen to
have been given the same name by their owners – Sandgrube (Sandpit).
The suffix '-er' added to the name of the village – Eltville, Eltviller –
is optional; it is equivalent to adding the definite or indefinite article
to the description of the wine – 'the Eltville' or 'an Eltville' wine.
Hochheim is sometimes said to be the origin of the word hock because
of the preference which Queen Victoria showed for wines from this
area. As hock appears to have been used to describe German Rhine

wine before the birth of Her Majesty, it seems likely that if it is derived from Hochheim it is for a less august reason.

Wines of the Rheingau are the aristocrats of German viticulture; they are firm wines, produced from the Riesling grape, and take longer to develop and live longer in bottle than other German wines. For me, some of their quality has disappeared nowadays in the attempt to meet the heavy demand from the public for younger and fresher wines. Therefore they are less austere and less dry than they used to be and altogether more amiable than impressive. The new process involves a speeding-up of the whole vinification and development, but it is commercially successful and the public have no means of knowing that they are missing anything. It is, in fact, a successful commercial compromise and in keeping with the times.

The Rheinhessen

The Rheinhessen is that territory bounded on the west by the rivers Alsenz and Nahe, on the north and east by the Rhine (which makes a right-angled turn at Mainz), and on the south by a line drawn roughly from Kreuznach on the Nahe to Worms on the Rhine. It is one of the biggest areas of the Rhineland, covering about fifty square miles of vines. The best vineyards are those on the banks of the Rhine situated in the parishes of:

Laubenheim	*Nackenheim*	*Oppenheim*
Bodenheim	*Nierstein*	*Guntersblum*

The vineyards around Bingen belong in part to Rheinhessen and in part to the Nahe. There are at least thirty more villages of less renown producing good wine in the area. There are many vineyards split up amongst these villages, but few large estates and none that have attained the renown of the great Rheinhessen estates. The predominating grape in the area is the Sylvaner and the wines of Rheinhessia reflect its soft, attractive qualities. They develop comparatively quickly in bottle and do not live as long as Rheingau wines, nor attain the intense flavour and bouquet of these. They provide a great variety of wine in the cheaper price range, from 80p to £1 per bottle, whilst still being represented amongst the high-priced wines by *Auslese* and *Trockenbeerenauslese* casks, produced in the best years.

Nahe Wines

The River Nahe is a tributary of the Rhine, which it joins at Bingen. It is a gentle, pleasant river, and the wines which grow on the hills lining both banks along the lower reaches of the river reflect something of the fragrance and friendliness of the surrounding country. They are wines which naturally develop quite quickly and which lack any of those aggressive qualities which tempt modern growers to produce a softening sweetness in wines which would otherwise take time to acquire the mellow quality that everybody likes. Nahe wines have perhaps suffered less from the effects of modern progress than most of their rivals. The hills on which the vines are planted consist of a porphyry rock quite different from the soil of other districts, and the distinctive flavour of Nahe wines is undoubtedly due to this soil. They are generally lighter wines and more 'streamlined' than other Rhine wines; they resemble the wines of the Moselle to some extent, whilst still being fuller than these and with a less pronounced acidity. They often develop a pronounced bouquet resembling that of honeysuckle and the best wines from individual casks of *Beerenauslese* wines can attain a balanced beauty equal to anything produced in the world. They are becoming better known in the U.K. than they used to be, and examples of Nahe wines are appearing in greater profusion on wine merchants' lists. The best wine-growing centres are:

Bingen	*Kreuznach*	*Schloss Böckelheim*
Münster	*Niederhausen*	

In area, the Nahe vineyard is about the same as the Rheingau and only one fifth that of the Rheinhessen. Like all German wine areas, it produces wines that are sold from 80p to £5 per bottle.

The Palatinate or Rheinpfalz

This is the other large wine-growing area of the Rhineland. It is about the same size as the Rheinhessen, having about fifty-five square miles under vines. It is the most southernly situated of the Rhine wine districts, although not the most southerly of German vineyards. Here the vines are not planted in close proximity to the river, but on the slopes of the Haardt Mountains, which run parallel with the Rhine a few miles from its western bank. The best districts consist of a sandy and silicate soil, with a certain admixture of calcareous clay, ideally suited to the production of fine white wine. The Riesling and the Traminer are grown here and produce a wine which, at its best, can compare in richness of flavour with the great Sauternes of France, whilst conserving the aromatic and penetrating qualities which are characteristic of the Riesling grape. The lesser wines of the area tend to have the same aromatic qualities, but less of the richness of flavour which they used to have, owing in some measure no doubt to the gradual disappearance of the Traminer grape from the district. It is seldom that wines from the Palatinate are offered amongst the lower price ranges on wine merchants' lists. They generally start at about £1·15 per bottle, rising as usual to the extravagant prices commanded by the finest casks. To obtain a true impression of these seductive wines the student should be prepared to spend between £1·50 and £1·75 on a bottle.

The main centres producing fine Palatinate wines are in the central part of the range of vineyards known as the Middle Palatinate, or Mittelhaardt; the best known in Britain are:

> *Kallstadt   Dürkheim   Wachenheim*
> *Forst* (with its famous Jesuitengarten vineyard)
> *Deidesheim* and *Ruppertsbeurg*

Ranking with these are Herxheim, Ungstein and Neustadt, all of course encompassing numerous vineyards which are indicated on the label in the traditional way – Dürkheimer Feuerberg, Förster Jesuitengarten, Deidesheimer Hofstück.

Other Rhine Wine Districts

There are no other areas in the Rhine wine country which produce wines of any importance to the export trade as still table wines. The officially recognized districts of the Middle Rhine, downstream, that is north of Rheingau, Hessen and Nahe territory, and the valleys of its two tributaries, the Lahr and the Ahr, produce some red wine much appreciated in Germany, and white wines often used for the production of German sparkling wine, or 'Sekt'.

The Moselle (Mosel)

This third largest of the German wine areas covers about thirty-five square miles of planted vines. It is at once both the most austere and the most charming of all districts. Austere because its clay topsoil is overwhelmed by broken slabs of slate from the rocks on which it is bedded and has a barren and forbidding appearance, which is, however, softened by the green of the vines that grow so successfully on it. The hillsides on which the vines are planted on terraced strips are so steep that earth erosion is continuous and has to be replaced by quantities of soil and broken-up slate carried up the steep steps that are the only means of access to the vineyards. The charm comes from the twisting, meandering river, bordered at frequent intervals by picturesque villages and the green of grass-covered slopes speckled with orchards. The river twists and turns back on itself to such an extent that vineyards planted on southern and south-eastern slopes are on both sides of the river, as are the villages. This is Riesling country *par excellence* – no other vine can produce quality wine from such thin soil and there exists nowhere else this combination of soil and hill-sheltered climate which enables this slow-ripening aristocratic plant to produce the exquisite wines that are grown on the Moselle in good years.

The river flows in a general north-eastern direction to join the Rhine at Koblenz. Vineyards are planted from the area of Trier along the whole of this stretch. The best vineyards lie along the first part of this stretch of the river from Trier to Reil, a distance of about thirty miles, and half-way to Koblenz. This part is known as the Mittel Mosel. South and north of Trier two important tributaries join the Moselle from the east – the Saar and the Ruwer, both prolific in vineyards producing fine quality wines. There are thirty-five villages, enclosing a large number of vineyards, on the Middle Moselle and nearly the same number, producing less fine wines, on the Lower Moselle – the name given to the stretch of river from Reil to Koblenz. One village at the very start of this section is more renowned than the rest. It is the village of Zell – with its famous vineyard the Schwartze Katz. The most famous of the villages on the Middle Moselle are:

Trittenheim	*Lieser*	*Erden*
Neumagen	*Bernkastel*	*Herzig*
Dhron	*Graach*	*Traben-Trarbach*
Piesport	*Wehlen*	*Enkirch*
Brauneberg	*Zeltingen*	

On the Saar:

  Ockfen   *Wiltingen*   *Scharzberg* (in reality
                      not a village but a
                      vineyard)

On the Ruwer:

  Eitelsbach   *Grünhaus*

The wines of the Moselle are lighter in colour than Rhine wines and often have a pleasant greenish tinge. They are lighter, too, in alcohol, and do not tire the system when drunk even in large quantities. They have a relatively high acidity, which in some measure accounts for their pleasant, refreshing qualities. They are, indeed, considered by many doctors to be positively beneficial to some conditions affecting the kidneys. It is even said that they are effective in disposing of excessive fat. The author takes no responsibility for this statement. A visit to the Moselle would seem to indicate that a large part of the population do not drink the local wine.

At their best, Moselles achieve a balance, a lightness and a dryness that permits them to be drunk with pleasure at any stage of a meal. In addition, they can achieve a flowery bouquet of such intensity and exquisite aroma that they blend well with the flavour of the most delicate fruits. They are quoted in London merchants' lists at 80p to £10 per bottle. Examples of well-bred natural Moselles of pronounced individuality can be found at between £1·15 and £1·50 per bottle, and good wines for ordinary occasions from 90p upwards.

Other German Wine Districts

As already mentioned, there is a group of wine areas generally referred to as Southern German wines, but starting in fact from the River Main, which flows into the Rhine at Mainz and stretching down to the Bodensee (Lake Constance) on the Swiss border. They are situated in the provinces of Franconia, Baden and Württemberg, all on the east side of the Rhine, and include an area known as the Bergstrasse on the same side of the river in Rheinhessia. With one exception, none of these areas produce wines for export. Nearly all are drunk locally – in Württemberg a big proportion of red wine – whilst the wines grown around Lake Constance have the right to the description 'Bodensee wines', irrespective of the provinces in which they are situated.

The exception amongst the above are the wines of Franconia, grown on the banks of the River Main, near Würzburg, the chief city of Franconia. They are known as Steinweins, and bottled in flat, flagon-shaped bottles called '*Boxbeutels*'. The name is derived from the Stein and Steinacker vineyards of Würzburg and strictly speaking should be confined to wines from these areas. The description 'Steinwein' is, however, used by other wine-producing countries to define wines grown on stony soil, and the German regulation is not strictly enforced by the authorities; it is used to describe all Franconian wines of the requisite quality. Types and quality vary a good deal because the soil of the area is very variable. There are only about 10,000 acres under vines and there are 10,000 proprietors, some admittedly associated in cooperative wine-making cellars; but conditions are still sufficiently fluid to produce many types of wine from this small vineyard. The Sylvaner grape predominates and it is a remarkable fact that this 'soft' grape produces such steely wines in this area. The most favoured vineyards are able to plant the Riesling and the most typical Steinwein is made from the few vineyards in which the Riesling forms at least part of the crop. These wines have a flavour of their own, they are firm and vary greatly in sweetness, but on the whole are very dry and for many a little austere. They are to be found on wine merchants' lists in the U.K. at about £1·50 per bottle.

DRYNESS AND SWEETNESS

Although hocks and Moselles do produce both dry and sweet wines, it should be remembered that the natural sweet wines only appear in the very expensive categories from *Auslese* upwards, where the fermented essence of the grape has left surplus sugar in perfect balance with the alcohol and acidity of the wine. The majority of German wines are dry or medium dry and can be drunk throughout the whole meal with pleasure.

SPARKLING WINES

Sparkling wines, known in Germany as *Sekt* (the word is used in the same way that 'Champagne' is used – 'a bottle of *Sekt*'), are produced all over Germany from both German and imported wines. In 1958 about 6½ million gallons were made, half from imported wines and half from German wines. Some German *Sekt* is made by the Champagne method (see p. 152) from all sorts of wines, more in *cuves closes*. The best qualities come from the Moselle and good Rhine vineyards, mostly in the Mittel-Rhein. Finest of all are the single vineyard sparkling wines made at Steinberg and Johannisberg from still wines containing at least two-thirds of wine grown on the estates. Red sparkling wine is also made, mostly from Württemberg wines.

The white sparkling wines are freely exported. They are sold on the British market at from £1·20 to £1·50 per bottle, nearly all of good quality, but varying in their individual characteristics just as Champagne does according to the blends of the various proprietors.

VINTAGES

Vintages of hocks and Moselles are important. The German vineyards are the most northerly situated in Europe and need all the warmth and sunshine that they are likely to get in a normal year. With modern knowledge, reasonable wines can be made in most years, but the finest qualities are still dependent on perfect weather.

During the last twenty years the most successful vintages have been:

Very Good: 1945, 1947, 1949, 1959.
Good: 1946, 1952, 1953, 1955, 1957, 1961, 1964, 1966, 1969.

but it must be emphasized that qualities of individual wines in single vintages vary greatly in a country where the greatest wines can only be produced by the perfection of highly skilled vinification techniques, and in which the finest qualities are sometimes made in quantities of only 250 gallons at a time.

ESTATE BOTTLING

Estate bottled wines of good vintages fetch anything from £1·25 to £10 per bottle, but they are guaranteed as regards both authenticity and quality. Because the law allows a certain controlled latitude in the description of vineyards and parishes based partly on contiguity, partly on quality and partly on blending, the working on a German wine label relating to proprietorship or place of bottling is rather more significant than the straightforward '*mise du château*' of France. It has already been explained how the quality descriptions *Spätlese*, *Auslese*, etc., can be applied only to natural, non-sweetened wines. In the same way, the words *Wachstum* (growth), *Originalabfüllung* (estate bottling), or *Originalabzug* (literally estate 'drawing off', meaning exactly the same as '*Abfüllung*'), cancel the latitude allowed by law and restrict the contents of the bottle to the unblended produce of the exact vineyard designated on the label. The word *Kellerabfüllung*, or *Kellerabzug*, does not, however, have this significance, since it indicates only that the wine has been bottled in the cellars of the merchant whose name appears on the label. The words *Originalabfüllung* and *Originalabzug* can logically stand by themselves on a label, since they must refer to the cellars of the vineyard named, but the word *Wachstum* will be followed by the name of the proprietor of the vineyard, and the wine, unblended and untreated, may have been bottled in the cellars of a shipper or merchant.

BOTTLES

The long-necked graceful shape of German wine bottles will be well known, or will probably quickly become well known, to most readers. Brown bottles are generally used for Rhine wines, blue were once traditional for Nahe, and green are now used for them and Moselle.

SUMMARY OF TYPES

It is impossible to generalize about the drinking qualities of different districts. The following summary is intended only to be a rough guide for the use of any reader who may find himself bewildered by the variety offered by wine merchants.

Rheingau: Firm, strong in alcohol, need time to develop in bottle and live a long time. Capable of great finesse and emphatic bouquet.

Rheinhessen: Softer, easier than Rheingau. Develop quicker and live less long. Provide most of the popular type of hock.

Nahe: Lighter, crisper than other three Rhine areas. Often a flowery flavour and bouquet. Can be drunk young.

Palatinate: Big, soft, aromatic, capable of great quality, most interesting in the higher price categories.

Moselle: Light, refreshing, lively wines. Can be drunk young. They also often have a flowery bouquet. Sometimes slightly *spritzig*, giving the impression of a light prickle on the tongue.

Greece

Greece, generally accepted as the originator of viticulture in Europe, does little today to keep abreast of her pupils. The mainland and the islands all grow the vine and most of them make wine of a kind, but a large proportion of the grape production goes to the making of dried grapes, largely exported to other countries for domestic wine-making, and eating-grapes. Viticulture is nevertheless a flourishing and expanding industry. There are nearly 600 square miles of vineyards in production, from which something like 88 million gallons of wine are produced, about the same as in the Bordeaux area of France, only about 10 million gallons of which is good enough to attract protective legislation. The remainder helps to supply the fifty bottles per head drunk each year by the population. Even the controlled wines seem a little carefree in their descriptions and their composition. A great deal of blending is allowed and a great deal of flavouring is permitted, controlled and presumably 'in accordance with local tradition and custom' as the international description of wine insists, but it is, nevertheless, an operation unthinkable to makers of fine wine. It is as though the mother of European vineyards mocked at the seriousness with which her children follow her teaching.

Both red and white wines are made, and in case the above remarks should have left a wrong impression, let me say at once that some of them are very palatable indeed and very cheap. They are, however, scarcely ever quoted on wine merchants' lists and therefore not generally known in Great Britain. Except for Retsina, which is the description of a wine flavoured with resin, Mavrodaphne, a fortified wine, and Samos from the island of that name where dry wines, resinated wines and sweet dessert wines are named, I have been able to find quoted only a red wine called Kokkineli, made in Crete, and two or three wines under brand names, one at least of which is a dry and pleasant white wine. Most of these wines sell between 70p and 85p per bottle, going up to £1 for wines bottled in Greece. The field is wide open to exploration for those in search of good everyday wines at reasonable prices.

Official figures for 1962 show the areas of main production in order of importance to be:

Central Greece	100,000 acres
Peloponnesos	100,000 acres
Macedonia	52,000 acres
Crete	38,000 acres
Ionian Islands	25,000 acres
Thessaly	17,000 acres
Cyclades Islands	15,000 acres
Aegean Islands	11,000 acres
Epirus	6,000 acres
Thrace	6,000 acres
Dodecanese	4,500 acres

Wine districts controlled by legislation are listed below:

Saint-Maure	Patros	Cephalonia
Paros	Tripoli	Zante
Corfu	Attica	Ithaca
Nemea	Eubée	Macedonia
Messina	Crete	Samos
Olympia	Santorine	

Probably the best place to start a search for Greek wines in Britain is the Soho area of London.

Holland

Holland produces about 100,000 gallons of wine from fruit and grapes – no separate statistics are available. Vineyards cover 1·5 square miles. Home consumption totals about 2·5 million gallons. Holland therefore imports wine and is not an exporting country. The situation is, of course, different for spirits and liqueurs, of which the Netherlands is an important producer.

Hungary

Hungary is a sunny country with a temperate climate. Its ancient vineyards were largely reconstituted 700 years ago and now cover

some 800 square miles, half of which is accounted for by the vineyards of the Great Plain, lying between the Danube and the Tisza.
Most of the rest lie to the west of this area.

A variety of good table wine is made, most of it white but with a
notable exception in the famous Bull's Blood of Eger commented on
below, and the red wines of Villany. The most famous of all Hungarian wines is not a table wine at all, but a sweet dessert wine made
at Tokay. Altogether an average of 66 million gallons is produced
each year, two-thirds of which is good-quality table and dessert wine
suitable for export, the rest *vin ordinaire*. Only about 10 per cent of
the production is in fact exported, mostly to the U.S.S.R. and Eastern
Germany, with smaller quantities to Austria and Switzerland and an
increasing trickle to the U.K. The soil of the wine-growing areas is
well suited to the production of good wine, being largely composed
of alluvial deposits from the mountain areas mixed with sand, clay,
slate and broken-up limestone, a heat-retaining soil that feeds the
vine and drains off excessive moisture. Nearly half of the good-
quality wines come from vineyards planted in the hills 800–1,000 ft
high; the production per acre is small compared to Germany and
Alsace, which use similar grapes and produce the same type of wine.
Partly for this reason and partly because of the soil, the wines have a
definite clean outline, without any of the woolliness that so often
comes from over-production. The name of the grape is often added
to that of the district or village either before or after the village name.
The grape varieties are easily memorized; there are one or two unusual names of original Hungarian vines, but for the most part they
are names to which any wine-drinker will quickly become accus-
tomed. The following is a list of regions: Badacsony, Somlo (a
favourite of Queen Victoria), Villany, Sopron, Debro, Mor, Eger,
The Great Plain, Tokay.

To these names the grape names are generally added: Riesling,
Szurkebarat (the Pinot Gris of Alsace), Furmint – probably derived
from the French Froment, which is allied to the Pinot Gris and
Traminer – Muskotaly (the Hungarian name for Muscatel), Kadarka
'an original Hungarian grape', Sylvaner, Muscadine, Veltellini,
Harslevelü, and the following original Hungarian grapes still grown
on the Great Plain: Kövidinka, Szlankamentha, Sarfeher. The white
table wines sold under these descriptions are well-made serious wines,
similar in character to German and Alsace wines.

There are laws governing the labelling of wines based on their district of origin which guarantee authenticity. None are more strictly applied than those governing Tokay.

Tokay is a wine of romance and majesty. Voltaire praised it, Schubert sang of it, Louis XIV called it 'the wine of sovereigns and the sovereign of wines', while Peter the Great of Russia is said to have sent a battalion of the royal bodyguard to escort his quota from Tokay to St Petersburg. History does not relate who protected the wine from the bodyguard. Tokay has more solid reasons for its reputation than the fame gained from royal and literary persons. It is made by a unique method and can claim with some justification unusual therapeutic qualities.

It is grown on a lava soil covering alluvial mountain deposits on volcanic rock. The grapes are the Furmint and the Harslevelü, ripened in the sun and concentrated by the same *Botrytis cinerea* (noble rot) as the wines of Sauternes. It is a richly sweet dessert wine, golden in colour, rich in sugar and no stronger in alcohol than a table wine. It has a suggestion of the taste of the volcanic soil from which it comes, reminiscent of some of the wines of Italy. Despite its high sugar content it is not fortified by the addition of alcohol and yet remains clear and stable in bottle for three hundred or four hundred years. It retains everything that it has drawn from the soil because it is not clarified by any artificial means, but left for four to eight years untouched in cask to complete its fermentation and to clarify itself. The concentrated richness of this wine is such that a small glass of it acts as a valuable tonic.

Those who have read the chapter on wine-making will remember that the fermentation of the grape juice is a natural, if complicated, process, which takes place through the action of the yeast cells that form on the skin of the grape. They will remember also that when the alcohol they produce reaches a strength of 14 or 15 per cent of the total liquid, the yeast cells die, fermentation stops and the liquid becomes stable. They will recollect further that in dessert wines like port and Madeira pure alcohol is added to the fermenting must to stop the fermentation and to give the wine sweetness and a high alcoholic content of anything up to 25 per cent. The Hungarians use a different method to produce their Tokay. To every hectolitre (22 gallons) of the fermenting must of the Furmint and Harslevlü grape they

add 3, 4, 5 or 6 *puttony* of the same grapes concentrated by the
'noble rot' and crushed in the small container called a *putt*. The *putt*
holds 30 lb. of grapes, equal to about 7 gallons of wine, its rich contents added to the fermenting must create a fermenting liquid with an
exceptionally high sugar content and at the same time permit a
perfect fermentation to a state of equilibrium. A must so rich would
otherwise be technically very difficult to ferment out if it started
from scratch. As it is, the fermentation can take many years to complete, and needs constant care and supervision, particularly of temperature. There are other highly technical problems connected with
the fermentation of a must of this richness that require the application
of the utmost skill during the whole operation. Tokay is sold and
described by the number of *puttony* that have been used in its production; the greater the number, the sweeter the wine. Tokay made
in this way is known as Tokay Aszu, a Hungarian word meaning the
same as the German *'Ausbruch'* – the purest wine from broken but
unpressed grapes.

There is a drier Tokay made from ripe and overripe grapes, pressed
and fermented together and known as Szamarodni, which can be
either sweet or dry. 'Maslas' in connexion with Tokay is used to
denote a secondary wine, made after the Aszu has been drawn off. It
is used for local consumption. Tokay Eszencia (as the name implies,
the very essence of Tokay) is made from the syrup-like liquid which
oozes out from a pile of overripe grapes, unpressed and untrodden,
but broken only by the weight of grapes in the container. It is used
for still further enriching the fine Aszu wine and is in fact almost a
syrup, since the very concentration of sugar prevents it fermenting to
more than 7° or 8° of alcohol. If sold on its own, it fetches an astrono-
mical price, described as 'the price of liquid gold', perhaps ten times
the price of a five-*puttony* Aszu. The amount of Aszu and Eszencia
made by a grower depends on the amount of *Botrytis cinerea* (noble
rot) with which his vineyard is favoured in different years. He needs
up to five or six *putts* of overripe grapes to every 22 gallons of must
from his ordinary ripened grapes and is normally left with an excess
of normal grapes for which he must save still more of his exceptional
grapes to make the lesser Szamarodni. Only in very exceptional years
can he afford to use botrytis grapes to produce Eszencia. In other
words, no Tokay can be made without the help of botrytis grapes
and the amount of the various types made on any vineyard each year

will depend on the amount of botrytis appearing in that vineyard and, of course, also on the market demand.

A Tokay bottle is only 50 cl. (half a litre), compared with a normal wine bottle of 75 cl. (three-quarters of a litre). The wine must, by law, be bottled in the district and every bottle is numbered and bears a vintage on the label. It can be kept in bottles that have been opened for many months without deterioration.

Bull's Blood (Hungarian – Bikaver) is the best known in Britain of all Hungarian red wines. It is said to owe its name to the men of the Hungarian Magyar army, who considered it to be the source of the strength and courage which enabled them successfully to defend the town of Eger, whence it comes, against the invading Turkish army during one of the many wars of the sixteenth and seventeenth centuries. It is made from the original Hungarian vine, the Kadarka, with the help of a small quantity of grapes of French origin It is a full-bodied, strongly flavoured red table wine, generally sold without a vintage. In the Eger district also is made a pleasant red wine known as Médoc Noir.

The finest red wines of Hungary are made in the Villany district from the red Burgundy grape – probably the Pinot. They are lighter and more delicate wines than the fulsome Bull's Blood, and are capable of development in bottle. On current British lists the table wines, including the red Bull's Blood, are quoted at 70p to 80p per bottle, whilst Tokay in its various qualities ranges from £1·10 for the Szamarodni to £1·80 for a five-*puttonyos* Aszu in half-litre bottles. The white table wines, such as Balatoni Riesling and Pecs Riesling, are listed at 70p to 90p. The Rieslings grown around Lake Balaton deserve a special mention; they are the finest made in Hungary.

Italy

Italy produces some 1,500 million gallons of wine per year, sometimes more and sometimes less than France, with whom she shares the position of the biggest wine producer in the world. Until recently there have been no widely accepted principles for naming wines or growing vines and only spasmodic attempts at making fine wine have been made, by dedicated individual wine lovers, or isolated communities. It is as though this gay, artistic, sensitive people are content to enjoy wine as one of the fruits of the earth and to reject the idea of making efforts to improve traditional methods that have proved satisfactory since the vine was first cultivated. In 1963, however, in order to fall in with the regulations concerning the production of wine in the rest of the Common Market a new law was passed by Parliament to control the production of quality wine and its description. Wine-producing methods that have survived for centuries cannot be changed overnight and it will be many years before the system becomes fully effective. But some areas have already been defined and identified with a particular type of wine, which must be made in a recognized way and of authorized grape varieties in order to be entitled to bear the name of its district, or claim to be of 'controlled origin denomination'. At the time of writing nearly 100 districts or vineyards have been recognized and there are some 30 others who have applied for recognition and whose application is at present being considered. Now that such legislation has been introduced it can be expected that in time all those vineyards that can pretend to producing wines of quality will be identified and controlled.

The wine-loving tourist who has travelled in Italy will have had plenty of experience of the difference between his ideas of quality, or even acceptable taste, and that of enthusiastic Italian wine-drinkers. And yet there are some remarkable fine wines made that never reach foreign markets, either because their price is too high to justify attempts to introduce them to countries like the U.K. where so little wine is drunk, or because not sufficient is made to satisfy the home market. An Italian vineyard may look like anything from the traditional rows of low-trained vines seen in France, to a garden of ten-foot-high pergolas, or an orchard of trees with vines trained amongst the branches. The yield per acre is sometimes prodigious; it is normal for a hectate (2½ acres) of ground planted with 1,000 vines to produce as much wine as a French hectare planted with 10,000. Accurate statistics are not to be had. Of the 14,500 square miles of planted vineyards (compare with 5,000 square miles in France), only about 4,000 square miles refer to ground planted solely in vines; the remainder to mixed crops in which vines are intermingled.

Piedmont and Venetia in the north were the two largest wine-producing provinces in 1960; in the first instance from large areas given up entirely to vines, in the second mostly from mixed-crop vineyards. Apulia in the south, however, generally produces more wine than either of the above two provinces, chiefly from unmixed vineyards. Thereafter the order of production runs: Emilia-Romagna, nearly all mixed; Tuscany (mixed) and Sicily (unmixed) on a par with one another; then Lombardy and Lazio, in each case with a predominance of mixed cultivation. As farming becomes more specialized and wine producing more controlled, much of the mixed farming is being abandoned and ultimately grapes will doubtless only be grown in those areas that are best suited, and there they will be grown intensively. Provinces vary in size and all that emerges from the above statistics, and those from other regions, is that wine production is at present spread fairly evenly over the whole of Italy. Most of the good quality wines that are known abroad come, however, from the northern provinces, particularly Piedmont, Venetia, Tuscany and Lombardy.

GRAPES

A great number of different grape varieties are used and since wines are often named by the grape, a list is given here to enable students to recognize them for what they are when seen on wine labels.

Red wine	*White wine*
*Nebbiolo	*Freisa
*Barbera	*Moscato (makes sparkling wine)
*Grignolino	*Vernaccia
Rossese	*Silvaner
Grappello	*Terlaner
*Sangiovese	Pinot
Lagreine	Riesling
Schiava	Termeno
Rossara	*Garganega
*Teroldego	Trebbiano
*Marzemino	*Albana
Corvino	*Verdicchio
Molinara	*Malvasia
Negrara	Greco
*Lambrusco	Drupecchio
Canaiola	Saint Nicola

Red wine	White wine
*Cesanese	Fiano
Serpentario	Falanghina
Mangiaguerra	*Aleatico
*Aglianico	Oliveto
Piede di Palumbo	Grillo
Soriella	Cataratto
Jaculillo	Insolia
Cannonau	Zibibbo
*Giro	*Naseo
*Monico	

* Grapes marked with an asterisk give their names to wines.

TYPES OF WINES

From this variety of grapes wines are produced by many different methods, varying from the crudest to the most highly skilled techniques. They produce table wines with the usual 10–14 per cent of alcoholic content, natural sweet wines from grapes dried for months after being picked in the manner of the *vin de paille* in the French Jura and then allowed to ferment slowly during the cold winter months. These wines can attain 15–17 per cent of alcohol whilst still conserving a lot of sugar as, for example, the Vin Santo made primarily in Tuscany but also in other parts of Italy. Similar wines are made by concentrating musts and straightforward fortified wines are also made, such as the well-known Marsala of Sicily. Wines over 14 per cent of alcohol are, however, not likely to be found easily in Britain, where the Customs Duty payable is almost doubled on wines with an alcoholic content above this level. Nearly all districts in Italy make their spumante, or sparkling wine. It is seldom made by the Champagne method, but generally by being bottled after a secondary induced fermentation has taken place in sealed vats. Sometimes the sparkle is produced by less legal methods. The result is often a somewhat fugitive sparkle once the wine is poured into a glass. Table wines are sometimes meticulously bottled as in France, but in general they are bottled as required and appear often to lose a good deal of their quality by overlong periods in wood.

VINIFICATION AND MARKETING

The grape gathering, like the vinification methods, varies according to local tradition and the possibilities of making fine wine. In some districts, such as Valpolicella in Veneto, grapes from the plains, middle slopes and top slopes of the hills on which they grow are fermented separately to make very different types of wine by complicated and highly technical vinification processes. The resultant wines, being eventually blended to make Valpolicella, a red wine, are sometimes found on British wine merchants' lists. There are, however, a great many qualities marketed, not all of them made by the complicated expensive method that produces fine Valpolicella. It is this lack of uniformity in making wines and lack of control in naming them that, combined with the fact that there are no simple property names comparable with the château names of France, make it difficult for foreigners to identify wines other than by the names of shippers or wine merchants. There exist a great many growers' cooperatives, who make and market their own wines; there are many large merchant firms who buy grapes to make and blend wines themselves to be marketed presumably under the name of the district from which they come or grape from which they are made. On a smaller commercial scale, good individual family wine merchants exist, who also buy grapes and make wine, always with the object of maintaining and furthering the reputation for quality of their firms. Apart from these, there are two groups of growers who make and market their own wines. These are the independent landlords of vineyards on a large scale, who can rely only on the quality of their wines to retain their clientele, and the associations of growers who have organized themselves into '*consorzii*' and imposed on themselves rules governing the growing, making and naming of their wines like the Appellation Contrôlée laws of France. Their products can be recognized by a badge or crest affixed to their bottles, issued by officers of the *consorzio* under strict control to those members whose finished wines comply with all the self-imposed regulations. The *consorzii* are not strictly speaking distributing organizations, since their wines are generally sold by their individual members through normal distributing channels, but they do afford to buyers a guarantee of quality which is especially valuable in the chaotic conditions under which wines are named and sold in Italy. It must be added that *consorzii* themselves are not controlled, so that it is still incumbent on the consumer to find out if a particular *consorzio* is serious and has imposed on itself any worthwhile restrictions to back up the value of its pretty crest. In the end, as usual, the only real guarantee of quality to the customer lies in the reputation of the wine merchant. In 1963 a law established the Denominazione di Origine Controllata under the Ministry of Agriculture. This applies only to wines in bottle. At the time of going to press only 83 wines have been given the right to bear the D.O.C. label. A further category, 'D.O.C. e Garantita', for the finest wines has not yet been awarded to any.

VERMOUTH

About 19 million gallons of vermouth, comparable to the total production of the Burgundy area of France, are made each year in Italy. Since vermouth has a basis of fortified wine, to which essence of herbs is added by various means, it is in its final form a man-made beverage and the many varying types are identified by the trademarks and names of the manufacturers.

WINES

The following list is of the better-known quality wines and includes those most often found on the wine merchants' lists in Great Britain:

Wines from Piedmont

Barolo. A red table wine. Alcoholic strength 12°–14° – about the same as red Burgundy. Made entirely from the Nebbiolo grape. Undoubtedly one of the best red wines of Italy. The Nebbiolo grape is widely used in Piedmont. 90p.

Barbaresco. Similar to the above, but develops quicker and lives less long. 90p.

Nebbiolo. A red wine, sometimes with a notable sparkle, named after the grape from which it is made. Listed in the U.K. at £1·20 per bottle. A still wine is available at 75p.

Freisa. A red wine of about the same strength as claret. Named after its grape. 65p.

Barbera. Dark-coloured red wine. Also made into sparkling wine. Strong in alcohol, sometimes above the 14° limit for Customs Duty on light wines. Named after the grape. 65p.

Grignolino. Light-coloured red wine. Sometimes quite sweet. Named after its grape.

Asti Spumante. Sparkling white wine. Made from the Muscat grape. It is made in the same way as the *mousseux* of France, but not often in the same way as Champagne. £1·15 to £1·35.

Vermouth. There are excellent vermouths made at Turin, sold as Vermouth di Torino, often under various brand names. In Italy the word Turin is often used as a synonym for Vermouth.

Wines from Liguria

Bianco delle Cinque Terre. A white wine grown on the almost vertical slopes of an inaccessible mountain. It can be dry or sweet, but in either case is a wine of real quality, personality, and vivacity. It is expensive and the production is very limited. Tourists should beware of imitations. It is estimated that the annual crop is drunk five times over. The white wine is known as Sciacchetra.

Dolceacqua. A strong, dark red wine, made at the town of the same name and surrounding villages, from the Rossese grape, which is mainly grown only here. Otherwise it has no great claim to distinction.

Wines from Lombardy

Frecciarossa. This vineyard is in the hands of a single, dedicated owner. Red, rosé and white wines are made. The dry white wine is of particular interest, being crisp, fragrant and refreshing.

Sassella. A fairly light, delicately flavoured wine of a claret type, made from the Nebbiolo grape.

Grumello. Very similar to the above.

Inferno. Very similar to the above.

Wines from Veneto

A great many varieties of red and white table wines. These include Caldaro and Marzemino red, and Termeno, made from Silvaner, Termeno and Riesling grapes, and white Burgundian made from the Pinot grape of Burgundy and Garganega, named after its grape. There is an affinity in this part of Italy between its vines and the vines of the southern Tyrol, with their inheritance from more northerly vineyards.

Santa Maddalena. A red wine of quality from the local grape Schiava.

Silvaner. A light white wine, made from the Silvaner grape.

Terlaner. A generally dry white wine, made from the Terlano grape, mixed with Sylvaner and Riesling.

Soave. A light, flavoury white wine, made with great care and generally bottled when two years old and allowed to develop in bottle. One of those wines for which grapes are selected from different parts of the vineyard to make varying qualities of wine. 80p to £1·05.

Valpolicella. A red, strong wine, made in different qualities, the best by a most intricate vinification process, involving the addition of strong red wine made from dried grapes from the best part of the vineyard. The wine is known as Recioto, a corruption of the word 'orecchio', meaning 'ears', and applied to the bunches of gathered grapes hanging up to dry for several months. The lower central part of the bunch is cut away and the remainder resembles two ears. Most of the Valpolicella imported is, however, a straightforward wine, fermented from grapes gathered on the middle or lower slopes. 65p to 80p.

Bardolino. Similar to the ordinary-quality Valpolicella. About 80p.

Valpantena. Like the above two, but also sometimes as good as fine-quality Valpolicella. Most of the vines in this valley are under one ownership.

Wines from Emilia-Romagna

Lambrusco di Sobara. Named after the grape. A red, rather ordinary sparkling wine.

Sangiovese di Romagna. A light red wine. Named after the grape, which is the same as that mainly used for Chianti. The wine has a certain delicacy and charm.

Albana di Romagna. Named after the grape. A white wine that can vary from dry to very sweet. Popular in the surrounding districts.

Wines from Marche

Verdicchio. Named from its grape. A white, dry, well-balanced wine. Protected by the rules of an effective *consorzio*. 80p.

Wines from Tuscany

Chianti. Red only. The whole area is now subjected to laws covering the production of wine and is the first of the Italian areas to be thus endowed. The area contains delimited zones, the best known being Chianti Classico which is also protected by an effective *consorzio*, whose crest is a black rooster. Good wines are also made in the other zones of Chianti. Usually, but not always, bottled in the familiar straw-covered flasks. The best Chiantis are delicate wines which can compare with medium-quality French wines. Sold in Britain in varying qualities, from 65p per bottle to £1·25 per litre (one and one-third bottles). The white wine may only be called 'White Tuscan'.

Vin Nobile di Montepulciano. From the Sangiovese grape. Not dissimilar to Chianti.

Vin Santo Toscano. Although made all over Italy the best Vin Santo Toscano, comes, not surprisingly, from Tuscany. It is a sweet wine made from grapes picked at the normal time but left to dry, often for several months, before being pressed and fermented. During the drying period the water content of the grape having been reduced through evaporation the proportion of sugar is increased. Having been pressed the must ferments slowly through the winter and is sometimes left for as much as five years in cask. Wines made in this way are called *passitos* or 'wines made from the *passito* grape'. They need all the art and skill of which the wine maker is capable, and the best can be a revelation, having a particular character not found in any other wine.

Wines from Umbria

Orvieto. Dry or medium-sweet white wine. Pleasant, rather full-flavoured and not the crisp type. The wines are in flasks but they are not litre flasks and contain about the same quantity as a bottle. 75p to £1.

Wines from Lazio

Castelli Romani. A crisp white and a red wine are made in the area south-east of Rome. Well-balanced, refreshing wines. The best known come from Velletri, Colli Lanuviani and (white only) from Frascati. The latter perhaps is the best quality of all.

Frascati. Makes other wines of less distinction as well. They are rather more full-flavoured, medium-dry white wines. About 70p to £1.

Est, Est, Est. Dry and medium-sweet white wines. The name supposedly derives from the well-known legend of the travelling bishop's servant, who chalked the word '*Est*' – an abbreviation for '*Vinum bonum est*' – on the door of inns suitable to receive his lordship and who found the wine in a particular inn to be triply good. 90p.

Wines from Campania

Ravello. Red and white wine from around Mount Vesuvius.

Vesuvio. A red wine from the same area.

Capri. A white wine, pleasant and dry if it can be found, but masquerading under many guises and officially made on the mainland as well as on the island.

Lacrima Christi. Red and white, and also grown on the foothills of Vesuvius, it has a flavour that comes from the strong soil. 80p to £1.

Falerno. A dry white wine from the Falanghina grape and rather dry red wine from various grapes. The white wine is the better known. It is rather more fleshy than some of the best Italian whites, but attractive to those who like this characteristic.

Gragnano. A dark-coloured red wine, smooth and light in flavour.

Solopaca. Red and white, no very distinct character, one of the many Neopolitan wines that are often sold as Capri.

Wines from Apulia and Lucania

Aleatico di Puglia. One of the natural sweet wines, made from dried grapes. Big, strong flavour. At one time very popular, now said to be less so. 80p.

Aglianico del Vulture. A red table wine, grown on Mount Vulture. Can be full flavoured and pleasant.

Wines from Sicily

Wine is Sicily's second crop and every type of table wine is made on the island. The most important wine provinces are Trapani and Catania, but wines are cultivated also around Palermo, Agrigento and Gela. Most of the wines are made at the huge co-operative wineries, which have done an important work in assisting the numerous peasant proprietors in what was formerly an extremely poor region, and they are developing markets outside Italy. It is said by chauvinistic Sicilians that at one time, before controls, the reputation of many north Italian wines was founded on base wine brought up from the south. There are some individual estates, notably those of the Conte d'Almerita and the Barone di Villagrande. The wines tend to be high in strength. Modern vinification methods have enabled white wines of definite quality to be made, pleasing, rather light red wines, and some rosé. The principal white wine grapes are: Inzolia, Grecanico, and Cateratto; red wine grapes are the Sicilian Nerello Mascalese, Frappato, and also the Pignatello. Experiments are being made with grapes from other classic wine regions of the world and promise interesting and profitable results. The Sicilians in wine, whether at the Wine Institute in Palermo or at the various establishments, are dedicated, serious men.

As yet only Corvo, from the Salaparuta Winery at Casteldaccia near Palermo, is widely available in the U.K. (£1·05 white and red), Sicilian bottled, but others are appearing on lists.

But undoubtedly the most famous Sicilian wine is:

Marsala. Marsala is a 'fortified' wine, a mixture of brandy and wine concentrate being added to the fermenting must to increase the strength and stop fermentation before all the sugar has been transformed into alcohol. It is then matured in casks for up to five years and blended, for continuity, through a 'solera' system, similar to that used in the making of sherry. Marsala is always sweet but may be flavoured either with egg yolk (the famous Marsala all' uovo) or, more rarely, with such flavourings as almonds, coffee, chocolate, mandarin, strawberry, or banana. Marsala is readily available in Britain at 85p to £1·05 per bottle.

Wines from Sardinia

Generally high in strength and strong in flavour, and often sweet. The best known are Vernaccia di Sardegna, Nasco, Monica di Sardegna, Giro di Sardegna, all named after their grape, and Oliena, named after its district.

★

The freedom with which names, until the introduction of the new wine law, have been used, the variations in the manner of vinification, the fact that the wines are often kept in cask until they are needed in bottle, and the frequency with which merchants blend their own wines, have all made it impossible to define with any certainty the quality of type of wine to be found for sale in shops. The new wine law will make it progressively easier to recognize a particular type of wine by how it is described on the label, but in the meantime the reputation of a foreign shipper or retail merchant is still the most reliable guide.

The labels on Italian wine bottles give a good deal of information apart from the alleged origin of the wine. *Secco* means dry, *abboccato* medium sweet. The contents of the bottle are stated on Italian bottled wines and are worth while noticing, because some flasks contain a litre – generally 97–99 cl. (centilitres) – and some only 73 cl. – the same as an ordinary wine bottle. Wines bottled in ordinary bottles are more easy to control because the different size of bottle is at once apparent in this familiar shape.

The majority of wine merchants list very few Italian wines, but there are Italian specialists in the Soho area of London who offer a wide choice in type, quality, price and value.

Luxemburg

Luxemburg is a tiny state with a tiny vineyard, covering not more than 5 square miles of hillside along the banks of the Moselle. It produces about 2½ million gallons of wine, which is a very substantial yield from 3,000 acres of vines. They are all white wines, made from the Riesling, Pinot Blanc and Gris and Rivaner grapes, and resemble the German Moselle wines. They are bottled in the same shape of bottle as German and Alsace wines.

The Luxemburgers drink about 8 gallons of wine per year per head per annum, which, with a population of about 300,000, seems to dispose of most of an average crop. They do, however, export about 25 per cent of their crop, nearly all to Belgium, and import from France, Italy, Spain and Yugoslavia a similar amount of red wine to replace it for drinking at home.

Production, marketing and particularly export are controlled by regulations to protect the quality and names. The authorized and protected descriptions cover: Vin de la Moselle Luxembourgeoise, Moselle, and the following villages: Schengers, Remerschen, Wintrange, Schwebsange, Bech-Kleinmacher, Willenstein, Remisch, Stadtbredimus, Greiveldange, Lenningen, Ehnen, Wormeldange, Ahn, Machtum, Grevenmacher, Mertert, Wasserbillig.

The name of the vineyard can be added to the label, as can the name of the grape, in the same way that they are in Germany. Wines destined for export must in addition bear the official control description 'Marque Nationale du Vin Luxembourgeois'. It is officially estimated that only about 20 per cent of the production is entitled to this description.

As can be imagined, holdings are very small and average two to three acres. At least half of the wine is made by cooperative press houses under first-class modern conditions. They are well-balanced, soundly constituted, refreshing white wines, capable of attaining a high individual quality and definition of character, but they are not cheap and are difficult to find on the British market.

Malta

Malta boasts a small vineyard of some 3,500 acres – about 5 square miles – and made 880,000 gallons of wine in 1960. Their quality is not impressive and the two white wines I have tasted, called 'Colena' and 'Colena Special White', did not compare well with other cheap white wines. The best wines of the island are Melita, Maltana, Flora, Hal Caprat.

Portugal

Portugal is a small country, with a total area of 35,000 square miles, but it has 1,280 square miles of its territory planted in vines. It produces about 220 million gallons of wine in an average year and has been selling wine to England for at least 800 years. It is today mainly associated with port wine in the minds of the British and unquestionably port wine and Madeira are wines which cannot be surpassed for quality. Their production, however, amounts to only some 5 million gallons and is restricted to a small, strictly defined area, port in the northern end of the country along the bank of the River Douro and Madeira to its island. The rest of the country is bespattered with vine-growing areas, except for a broad strip across the centre, where no vines are grown.

In the northern half vines are, for the most part, grown in the mountainous central area, whilst the more southern vineyards are in the plain between the sea and the mountains. The greater part are table wines, solid, pleasant and well made, for the most part either drunk in the country itself, where the consumption averages a hundred bottles per head per annum, or exported to Portugal's colonies. Except for the Douro, where port wine is made (nearly 4½ million gallons, of which Britain buys about 1½ million), Madeira (600,000 gallons of fortified wine), Setubal in the south, where a small amount of dessert wine is made from Muscatel grapes, and a negligible amount of fortified wine at Carcavelos, just north of Lisbon, the wines of Portugal are red, white and rosé table wines. Some areas have established a high reputation for consistent high quality and these are protected by an efficient wine law. The areas at present listed are the Vinho Verde (green wine) area in the north, and Douro, where the table wines outnumber the fortified by about three to one, Dão in the middle, Colares and Bucelas in the south. Consideration is being given to the claims of some other areas to protection, notably Lafoes, where a wine similar to the green wine in the area slightly north of this district is made, Meda, Pinhel, Agueda, Barba and Lagoa. The soil and climate vary considerably from area to area and the wines each have their own sturdy characteristics; few of them are known in Great Britain, although thirty years ago reasonable quantities were imported under the name of Lisbon wines. Bucelas was a popular wine, rich and golden, about a hundred years ago, but is now a dry wine. For those interested in the relative importance of the different types of wine produced in Portugal the following are the approximate production figures for each area or type:

Ordinary table wine	200 million gallons
Controlled table wine	100 million gallons
Port	6 million gallons
Madeira	1 million gallons

Vinho verde is deliberately made from grapes that have not attained their full maturity, in order to give the wine the light, refreshing quality for which it is famed. It is often a slightly sparkling wine. The vines are grown on a granite soil and trained on high trellis fences and trees. The white wines are available in the U.K. at about 95p per bottle. Red, but not rosé, is also made. The sparkle is derived from a natural secondary but non-alcoholic fermentation which takes place in bottle. In Portugal they are usually very dry and crisp, but some are 'softened' and made less dry for Britain. All are bottled in Portugal and all must bear the seal guaranteeing their origin.

Dão. Red and white are obtainable at about 40p. They also are grown on a granite soil. The wines are fragrant, well made and reliable. The red are the best known.

Bucelas as made today in Portugal is known mainly for its white wines. They have a special bouquet and are very dry light wines with a high acidity that is not very popular in Britain. They often acquire a slight sparkle with age.

Colares. Grown on a sand and clay soil. The red wines have a pleasant distinctive taste of their own. The clay can be as much as 9 or 10 ft below the sandy topsoil and the vines have to be planted a few inches below the clay surface.

There are other table wines from uncontrolled districts which are worth tasting as opportunity occurs.

Lafoes on the River Vouga produces wines similar to the Vinho Verde, both red and white. Like the Vinho Verde vines they are grown on high trellis structures.

Pinhel on the Coa River, *Agueda* on the river of that name, *Alcobaca* in the Estramadura, north of Lisbon, all produce light, fragrant red wines and some white.

Bairrada in the northern plains produces full-bodied red and white wines, the white largely used to produce sparkling wine.

Torres Vedras south of Alcobaca produces red wines for early consumption, rich, red and strong in tannin, giving them a rough taste, whilst *Ribatejo*, the area on the Tagus north of Lisbon, is a large producing area of full-bodied red wines.

Wines from these and the controlled areas are widely sold in Britain, under brand names or general descriptions, at 60p to 70p per bottle. Sometimes the area of production is named, sometimes not, but in any case it is better to select wines by their brand names, because the variation in types produced in the districts is considerable.

Rosé wines are also freely made all over the country and are available at between 60p to 80p per bottle.

PORT

No wine is more strictly controlled than port. The area in which the grapes may be grown was last defined in 1907. The situation of the vineyards themselves is controlled: they must be at a height of 1,500 feet above sea level; and in addition to the usual controls governing the varieties of grapes permitted and the strength of the wine, there are regulations governing the place in which the wine matures, its movement from vineyard to cellar, and the port from which wines destined for export to Britain are shipped.

The area is in the hills surrounding the valley of the River Douro and is known by that name. The wine must be matured in the lodges, as the one-storey ground-floor warehouses are called, in the town of Vila Nova de Gaia, on the River Douro opposite Oporto. Vila Nova de Gaia is at least forty miles from the nearest 'quinta', or farm, the Portuguese word used to describe vineyards, and it is a hundred miles from some. The movement of the wine from quinta to lodge is controlled and supervised. These and the regulations covering the actual making of the wine on the *quintas* are largely responsible for the impeccable standard of quality maintained by port wine from year to year. The climate and the soil play the important part they do in any vineyard, but the Douro is particularly favoured both in the position of its vineyards and the granite rock which forms their sub-soil and enables the land to drain off excess moisture. The topsoil consists of clay and disintegrating rock, rich in minerals and mixed in such proportions that the roots of the vine are both well nourished and well aerated. It is a soil particularly suitable to the production of full-bodied red wine and not very suitable for white wine.

There are several varieties of vines planted. The basis of port production seems to be a grape called the Maurisco, but others resembling the Pinot of Burgundy and the Cabernet of Bordeaux are also freely used as well as a dozen others, some of which are planted to produce white port. The vineyards, being situated on the steep mountainside, have to be terraced, both to conserve soil from erosion and to enable the necessary work of cultivation to be carried out. The Douro vineyards demand a great deal of manpower.

The vintage starts towards the end of September or beginning of October, when the grapes in the inaccessible vineyards are picked and transported by manpower to the 'lagars' where they are pressed. These lagars are large 3-ft-deep stone troughs, about 15 ft. by 18 ft. in area, which, during the course of the day, are filled with the picked grapes. It is in these flat troughs that the wine is made and in which the fermentation takes place, unlike any other red wines that I know of. The reason possibly lies in the need for the wine to acquire its deep red colour quickly, since a special method of vinification is necessary to obtain the sweetness which is one of the characteristics of port. It is without a doubt the particular method employed for making a sweet wine which makes port supreme in its class. Once the lagar is full of grapes, a team of barefooted (well-washed) men link arms and methodically move backwards and forwards over the thick carpet of grapes. There is no danger of pips or stalks, with their high acid content, being crushed by this method, but the grape skins are broken and the juice expelled by the weight of the men. The white juice comes into immediate close contact with the purple or black grape skins and the yeast ferments with which they are covered;

fermentation starts quickly. Not only is a larger part of the juice in contact with the skins in the flat lagar than would be possible in the normal upright fermenting vat, but, as the colour of the skins is squeezed out by the pressing process, it is immediately absorbed by the juice. Consequently, after three or four days in the lagars, the wine has obtained as much colour as Burgundy can obtain in ten days from its contact with broken but unsqueezed skins in an upright vat. This is a fact of the greatest possible importance to port, because after three or four days the fermentation has converted so much sugar into alcohol that what remains is needed to give the sweetness characteristic of port, and the fermentation must therefore be stopped. To do this, alcohol must be added to the partially fermented juice, for alcohol kills the ferments that produce it. But the juice is at present in contact with skins and twigs and if the purity and clean taste of the wine is to be preserved it is desirable not to let pure alcohol get into contact with skins and stalks from which it would quickly extract the bitter flavour they contain. So the alcohol is poured into casks holding 116 gallons, known as pipes – about 25 gallons in each cask – and the wine, or fermenting must as it really is, is transferred from the lagars on to the brandy in the casks, and so leaves its colour-rich skins and has no more chance of acquiring any colour. The only alcohol allowed to be used in this process is pure Portuguese grape brandy, another sensible regulation designed to make port a pure wine of the highest quality. Mechanical processes, eliminating some of the foot pressing, are being carefully and gradually introduced nowadays, with considerable success. The wine, for such it now is, is still raw and full of impurities. It is stored at the *quinta* and during the cold of the winter in the mountains will throw off many impurities; these, together with any other solid matter from pulp or skin that may have been transferred from the lagar to the cask and the now dead yeast cells, will fall to the bottom of the cask. The clear wine is now, at the end of the winter, racked off the deposits (lees) into a fresh, clean cask and in the spring it is transferred, still under strict official super-vision, by road or river to the wine lodges at Vila Nova de Gaia. Here, in the cool lodges, it will gradually come to terms with the brandy, clean itself of further impurities and within twelve months have become an individual wine with its own character and person-ality. It will, however, not have been left undisturbed in its original cask during all this time. Soon after its arrival it will have been blended with other casks from the same vintage in a big vat, and then transferred back into pipes (116-gallon casks).

Vintage Port

Ports are not, or are only very rarely, sold under the names of their *quintas*. They are sold as various types of port (vintage, wood port, ruby, tawny, etc.) and the shipper will, each year, blend his new vintage wines together according to their different qualities and their suitability for one of his different types. He knows, of course, which are the wines from the best *quintas* capable of reaching the highest standards, but he will not know for some months after receiving the wines in his lodges whether they are going to reach such a high standard that he feels justified in declaring a vintage. Three or four times in each decade he is able to do this. If he does decide to declare a vintage, the blend of his best wines on which he has based his decision will be cared for in cask until they are two years old, and then shipped to his customers in Britain (the only country that makes a practice of bottling vintage port), where they will be carefully bottled into specially prepared bottles. They will then be laid down in wine merchants' cellars, either to remain there for about fifteen years or so, until they are ready for drinking, or to be transferred to private cellars for the same purpose. As vintage port, containing as it does about 22 per cent of pure spirit, needs such a long time to develop all its qualities, it has to be bottled whilst the wine has all its fruit, which it needs to conserve its flavour in age, since otherwise, as it ages and becomes lighter, it would be overwhelmed by the alcohol. Consequently it is bottled early, at a time when it still contains a good many of the impurities which otherwise would have been deposited in cask and never reach the bottle. Vintage port has to deposit these impurities in bottle and it does so in the form of a crust, which adheres firmly to the sides of the bottle and leaves the wine bright. For various reasons this crust may slip and greatly complicate the business of decanting. One of the most usual reasons for a slipped crust is the movement of the bottle from cellar to cellar after the crust has formed. It is useful, therefore, either to buy young vintages and lay them down or to get the wine merchant to decant if the wine is needed for drinking at once. A slipped crust generally breaks up into largish pieces which can be eliminated by decanting through a silver sieve, but if the wine has travelled much it may have broken into small particles and it is necessary to decant through clean, unstarched muslin washed in water only, with no soap or detergent. Port with a broken or crumbled crust can be decanted in the ordinary way if there has been time to rest it, upright or horizontally, in one position for twenty-four hours. Because of the thickness and colour of a port bottle it is, however, not usually possible to use the decanting light in the normal way. An alternative method is given in the notes on decanting in Chapter 5, as is also a note on how to deal with the corks of very old bottles.

Late Bottled Vintage

To meet the requirements of many consumers who would like to enjoy the qualities of vintage port without the trouble of storing it or decanting it, many shippers now market a Late Bottled Vintage (L.B.V.). This is a vintage wine, kept for five or six years in cask, to enable it to develop at a quicker rate and to get rid of its impurities before being confined to the bottle. It is therefore lighter than traditional vintage port in both body and colour, but is free of all deposit and ready for the enjoyment of this hurried generation.

Crusted Port

A vintage port is available only in limited quantities, being the product of one vintage only. As there is a big demand for this type of wine, most shippers sell the immediate following quality, the wines not quite up to vintage standard, under the description 'crusted port'. These, treated in exactly the same way, but not sold as a vintage, can be a blend of different vintages. They enable the shipper to maintain a continuous supply of fine ports suitable for maturing in bottle to sell at a slightly lower price than vintage port. Qualities vary naturally with shippers, but a good crusted port, which needs only seven to ten years to reach full maturity in bottle, can be considered in the same bracket as vintage wines. Crusted ports can be bought at about £1·45 per bottle. Old vintages, ready to drink, are hard to find and can cost between £2 and £2·50 per bottle, whilst young vintages, not yet ready, such as 1966, cost about £1·35 per bottle.

Ruby Port

A wine that is not of high enough quality to need a long time in bottle can be matured by a longer stay in cask, so that it gets rid of its impurities before it is bottled and therefore forms no deposit in bottle. It will lose some of its dark colour, but still retain a rich ruby, varying according to the time it has been left in wood. Such wines, matured in cask for two or three years or even longer, are known as ruby ports. They are fully matured when bottled and can be drunk at once if desired, although they take no harm and may indeed improve their bouquet if kept a few years in bottle. They are, however, not generally of a quality that has much to gain by further ageing. They have all the softness and generous flavour of port and can be bought at £1 to £1·25 per bottle.

Tawny Port

A different type of port altogether is made by maturing fine wines in cask for about fifteen years. They become very light in colour, but can develop exquisite flavour and bouquet and attain a velvety consistency that is very attractive. Tawny ports vary a great deal in quality, because they can be made from poor-quality wines by blending red and white, as well as from fine wines that acquire their colour from age in cask. To mature a wine for such a long period in cask, entailing as it does continual filling up to make good wine lost by evaporation, and the tying up of capital for fifteen years, costs a lot of money and genuine old tawny is very expensive. It can cost as much as £1·25 to £1·50 a bottle. It is quite legal to produce a tawny port by blending red and white ports. Such wines are, however, not of a quality that needs years to mature, but are young wines, generally superficially pleasant and sound. They can be bought from £1 per bottle.

White Port

A certain amount of white port is made from white grapes fermented out to produce a dry wine and fortified in the ordinary way. They are intended for use as aperitif wines, but find it difficult to compete with sherry made from vines grown on the calcareous soil of Jerez. In themselves they are pleasant, clean wines of no great distinction and lacking that liveliness which only a suitable soil can give to white wines. They are sold at about £1·15 to £1·35.

Labels

Up to a few years ago vintage port bore no label. The bottle was marked by a white smudge to show which way up it should lie in the bin so as not to disturb the young newly forming crust and the vintage and name of the shipper was embossed on the capsule or the wax seal. These particulars were also branded on the side of the cork and acted as a good identification of the contents of the bottle, provided that the cork had not crumbled by the time the bottle was opened. After twenty years in bottle corks generally begin to disintegrate and it was no uncommon thing in the days before the last war for bins of old vintage wine to be recorked. It is a practice frowned upon by the port trade, who maintain that to recork is to allow the accumulated bouquet to escape, and suggest that when the cork is too old the wine should be drunk – and presumably replaced by a new purchase. To-day, stocks of very old port are a rarity and the question of recorking arises less often. Present regulations make it compulsory for a bottle to be labelled to show the country of origin and the responsible shipper or bottler. Ports other than vintage ports are generally fully labelled with a brand name of either shipper or bottler and a description of the type.

Vintages

Recent port vintages: 1967, 1966, 1963, 1960, 1958, 1955, 1954, 1950, 1948, 1947, 1945.

Older vintages sometimes available: 1942, 1935, 1934, 1927, 1924, 1922.

The war years of 1942 and 1945 were bottled in Oporto. This was unheard of up to that time, but the results were considered satisfactory by some wine merchants and shippers and the practice has not been entirely abandoned since the war.

MADEIRA

Of the comparatively small amount of wine made in Madeira, half is bought by France, Sweden and Denmark in about equal quantities. It has always seemed to me strange that this remarkable wine is not more popular than it is in Britain. The reason is perhaps to be found in the small quantity and the consequent high price of the fine qualities. The chief buying countries use Madeira as we use port and therefore buy the younger, cheaper varieties for immediate consumption. We remain faithful to port for our daily consumption and buy fine Madeiras for their particular virtues and for use on more special occasions.

Madeira is a small and hot island lying in approximately the same latitude as Morocco. Its vineyards, which are planted on both the northern and southern slopes, look more like the picturesque garden vineyards of Italy than the regimented rows of France. The vines are trained over wicker platforms supported by poles five or six feet in height and underneath grow vegetables to give a second crop from the precious land. The 'trees' of vines are grouped here and there and the grapes hanging below their umbrella of leaves are protected from the fiercer rays of the sun. There are four main varieties of grapes grown and a different type of wine is made from each variety. The wines are named after the grapes that produce them.

Malmsey is the English equivalent of the grape-name Malvasia and is the finest and richest of the Madeira wines. The production is very limited indeed and a true old Malmsey wine is difficult to find and can cost anything from £1·25 to £3 a bottle, depending on whether it is a genuine old solera wine or a blend. It is generally dark brown in colour.

Bual (Portuguese Boal) is a less rich wine, golden-brown in colour, fragrant, velvety, well balanced and satisfying, a perfect dessert wine or a wine to be drunk on its own. It varies in price from £1·15 to £1·50 per bottle, depending on its quality and age.

Verdelho is a lighter wine than either of the above, golden in colour, less sweet than Bual, silky and pretty on the palate rather than velvety and grand. It can be quite dry or distinctly sweet. It is a particularly graceful wine and might be considered to be to Madeira what Amontillado is to sherry. It varies in price from £1·25 for a blended wine to £2·50 for a genuine old solera.

Sercial is the driest of the four. It can be quite dry and is different from other Madeiras as Manzanilla is different from other sherries and, in a way, for the same reasons. It is grown on higher ground than most Madeira grapes, just as Manzanilla is grown near the sea in vineyards separated from the bulk of the Jerez wines. It is light in colour and is an excellent aperitif wine. It is sold at £1·15 a bottle to £1·75 for an old solera wine.

There are two common exceptions – commoner in the United States than here – to the practice of naming Madeiras after their grape varieties. One is Southride, a name which refers to the southern slopes of the island from which the best qualities are said to come, and the other is Rainwater, which is used to indicate a blend of Sercial wines, therefore a dry wine. There are several theories explaining the origin of the name; Rupert Croft-Cooke, in his fascinating book on Madeira (see page 276), suggests that it indicates wine made from the higher slopes, as Sercial should be, on soil depending on rain for its moisture and not irrigated by the rivers. It sounds a likely explanation, although to me the name has always seemed an unhappy choice. The only definite place-name I have come across on a Madeira label is that of the district Cama de Lobos, applied to an 1864 solera and sold in 1964 by a London merchant at 25s. per bottle. It is described as a 'dry old wine'.

Making Madeira

Although a fortified wine, Madeira is not made in the same way as either port or sherry. The grapes are pressed by foot in wooden lagars – about 10 ft by 10 ft and 3 ft deep – in a similar way to the port grapes, but the juice runs out of the lagars into casks and is thus immediately separated from the skins. After the foot pressing, a further mechanical pressing of the grapes is carried out by a wine press mounted on the lagar. The must is immediately transported to the lodges in Funchal, where the fermentation takes place. Brandy is added to the casks when all the sugar that is not needed to give sweetness to the wine has been turned into alcohol. The amount varies according to the type of wine to be made. Once the brandy has been added the unfermented sugar remains in the wine safe from further fermentation because the brandy has killed the yeast cell ferments.

For the dry wines in which little or no sugar is desired, a much smaller dose of brandy is administered at this time, in order to reduce the tempo but not entirely stop the process of fermentation. If sufficient spirit cannot be added to the fermenting must to give the finished wine the alcoholic strength required for foreign, or indeed home markets, the amount needed is made up when the fermentation is over. But this does not happen until the wine has gone through the unique process which makes Madeira different from all other wines. As soon as it is made, it enters upon a six-months-long Turkish bath.

The casks are stored in heated rooms called 'estufas', in which the temperature is gradually raised to between 90° F. and 140° F. according to the quality of the wine (high for the lesser qualities, low for the best) and lowered again before the wines are removed at the end of the period. This special treatment is unique to Madeira and is responsible for the particular Madeira taste. The duration of the treatment can also vary from three to six months. The wine is now ready for any necessary adjustments of the alcoholic strength and for a long rest in cask to acclimatize itself to its new condition. Within the next few months it will be blended with other casks and stored, either in butts or vats, to rest for at least two years. The cheaper Malmseys and Buals cannot be fortified in the normal way, because too much is lost during the *estufa* period by evaporation to make it possible to sell at low prices. They are therefore fermented out before being placed in the *estufa* and then sweetened by the addition of a concentrated must preparation and further fortified. The Malmseys, Buals, Verdelhos and Sercials of the cheaper kind, those destined to be sold at £1·15 to £1·40 a bottle, once blended are stored and cared for in their casks or vats until after three years or so they are ready to be shipped or bottled and consumed. The finer qualities may be assigned to soleras, which in Madeira are maintained in a similar way to those in Jerez, or in rare cases they may be conserved as single wines for the delectation of future generations and be entitled to a vintage on their label. Madeiras have been known to live and improve in cask, unrefreshed, for fifty years and if bottled can survive for another hundred years and acquire in the process an exquisite bottle flavour. Generally, however, fine old Madeiras are the product of soleras and are true representatives of the best wines that can be made. It should be remembered that it is the custom in Madeira to identify soleras by the date they were established, and this may lead to some confusion. A Malmsey solera 1810 does not mean that the wine in the bottle was vintaged in 1810. It means that the solera was established in 1810 and the proportion of very old wine in it will depend on the number of 'scales' in the solera and the rate at which it has been sold. It can be safely assumed that a solera of fine wine established by a shipper will have been carefully nursed by him, for it is a precious possession. Its quality will remain constantly as good as it was when he first started to sell it.

There are, then, three classes of Madeira: young blends from three to seven years old, soleras of the finest wines the island produces, and the occasional single-vintage Madeiras which are too good to keep and too precious to drink.

Rumania

Rumania is making great efforts to improve both the quality and quantity of its wines. During the last ten years it has planted new vineyards and installed every kind of modern apparatus for making wine and for knocking it into shape after it is made. In 1944 the vineyards covered 169,000 hectares (2½ acres to 1 hectare); the Rumanian People's Republic announce that very soon they expect this to be increased to 400,000 hectares (about 1,500 square miles); in 1959 it was 240,000 hectares, which produced about 130 million gallons of wine and a large quantity of table grapes.

The vineyard areas are dispersed over the whole country, from the foothills of the Carpathian Mountains in the north-east, the Dobrudja in the south-east, the area around Arad, known as the Banat, in the south-west, and the Valea Calugareasca (Valley of the Monks), a newly planted area, in the south. In the centre of the country vines grow in Transylvania on the slope of the Tirnava valley, at Dealul-Mare in the Prahova county, and at Odobesti. The soil as usual varies with the districts. In some parts, at any rate, it appears to be very suitable to vine culture, as for example, the chalky soil in the Black Sea area in the south-east, where a white wine called Murfatlar is made, and the rock and like soil of the Odobesti and Focsani area, where wines of differing qualities are made, including some of those which the Rumanian People's Republic recommend as being amongst the best of their white wines. The vines are largely the classical French varieties, with the notable addition of the Italian Riesling and the Hungarian Furmint and Kadarka. There are also a number of original vines, particularly in the Odobesti region, the most productive of all the wine-growing areas, the Tirnave area, recognized by the Rumanians as a wine of quality, the Banat area and some of the older vineyards of the now extended Valea Calugareasca.

Wines are named either by their place of origin or by the grape variety, or by a combination of both. There is no rule about the order in which they are used, but generally the place name seems to precede the name of the grape. At present the Rumanians consider only about

30 per cent of their production to represent their best qualities; the more ordinary wines are sold under the name of either the grape, e.g. Cabernet Sauvignon, Kadarka, or broad areas such as Rumanian red wine, Moldavian red wine, etc.

The vineyards recommended by the Rumanian state export organization are:

Cotnari. Producing 154,000 gallons in 1959, predominantly white dessert wines, including one from the Muscat variety, called locally Muscat Ottonel.

Murfatlar near the Black Sea, about 130,000 gallons in 1959, producing wines similar in type to Cotnari and with the same vine varieties.

Dealul-Mare in the middle south-east region, 550,000 gallons in 1959 of good white table wine.

Dragasani in the south, 170,000 gallons in 1959. A light white table wine, made almost entirely from original Rumanian vines.

Odobesti in the east, 600,000 gallons in 1959. This is the area of the Putna Basin. Both red and white wines are made, the most highly prized being a light dry white table wine of good quality. More ordinary wines are also made here and generally sold as Moldavian white or red wine.

Tirnave in the middle of the country. No information about production. Vineyards are on the slopes bordering the rivers that rise a little to the north, in the Transylvanian Alps. Vines are mostly noble varieties of Western Europe – Riesling, Traminer, Pinot Gris and Sauvignon, with some of the best Rumanian varieties – Furmint (from Hungary) and the Muscat Ottonel, with some original Rumanian varieties. The wines are considered to be amongst the best white wines produced in the country.

Teremia in the south-west Banat area near Arad. In 1959 220,000 gallons produced in this and the surrounding area. Both red and white wines are made here, mostly for blending together to maintain regular established types. The Kadarks grape (of Hungarian Bull's Blood fame) is grown, as are several local varieties. The Cabernet Sauvignon of Bordeaux and the Pinot of Burgundy help to make good red wine, dark in colour and strong in flavour, mostly in districts to the east of Teremia itself. The white wine is said to be an all-purpose wine of medium quality.

Valea Calugareasca in the south-west corner. One of the new wine-growing areas which includes some traditional vineyards. Those of Segarcea produce red wines that have gained a reputation within the country and now are obtainable in the U.K., as well as a white Muscat Ottonel also listed by some British wine merchants.

Various fruit cordials, such as plum brandy, are also exported from Rumania; there are two types, called Tzuica and Slibovitza which, according to official pamphlets, are exported to France, Germany, Finland and the Far East. Both are said to be made from the distilled juice of plums, but the alcoholic strength is different, being 36 per cent for Tzuica and 45 per cent (that is almost 'proof' spirit by British measurements) for Slibovitza. It seems possible that the weaker of the two may be obtained by the maceration of plums in brandy, as with some cherry brandies, and the stronger by direct distillation – but I have been unable to get any clear information about this. The Rumanian wines are exported not only to the above countries but to the U.S.S.R., some Scandinavian countries, Holland and Switzerland – in 1959 exports amounted to about 5 per cent of the total production. Home consumption of wine is as much as forty bottles per annum per head of the population according to available statistics.

I have the following tasting notes:

Muscat Ottonel: Restrained Muscat flavour. Sweet.

Tirnave Riesling: Does not taste like a Riesling. Over-pressed.

Tirnave Perla: Pleasant white wine with a strong flavour.

Sergacea Cabernet: A rather sweet, soft and agreeable red wine of straightforward flavour.

All these wines sell at 65p to 70p per bottle. They are listed by nearly a hundred retail shops in various parts of Britain. A great deal of interesting information about them is obtainable from Messrs Norton & Langridge Ltd, Wood Street, London, to whom I am indebted for much of the information from which these notes are compiled. The place of these wines in the lower price ranges can only be determined by personal taste and comparison with other wines available at these prices.

Spain

Spain is the third largest producer of wine in the world, ranking after Italy and France. Although she has nearly 6,000 square miles of planted vines, compared with 5,000 in France, Spain produces only about one-third of the quantity of wine that France produces. The Jerez area which produces the sherry for which Spain is best known accounts for only 4½ million gallons out of the average 400 million gallons total produced each year; the rest is mostly red and white *vin ordinaire* for home consumption, with a few table wines of better quality from one or two favoured areas which are exported. The vine is grown all over Spain, but the production per acrea calculated on the basis of published statistics is remarkably small and not too much attention has been paid to them here. A large part of the country suffers from insufficient and spasmodic rainfall, so that vintages vary greatly in yield from year to year. The overall picture, however, is one of small production per acre, with the unusual variation of the best wine, sherry, being produced more prolifically than the cheap wines.

WINE LAWS

There are laws controlling the naming and production and treatment of wines which cover about 30 per cent of the production, but not many of the wines affected are to be found easily in foreign markets. Leaving aside the sherry names, which are dealt with more extensively below, the most generally exported of these controlled wines are Rioja, Tarragona, Valencia, Alicante and Malaga, all names of the chief towns in the areas in which the vines grow.

WINES SOLD TO GREAT BRITAIN

Rioja. Is a light table wine, both red and white. It has no pretensions to fine quality, but is a good, clean wine, listed on most wine merchants' lists at between 55p to 65p a bottle.

Tarragona. Was at one time shipped to Britain as a fortified wine, strong in alcohol and comparable in this respect to port. Today, however, the wine exported to the U.K. is a low-priced, sweet table wine, comparatively low in alcohol and high in sugar content. It sells at 60p to 70p per bottle. It is, in fact, that unusual thing – a sweet red wine. Besides these wines, described as Tarragona, a big proportion of the red and white table wines shipped to Britain under brand names simply as Spanish red or white wine come from vineyards in this area.

Alicante and *Valencia*. Both sweet red table wines, scarcely ever quoted on lists in the U.K., but both popular in Spain and in some foreign countries.

It is not possible to identify the origin of most of the red and white Spanish table wines on sale in Great Britain. Other names are sometimes found, such as Valdepeñas, Alella, etc. The word '*tinto*' after a wine indicates it is red wine and is the origin of the word 'tent' sometimes still applied to cheap red Spanish wines. Most Spanish table wines range in price from 55p to 65p per bottle. For the most part they masquerade under such names as Spanish Chablis, Sauternes, Graves and Burgundy, although they have no connexion at all with the wines produced in these French areas. They are often palatable cheap wines that should be drunk young and fresh and represent sound value at their price.

Malaga

Here in the hills surrounding this old town in southern Spain – not so very far from the sherry district – is grown the same Pedro Ximenez grape which enters largely into the production of sherry. Like sherry, Malaga wine is produced in a variety of types. That best known in Britain is a sweet, straightforward table wine, unfortified, with a natural alcoholic content about equal to that of Sauternes and a heavy, powerful flavour. It can be bought for about 65p per bottle, although it is not listed by all wine merchants. About 22,000 gallons were imported into Great Britain in 1958. Most of the wine produced in Malaga is, however, fortified and strengthened and sweetened by the addition of concentrated wines of unfermented grape must to produce big sweet wines, dark in colour, that can live for as much as a hundred years and develop well in bottle. Different types are made to satisfy various export markets, the most important of which are Switzerland, which uses something like 400,000 gallons per annum, and Germany; then come Belgium and Poland, which take about

60,000 gallons each. Tourists to any of these countries may well add to their wine experience by taking the opportunity to taste a type of Malaga not easily obtainable in Britain. The wine known as Malaga Lagrima, a wine of great finesse, must be tasted in Malaga itself, since it is scarcely ever exported. A fortified wine from Malaga known as 'Mountain' used to be exported to Great Britain, but has now been replaced by the wines of Portugal.

EXPORTS

In the main Spanish wine exports consist of sherry to most countries of the world, but to the U.K. in particular, and inexpensive table wines particularly to West Germany, Holland and the U.K. Exports have grown steadily over the years, reaching 57 million gallons in 1969. Of this Britain took 12 million, Western Germany 6 million, and Holland 5 million.

With the falling off of home consumption (67 bottles per head per annum, only half of what it was fifty years ago) and the fact that it is estimated that as much as 15 per cent of the population depends on the wine industry for its livelihood, the export trade is of vital importance to Spain, and efforts are being made to improve the quality and increase the appeal of the table wines. This is becoming increasingly important as Spanish production costs have at least partly caught up with those of other European countries, and the price advantage is rather less than it used to be.

SHERRY

Without any doubt the vinous glory of Spain depends on those thirty square miles of vineyards planted in the chalk-rich soil around Jerez de la Frontera in the south-west of Spain just north of Cadiz. As usual the reputation for quality established by the wines of Jerez is due to a combination of soil and climate. The value of calcareous soil in the growing of fine white wine has already been referred to several times; the climate of Jerez, unlike that of much of Spain, is reliable from year to year – the rain and heat come regularly and at the right time; each vintage resembles the last, so that regular supplies of wines identical with their predecessors are available for blending each year; this is the foundation on which sherry as we know it is built, and which enables the solera system to keep a constant balance between young and old in blends or to produce an annual supply, depending on the size of the solera, of a blend of any desired average age. The regular quality and character of shippers' blends make it easy for the public to select the most suitable wine and to be sure of future supplies without having to buy large quantities.

Sherry is drunk when matured in cask, except for very rare wines, and the layman has none of the difficulties he experiences in choosing fine claret or Burgundy; he does not have to estimate the time needed to obtain full maturity in bottle or the form that maturity will take. The shipper can use his knowledge of public taste to blend exactly the type and quality he wants and go on producing identical wine year after year; he is not at the mercy of widely differing vintages as is the shipper of high-class table wines. Because it is a blended wine, sherry is not known by the names of vineyards or even by the names of the grapes from which it is made, but is always described by the type of solera from which it comes. These are in the main:

Vino de Pasto – Medium quality, low priced, medium sweet.
Fino – Dry, light-coloured wines of finest quality.
Amontillado – Less dry, slightly darker coloured, fine quality.
Oloroso – Fuller, sweeter wines, darker.
Amoroso – Name often given to gentle olorosos.

There is one main exception to this rule: the wines made in the area around Sanlucar de Barrameda, which have a different flavour and a lighter character than those of other districts, are known as Manzanilla, a name which Julian Jeffs in his masterly book on sherry attributes to the taste of camomile, which in Spanish is called *manzanilla* and which the taste of the wine is said to resemble.

Although sherry is a blended wine and, in a way, because of the opportunities blending gives the shipper, it is available to the public in an infinite variety of quality, type and character. Each of the four main types mentioned above are subdivided into several qualities that can vary in price from 95p to £1·50 per bottle, whilst amongst wines of the same quality there are differences in flavour, character and sweetness that give the buyer an immense variety to choose from. They are identified by labels, which bear either one of the above names to indicate the type of wine, or sometimes the word 'Cream', nowadays often used to indicate an Oloroso (the word 'Milk' is applied only to sherry imported through the port of Bristol) or some other descriptive word, such as 'pale', 'golden', 'brown', or perhaps only a shipper's or importer's brand name. In addition to this indication of the type of wine, Fino, Amontillado, etc., the label will bear the name of the shipper or importer, so that the customer may ask for 'A's Fino', or 'B's Fino', or 'X's Amontillado', etc. Brand names are increasingly used, both by importers who either blend their own wine or use a shipper's blend under their own name, and by shippers who ship large quantities from their own soleras under brand names. The solera system is explained later in this chapter and the reader will easily understand that the blending of wines that takes place in a solera over a number of years – wines of different ages that grow up together in a cask – is a very different operation, and produces a very different result, from that of mixing two matured wines and bottling them immediately. Most wine merchants' brands are, in fact, shippers' soleras sold under the wine merchant's name.

There are many different grapes used in the production of sherry, but the three most important are the Palomino, Pedro Ximenez and Moscatel. The two last are sweet grapes, used for making sweet wines mostly consumed in Spain, or for blending with export wines to suit the taste of various countries. The vintage generally starts during the first half of September. The grapes when picked are left to dry in the sun for various lengths of time, depending on the wine that it is hoped to make from them. The Palomino, which makes a dry wine, may be left for no more than a day, whilst the Moscatel and Pedro Ximenez may be dried for as long as three weeks until all moisture has evaporated. The pressing is done by foot, by men wearing special nailed boots to prevent the pips being crushed and adding their high acid content to the wine. A light mechanical pressing follows and the juice from this is also normally used for the making of fine wine. The juice resulting from subsequent severe pressing is not used in the production of sherry. The wine is fermented, not in vats, but in casks known as butts, and holding 140 gallons of must. They are bigger than the butts used for shipping, which hold 110 gallons. The casks are, however, not filled up as the process of fermentation needs both space and air. Once the main fermentation is over, in about three weeks, the must has technically been turned into wine, although in Jerez they still call it must, presumably because it still has further development to undergo before it can be considered to be sherry.

The new wine is left on its lees of grape pulp and bits of skin and pips that have been sucked up into the butt from the pressed-out juice, and in another six weeks or so the dead ferments and other impurities that cloud the wine have sunk to the bottom and the wine is more or less clear. But the young wine is still left lying on its impurities because it cannot be moved until the unusual properties of the Jerez climate have had a chance to start the wine along the path it is to follow during its maturing period. It is left for another three months and only then is it examined to determine the type of wine that it will finally turn into. It is classified into four categories, the casks are marked with signs to indicate the category, and at last the 'must', as it has been called up to now, is racked off the lees into clean casks and recognized as wine. Each butt will have developed differently. Those grouped as light, dry wines will possibly have begun to grow the '*flor*', the growth of yeast cells on the surface of the wine which gives a particular character to fine sherries, and which cannot be artificially induced but must appear or not appear naturally. Such wines are destined for the 'fino' type, but no two casks will be exactly alike; the next category, probably similar in type, may develop *flor* by the following spring, or may never become a 'fino'; the third category is a fuller wine and the fourth a clumsy wine, unlikely to achieve quality. At this point the wines are fortified with pure alcohol, not necessarily grape spirit, and left to rest for a further few weeks before they are again classified into more definite categories.

The first classification has enabled the grower to determine the degree of fortifying that is necessary – slight for the *flor* growers or possible *flor* growers, heavier for the fuller wines; and the second has given him an idea of the quantities of new wine he has available for the refreshing of his different soleras. The wines are examined at regular intervals during the following months; some of them will develop as expected, some not; some will be attacked by bad ferments and be lost, others will develop in an unexpected way and change their category and some will remain borderline wines, fitting into none of the established soleras. After two or three years the wines will have developed their final character and be assigned to their various soleras.

The solera system is nothing but a well-tried method of refreshing delicately flavoured old wines still in cask with small quantities of slightly younger wine of the same character in order to keep a continuous stock of mature wine of one type and character always available. The matured wine is referred to as 'the' Solera (with a capital S), often given a number or name to identify it amongst the shipper's stocks. The whole group of casks of wines of varying ages earmarked for the refreshing of the old wine is also referred to as 'a' solera (with a small s). Although the function of the young wines is to refresh the older 'scales' (q.v. below) and maintain a regular average age of the final Solera wine, the system is based on the same principle as that used in taming young elephants. It could not be successful were it not for the fact that a young wine, of suitable breeding and character, can be influenced by the medium in which it finds itself. It can, in the course of time, adapt its own individuality to the general character of the company it keeps.

Imagine a single cask of ten-year-old wine in your own possession. It could hold about six hundred bottles. Suppose you use about fifty bottles a year. On the first of January you could draw off fifty bottles and store them ready for use. You could replace the wine drawn from the cask with an equal quantity from another cask of similar type and character but three years younger and continue replacing until you come to the youngest cask, which you would then fill from fifty bottles of newly purchased young sherry. The 'scales' of a solera are known as '*criaderas*'; unblended wines used for refreshing the youngest scale are called '*añadas*'. It is not always *añadas* that are used as the young refreshing wine. The type of Solera A may have been initially started from one of the *criaderas* of Soleras B. In that case that same 'scale' or *criadera* of Solera B will serve as the refresher for Solera A. As the small quantities of slightly younger wine are blended with the large quantities of older wine they take on the character of the older blend, which in return is refreshed by the younger.

A solera is normally started by buying from other firms who specialize in the accumulation of stocks for this purpose the wines necessary to start a complete solera of, say, four or five scales. Since the basis of the system is that there shall not be more than two or three years between the refresher and the refreshed, it follows that the older the final solera is to be, the greater the number of scales required, since the youngest refresher wines will have to be gradually blended with wines not more than two or three years older than itself for ten, fifteen or twenty years, whatever the average age of the final Solera is to be. Similarly, for a young, fresh final Solera, the age gap between the first and the last will be small and perhaps only three scales needed to cover it. There are other factors to be considered, such as the permissible gap for various types of wines, but the principle for setting up a solera remains the same.

When the wine is ready to be sold, an equal number of gallons is drawn off the final Solera into shipping butts of 110 gallons, which are filled right up and stored ready for shipping. Perhaps fifteen butts a year are taken out of the fifty solera butts, or only two or three if the shipper wants his Solera to get older. The Solera butts are then refreshed from the wine in Scale 1 and those in their turn refreshed from Scale 2 and so on, until the last scale is refreshed from stocks of young wine, either blended or unblended. For some markets, very dark, sweet sherries are required, and although a sherry acquires colour during its maturing process in cask, it becomes necessary to darken it still further. This is done by the addition of dark, sweet, syrupy wine, made from must concentrated by heat, blended with natural must and fermented together. It produces a heavy, dark, very sweet wine, which is used in small quantities to sweeten and darken normal wines when needed to satisfy the tastes of particular markets.

The district of Montilla, immediately to the north of the Jerez area, is no longer officially part of the sherry district. The quality of sherry-type wine made there is good, though said to be less good than the natural product of the Jerez vineyards. It is sometimes quoted on wine merchants' lists and is freely sold in Spain, when the growers of the district, not unnaturally, consider it to be rather superior to the wines of Jerez. The climate of the district is, however, less kind than it is in the sherry area proper, and the excessive heat tends to produce wines lacking in acidity, and consequently in subtlety. The description Amontillado is derived from the similarity of this type of sherry to the wines grown in Montilla.

Drinking Sherry

Many other descriptions are used in Spain to name the intermediary stages through which young wines pass and even to describe their final character, such as *palo cortado* for a wine that is not quite a fino, *palma* for a fine fino, etc., but since these are seldom part of an established solera but single casks that have developed in this way, they are seldom available in sufficient quantities for export, and although much appreciated in Spain are most likely to take their place in one of the 'scales' of an amontillado solera. Soleras which are exported are classified in the practical manner already mentioned.

Vino de Pasto. Light wine of no great quality and more often than not an *ad hoc* blend rather than a solera. It is seldom offered in the U.K.

Fino. A light-coloured, dry wine that can only be produced by musts that have grown the *flor* and on which the *flor* has continued to grow until the wine is ready for drinking. The description is, however, used in Britain rather freely to describe any dry pale sherry, and is quoted on lists from as little as 95p to £1·71 for a well-known fine natural fino with a branded name. The student will generally find the quality is faithfully represented by the price.

Amontillado. An amontillado is a fino that has aged in cask. That is to say that a true amontillado can only evolve from a fino, but not that all finos turn into amontillados as they get older. Some preserve their dry fino character whilst still gaining both in alcoholic strength (through the evaporation of water in the dry climate) and in colour, as all sherries do during their years in cask. An amontillado is then a fino that has not retained its dry characteristics but has become softer, fuller in flavour and sweeter. How or why this happens nobody knows and no sherry shipper can tell what his young fino is going to turn into. If all amontillados were limited to finos that had been kept for ten or twenty years in order to turn into amontillados, the price would be astronomic, and so the description amontillado is used to define wines from soleras established with the definite object of producing this type of wine. It does not mean that the wine is younger or untrue in its quality, but simply that instead of leaving the development to chance, the wine is given the material necessary to enable it to become an amontillado with time. The finished product can vary quite a lot in sweetness. Some amontillados on the market are quite dry, although with an unctuous cloying character that finos do not have. Some are quite sweet whilst remaining light and soft on the palate. There is the usual big price range, from £1·05 a bottle to £2, for that rarity, an old bottled sherry.

Oloroso. Is the term used to describe a fairly full-bodied, generally dark-coloured and almost always sweet wine, even though the sweetness has been acquired by blending. It is a wine that, from the time it was made, has never grown the *flor* and never could have turned into a fino or amontillado. It can still attain a remarkable perfume, which is what the Spanish word means, but is generally a clumsier wine than the two previous. It varies in price from 95p to £1 per bottle.

Amoroso. Is a description sometimes used to describe the softer type of oloroso. Wines of this nature are often described as 'cream' sherries and sold under brand names. They are big, sweet, attractive after-dinner wines that can vary a lot in quality, although in this case, since part of their attraction is the luscious flavour which, in all but the rarest cases, is acquired by blending, the price is not always a reliable guide to the quality. Prices vary from £1·20 per bottle to £1·50 for wines sold under established brand names.

Manzanilla. This is the only sherry which has a definitely limited geographical origin within the sherry area. It is made on the coast, at Sanlucar de Barrameda It is a dry wine of the fino type. Although like other wines of the fino type it can develop into an amontillado type, the Sanlucar wine remains a manzanilla in name. Experts say that it has a tang of the salt sea air in its flavour and undoubtedly some blenders make it easy for the layman to recognize this well-known characteristic. It is paler in colour than most sherries, which is natural for a wine that is drunk comparatively young to preserve its fresh, stimulating flavour. It ranks in quality with good finos and is sold at about £1·15 in London.

Intermediate types of sherries are described as brown, light golden, pale, etc , and are for the most part excellent wines, blended to the taste and needs of importers.

Old Bottled Sherry

Probably 99·9 per cent of sherry is drunk when it has been matured in cask and very little is deliberately laid down in bottle to develop bottle age. Now and again parcels of sherry develop bottle age by accident in private cellars inherited by unappreciative heirs, and a few traditional wine merchants lay down small parcels of amontillado and amontillado-type wines to be sold at about £1·75 per bottle to the connoisseurs amongst their customers. All fortified wines take a long time to develop in bottle, because of the stabilizing influence of the relatively high proportion of alcohol which they contain, but like port, vintage sherry can attain very high standards, with powerful and very attractive bouquet and great generosity and delicacy of flavour. The high cost of keeping wines for the fifteen or twenty years minimum that is necessary to show good results, and the small demand for wines at these high prices, preclude most wine merchants from laying down sherry. Old bottled amontillados and olorosos are difficult to distinguish from Madeira, but at the end of a meal or with a fat turtle soup at the beginning, they find their full justification. A vintage sherry is, or should be, dated from the time it goes into bottle and is therefore not a vintage in the true sense of that word. A wine that is produced by any system such as the solera system can obviously not be the product of any one year and the word vintage has nothing to do with the bottling date. Most wine merchants refer to sherries laid down in bottle as 'old bottled sherries' and often give the date of bottling as a guide to the consumer instead of the vintage or date of making.

Temperature

Many wine merchants suggest that sherry should be drunk iced, like white wine. It is a matter of taste and a matter also of the qualities and character of the wine. The principles governing the temperature at which wine should be drunk have been suggested in Chapter 5. They apply to sherry as well as to table wines. The freshness of a fino or manzanilla is one of their prized qualities and can well be maintained by slight chilling. Over-freezing will kill both the bouquet of the wine and the sensitivity of the palate. Less dry wines also should not be warm or give the impression of flabbiness, but there is a comforting warming quality about fine amontillados and this can easily be destroyed by over-chilling; probably, as a general rule, sherry should be served cool but not cold.

Sherry is produced in such variety that it is possible to find one to suit almost any palate or occasion and almost any pocket. Its most general use is as an aperitif immediately before a meal; the richer types can well take the place of port at the end of a meal. It is an excellent accompaniment to egg dishes and with the stronger-tasting cheeses. As a mid-morning refresher the 'sherry and biscuit' is hard to beat and strong-flavoured old amontillados can be an excellent partner to the more acid fruits such as strawberries. Whole dinners have been organized round sherry, but this is an exercise perhaps best left to adventurous enthusiasts.

Switzerland

Vines grow on the borders of the lakes, on the hillsides and on mountain terraces, in the south-western canton of Switzerland, in Geneva, Neuchâtel, Vaudois and Valais, and they have grown there from time immemorial. A few, very few, of the original vine varieties are still cultivated and highly prized, but for the most part the vines are the well-known types imported during the past two hundred years from France, Germany and Austria. Altogether, they cover an area of about 50 square miles and produce a variable quantity of wine, which averages out at about 15 million gallons per annum.

The variations of production are big, as they must be in vineyards depending on a variable climate. The soil is eminently suitable for producing white wines, which account for 70 per cent of the total crop; it is alluvial from the mountains and consists of stony slabs and schist of granite and calcareous rock. These four cantons, known as La Suisse Romande, produce 90 per cent of the total crop, the white wines from the Chasselas grape, the Pinot Gris, Marsanne (from the French Hermitage district), the Riesling, Sylvaner and Traminer, and the red wines from the Burgundian grapes Gamay and Pinot. The wines are named generally by the villages from which they come, often allied to a 'type' name. The two best known, from the canton of Valais, are 'Fendant', a light, dry white wine made from the Chasselas grape, and 'Johannisberger', made from the Sylvaner grape (unlike the German Rhine wine of that name, which is only made from the Riesling). The Swiss also use a grape called 'Rhin', which is probably originally the Rheinriesling, in the production of Johannisberger. 'Ermitage' is a third wine from the Valais, with an imaginary name, based this time on the Marsanne grape from which it is made and which was imported from Tain l'Hermitage. There is also a sweet white wine known as 'Malvoisie', presumably because it is made from the Pinot Gris – a grape known also as the Tokay d'Alsace – and similar in properties to the Malvasia grape that makes sweet wines in Madeira, Greece, Cyprus and Italy. Finally, in the Valais is the only red wine of Switzerland that has attained any reputation. This, Dôle, is made from the Burgundian Pinot grape or the equally Burgundian Gamay, or from a mixture of both, in which case it is comparable to the Burgundian Passe-tout-Grains, made in the Côte d'Or. The Pinot is the grape of the great Burgundies, the Gamay the grape of Beaujolais. The Dôle wines are often pleasant, highly scented, soft and similar to Beaujolais in character if not in flavour. The name comes from a town in the Jura *département* of France, not far from the Côte d'Or from where these vines were imported.

The canton of Geneva has a white wine known as Mandement, which claims to have a taste of hazelnuts. The vineyard belongs to the Priory of Satigny and includes two other villages within its boundaries – Peissy and Russin.

The remaining wines from the Vaud and Neuchâtel cantons usually bear the name of their village or the grape – e.g. Gamay (grape) for the red wine made in the Vaud, or Dézaley, a mountain slope in the Lavaux area; the most famous of Neuchâtel calls its rosé 'Œil de Perdrix' (partridge eye), a name used in some French wine districts.

A complete list of the names of Swiss wines would serve no purpose, even if it could be established, for many are made in such small quantities that they enjoy no more than a local reputation. The following table is a guide to those most likely to be found on British lists or in the Swiss tourist centres.

Canton of Geneva. Mandement (white), often with village name added to the description.

Canton of Neuchâtel. Œil de Perdrix (rosé).

Canton of Valais. Fendant and Johannisberger, and, rarely, Arvine and Amigne, the two last made from a variety of ancient indigenous vines, and the red Dôle. Some of the highest vineyards in Europe are in this area, the highest being 4,000 ft above sea level. All are on terraced steep slopes and require a great deal of hard manual labour to cultivate them. Ermitage and Malvoisie come from the Valais.

Canton of Vaudois. The district of La Côte along the bank of Lake Geneva, roughly from Geneva to Lausanne; the district of Lavaux from Lausanne to Montreux; the district of Chablais at the western end of the Lake, along the banks of the Rhône from Villeneuve to Saint-Maurice. Mont Vully is an isolated small area in the northern end of the canton, between Lake Neuchâtel and Lake Morat. These are nearly all gentle slopes, less steep and difficult than the mountains of the Valais.

The famous 'glacier wines' can be tasted only in the mountain villages, where they remain for ten to fifteen years in cask; they are not available through the usual commercial channels. Wines known as '*vins flétris*' are also made. They approximate to the *Spätlese* wines of Germany – the word meaning 'dried'.

The Swiss drink about fifty bottles of wine per head of the population per annum, largely bought by the glass as aperitifs. Nor many of these wines find their way to the U.K., but they do appear on the price lists of a few wine merchants as follows:

Fendant: 80p

Johannisberger: 85p

Neuchâtel: 75p to £1·15

Dézaley: £1·25

Dôle: 85p to £1·05

The Fendant and the Johannisberger seem to me to represent the best value amongst these. Œil de Perdrix at £1·35 and Malvoisie at £1·30 are among other wines being shipped, and also two 70p wines from the Vaud, but I have not been able to find them on retail wine merchants' lists. Delicate white wines such as these are often best bottled in their country of origin and must therefore be more expensive than robust types which can be bottled here.

Turkey

Wine production in Turkey is now a state monopoly, but it is only a small part of the nationalized vine culture industry. The area under cultivation has increased rapidly during the last few years and is officially given as 710,000 hectares (3,000 square miles), an area which would produce about 700 million gallons of wine in France. But Turkey appears to have made only 5½ million gallons of wine in 1958, the year for which the area figures are given, the majority of the grapes being either eating-grapes or used to produce non-alcoholic beverages, such as Boulama, Peknez and Soudjouk. The home consumption in the whole of Turkey is reported as 50 lb. of grapes per head of the population per annum and, according to my calculations from the somewhat indefinite figures at my disposal, about 2 pints of wine.

Wine is not a popular beverage amongst Musselmans, and was in fact only made respectable (for export) by Kemal Ataturk, so that the intriguing regulation which forbids wines to be named by the grape from which they are made must have some object in view other than the protection of the population from phoney Rieslings. Perhaps it is a question of control by a Government that appears to be doing all it can to build up an export market for Turkish wines. Those described as 'wines of quality' are called Izmir (Smyrna), Tekirdag, Mürefte, Bozcaada, Ankara, Tokat, Elazig and Antep, which are names of places and therefore easy to control. The three Turkish wines that I have been able to taste have none of these names. They were:

Trakya (kirmizi), a place name. The same word as that used by the Bulgarians to denote Thrace. This was a pleasant, well-made red wine of claret type, with a soft, good and gentle flavour.

Trakya (sec), bearing on the label a sub-title indicating the grape from which it is made. These include the Sémillon, one of the two main white grapes of Bordeaux. This again is a well-made, clean-cut wine, medium-dry and medium-full in flavour, with a well-defined taste of its own and a suggestion of Muscat.

Buzbag (kirmizi), again with grape names on the label. A red wine of real merit, the weight and shape of a Burgundy, but a taste that reminded me of the red wines of Hungary and Bulgaria. It is a beautifully balanced wine, with an air of breeding that speaks well for its future development, and an attractive bouquet. As a west European wine, it would sell easily at 70p to 75p per bottle.

Turkey already has a certain export trade, her main customers being Germany, Sweden and Finland. The wines mentioned above sell at between 45p and 50p per bottle.

U.S.S.R.

In 1968 the U.S.S.R. had just over 1 million hectares (4,000 square miles) under grape cultivation. This puts them in fourth position (to Spain, Italy and France). Most of the production is, however, of raisins and table grapes and in spite of having nearly four times as much land under vine as the Argentine, at 400 million gallons it is number five in the wine production league table. Most of the wine-producing vines are hybrid, and nobody has yet been able to produce high quality wine from such vines. The Russian production is therefore of relatively ordinary wine and though it is reported that they are interested in increasing both the quantity and the quality of their production it is not clear whether it is intended to adapt the hybrid vines or whether grafted *vitis vinifera* will be planted.

The main production areas are the Ukraine, Moldavia, Russian Georgia, Uzbekistan and Armenia, in that order, with several other areas producing small amounts of wine.

There are a few Russian wines on sale in the U.K., but so far they do not seem to have been very popular. The following are quoted, all at 65p per bottle:

Tsinaldali, Gurdzhani, Riesling white wines, and Mukazani, Saperavi, and 1957 Negru de Purar red wines, the last one from Moldavia, all the others from Georgia. Those I have tasted have not reached the standard of other wines at the same price.

Yugoslavia

Yugoslav wines have become popular in Great Britain over the last ten years. They are the product of vineyards formerly belonging to Austria-Hungary and Serbia, some of them claiming to be amongst the oldest vine-growing regions of Europe. The country is well suited to wine-making. The soil and climate and the ancient tradition combine to produce wines that are well balanced, pleasant in flavour and well made. The majority are white wines, resembling the lower-priced categories of German, Alsatian and Hungarian wines, and made sometimes from the same grapes. The red wines are less well known and mostly made from indigenous vine stocks.

Altogether the Yugoslav vineyards cover about 1,000 square miles, with an average annual production of about 90 million gallons. Over half the grapes grown are eating grapes, but even so the total amount of wine produced from the remainder is modest and an indication of the sacrifices made to produce wines of good quality. The vineyards are spread over the whole country. The largest producing province is

Croatia in the north, then Serbia in the east, and Slovenia in the extreme north; then come Macedonia, Bosnia and Herzogovina and Montenegro. The vineyards are on hillsides or in plains fed by streams and rivers rising in the Alps and central mountain ranges, providing the friable nature as well as the chemical elements in the soil which are needed to make good wine. The wines are generally named by the grape and the region from which they come, as, for example, Lutomer Riesling, a wine made from the Riesling grape at Lutomer in the north-east corner of Slovenia.

Most of the wines so popular in the U.K. come from *Slovenia*, the northern province in which, in addition to Lutomer, the districts of Maribor and Brda have become well known for their vineyards planted on the foothills of the Alps. The Riesling, Sylvaner and Traminer grapes are all grown here and provide most of the Yugoslav white wines drunk in England. The Sauvignon is also grown in Slovenia, rather surprisingly, since it flourishes most successfully in the very different soil of the Graves and Sauternes areas of Bordeaux and on the banks of the Loire. A local grape – the Ranina – produces a sweet white wine from overripe grapes sold as Tiger's Milk, and another Bordeaux grape, the Merlot, produces red wine at Brda which can be bought here at 70p per bottle.

Croatia, south of Slovenia, is the largest producing area and rapidly increasing. The Riesling grape is its mainstay.

Bosnia and Herzogovina, one of the smaller producing provinces, is represented on English lists by Zilavka, a dry white wine made from grapes of that name, whilst the neighbouring *Dalmatian* provinces produce a wine named Dinjac, a red wine, which one British importer at least quotes at 65p per bottle, with the recommendation that, for a table wine, it is rich in alcoholic content.

The central province of *Serbia* seems to be decreasing its production, although its main grape is the white Riesling. The indigenous red grape Prokupac also makes a rosé wine called Ruzica, which I have not been able to find on U.K. merchants' lists.

South of Serbia, *Macedonia* claims to be the oldest of all the vineyards of Yugoslavia (it is in the same latitude, 41° N, as that area of Turkey which claims to be the original home of *Vitis vinifera*, so it may have some justification) and is mainly known for its white Zilavka grape and red Prokupac, as well as other original varieties.

There is no doubt that the Yugoslav vineyards are amongst the oldest in Europe, a great variety of indigenous *Vitis vinifera* are still producing wines; the whole industry may be described as progressive-conservative and the wines are freely imported by British merchants. Whilst they do not claim to produce wines of the breed and elegance of classed-growth French wines, or the finest Rhine wines, they do offer, at low prices, wines made with all the skill and care necessary to display the charm of their natural qualities. All are sold at between 65p and 80p per bottle.

NON-EUROPEAN WINES

Algeria

Algeria has the distinction of not being 'one of the most ancient vineyards in the world'. It could, in fact, celebrate its centenary in 1965, having planted its first vines just a hundred years ago. French colonists saw the possibilities of vineyards planted on eminently suitable soil on land which could be bought for very little and cultivated by cheap and plentiful labour. By the time the French home vineyards were being decimated by the Phylloxera in 1880, Algeria was producing 1½ million hectolitres of wine (33 million gallons) per annum and did very nicely. In 1960 the figure was 350 million gallons from 1,200 square miles of vineyards, nearly all red wine and two-thirds of it good enough to be protected by an appellation law. At least 85 per cent of the crop is exported, most of it to France, although 'export' is not the right word, since Algeria formed part of metro-politan France until she won the benefits of independence. Today, French imports of Algerian wine are strictly regulated by French needs.

The vines of Algeria are similar to those of the Côtes du Rhône and Burgundy. Planted in the two provinces of Oran and Algiers, they are capable of producing strong, satisfying red wines which today, by special dispensation, enjoy their former privilege of being classified as French *vin rouge*. Under French jurisdiction the appellation laws of France applied equally to Algeria and although none of her wines were sufficiently individual in character to merit full Appellation d'Origine Contrôlée status, the two-thirds mentioned above were classified as V.D.Q.S. (Vins Délimités de Qualité Supérieure). The delimited areas involved are the following:

Département of Algiers: Medéa, Haut Dahra, Ain-Bessem Bouira, Côtes de Zaccar.

Département of Oran: Coteaux de Mascara, Mascara, Coteaux de Tiemcen, Monte de Tessalah, Ain el Hadjar, Mostanagem, Oued-Imbert.

There is control also over the description 'Vin d'Algérie', mainly by a tasting test, with a minimum alcoholic content varying with different districts controlling both these and the lowest classificotion of all – 'Vin du pays'. The V.D.Q.S. wines coming from the delimited areas mentioned must all contain at least 12 per cent of alcohol by volume, and some 12·5 per cent. The vineyards are for the most part sited on the slopes of the Atlas Mountains, and produce wines with a distinctive pleasant taste of the grape and full, mature flavour. The best of them are good wines by any standard, far superior to most of those which came to England during the Hitler war under government auspices, and proved unsaleable even in wine-starved Britain until Germany was defeated and kindly bought them from us for her own home consumption. Nevertheless, there were good wines amongst the first shipments which arrived in 1943, in cask as ballast on returning transports, the best of which proved capable of great improvement in bottle and made good drinking in 1958 or 1959.

Having disappeared from the lists of British wine merchants since the late 1940s they are now creeping back, and are to be found occasionally at about 65p. Having outlived their unflattering reputation of the immediate post war years, and no longer able to enjoy a privileged position on the French market, it is possible that they will one day compete with Portugal, Spain, and other large producers, for supplying good, sound wine at a reasonable price.

Egypt

Egypt has a climate suited to the vine but produces very little. Ten per cent of her 31 square miles of vineyards are owned by one company and by far the larger part produce table grapes. Only 660,000 gallons of wine per annum are produced, compared to the six million that might be expected from such an area. This was the position in 1960. There are very few regulations governing wine-making – a liquid containing only 7 per cent of alcohol by volume is allowed the description and those wines that are made are known by brand names. They are not sold in Britain.

Iran

The vine grows prodigiously and prolifically in Iran. It grows naturally as the bush or tree which it is, but it bears forbidden fruit for the inhabitants, forbidden, that is to say, when turned into wine. Consequently wine may be made only under special royal permit. The output is in fact minimal: 300 square miles of vineyards, producing only 40,000 gallons of wine. One of the wine areas is Schiraz, the origin perhaps of a strong red grape known as Shiraz and found in some Australian vineyards, apparently closely allied to the Syrah of Côtes du Rhône fame.

Israel

Israel has altogether about 30,000 acres of vineyards, 48 square miles planted in the hills of the centre, as well as the west-coast plains. The area is less than that planted in the whole of Palestine before 1948, but is being increased, and the ancient vine-bearing areas which had been allowed to die out during the centuries of Arab occupation are being replanted. Only about one-third of the grape production is used for wine; the remainder produces table grapes, which are largely exported. Of the wines made, the table wines are mainly white, medium dry and sweet, and the red wines appear to be mostly light, sweet wines, like the Valencia and Alicante wines of Spain or the Commandaria of Cyprus. They are well made and pleasant and in various qualities vary from 65p to 90p per bottle. On the whole, they are more successful than the white table wines, which often have an intensity of flavour which overrides the taste of English or French cooking and lacks the gentle approach to the palate that makes wine attractive. They are quoted at 75p or 80p, prices at which many other countries can offer their traditional fine wines. The flavour of the Israeli wines I have seen is by no means unattractive in itself and the final judgement must, as usual, rest with the drinker. They are identified by place names, which however refer to the shippers' cellars rather than to the vineyard location.

In 1960 Israel made about 3½ million gallons of wine, of which 150,000 gallons were exported. The home consumption is at the rate of six bottles per head of population per annum.

Jordan

This is a 'nil return', included only because, in view of its position, it ought to make wine. In fact 75 square miles of vineyards produced 40,000 gallons of wine in 1962 – the crop of grapes being used almost entirely for eating and for distilling into local 'Cognac'.

Lebanon

I have tasted a very pleasing red wine from the Lebanon in a Persian restaurant in the City of London, but have found these wines no-where else in Britain. Ninety square miles of vineyards produce grapes of which 90 per cent are used for table grapes; only 700,000 gallons of wine are made.

Morocco

There is a well-organized and well-controlled effort being made by the Government to create a wine industry based on quality. Vine-yards are classed into two categories, traditional and modern. The traditional, of which there are some 15,000 hectares (60 square miles), produce mainly eating grapes for the home demand and raisins, whilst the modern vineyards, 600,000 hectares (235 square miles), are cultivated for wine-making. The modern vineyards, which were only started in 1912, already make about 44 million gallons of wine from vines imported from France, mainly from the Rhône region, like those of Algeria. Nearly all is red or rosé and benefits from a low natural acidity. The consequent softness of texture allows the full warm flavour of the wine to be comfortably appreciated whilst it is still young. The wines are identified by brands or by place names but not by individual vineyards.

Seventy per cent of the production is exported and 85 per cent of the exports go to France or other French possessions. Being a modern, planned industry, the vineyards are situated in well-defined areas, chosen for the suitability of climate and soil. There are three along the coast, at Casablanca, Rabat and Kenitra, and four others inland, at Marrakesh, Meknes, Otaza and Oujda. The Moroccans consider that their best wines come from Casablanca and that wines from that area are capable of improvement in bottle. The *gris* (grey) wines, which are highly thought of in Morocco, are also made in this region. They are dry, strongly flavoured wines, with a slightly grey colour, which, however, do not appear to be available in the U.K. The red wines are quoted by some wine merchants at the low price of 55p to 60p per bottle and should be of interest to any reader who makes a small daily ration of red wine part of his diet.

Syria

Syria has 270 square miles of vineyards which produce 400,000 gallons of ordinary wine; most of the grapes are used for eating.

Tunisia

The Tunisian vineyards, like those of Algeria, have acquired their modern shape only since 1912. The area under cultivation has increased since then from 16,000 hectares to 50,000 hectares (195 square miles). The manner of their cultivation and of their control is very similar to that in Algeria. Most of the 42 million gallons of wine made is red *vin ordinaire*, but a small amount of superior white wine made from the Muscat grape enjoys the protection of an Appellation Contrôlée as Muscat de Tunisie, or the delimited areas of Thibas, Radés and Kelibia, whichever is appropriate.

Like Algeria, Tunisia's export trade has undoubtedly suffered as a result of losing its privileged position on the French market. Tunisia used to export 70 per cent of its production, and the wine industry, if it is not to decline, will have to find other markets to replace what was overwhelmingly its largest customer. British wine merchants are beginning to list Tunisian wines and they are worth considering for inexpensive drinking. They are also being used, anonymously, by importers under their own brand labels of inexpensive 'vin de table'. They sell at about 60p per bottle.

Australia

The first vine was planted in Australia near Sydney in New South Wales in 1788. Forty years later, samples sent to the Society for the Encouragement of Arts, Manufactures and Commerce, later to become the Royal Society of Arts in London, obtained favourable mention, and about twenty-five years after that, in 1854, the first commercial shipment of Australian wine was made to Britain. Since then progress has been steady, despite the occasional setbacks that afflict all wine-exporting countries.

Britain is still Australia's biggest customer by far, taking about 50 per cent of the 1·8 million gallons exported in 1969. The quantity is made up of almost equal parts of fortified, dessert-type wines and of light table wines, with a small amount of brandy – 2,200 proof gallons, amounting to only 2 per cent of Australia's total export of brandy. The remainder of wine exported goes mainly to Canada and New Zealand, whilst the brandy goes to Canada (50 per cent of the exports), Malaya and Singapore (30 per cent of the exports), and a small quantity to New Zealand. Thirty years ago total wine production was about 16 million gallons; in 1960 it was 29 million and in 1964 it is estimated at 40 million. The Australians themselves drink about 1·6 gallons per head annually, accounting for some 20 million gallons a year; the seeming over-production which might be expected from these figures is regulated by distillation of a large part of the crop to provide the fortifying spirit necessary for making dessert wines and selected spirit destined for maturing as brandy. On an average the crop is used in the following proportions: 16 per cent to produce table wine, 27 per cent fortified wine, 14 per cent brandy, 36 per cent fortifying spirit. The table wine proportion is increasing steadily as these become more popular in Australia itself. Production has doubled over the last twenty years, reaching 52 million gallons in 1969.

Most of the vineyards are in the southern part of the continent, in the latitude of about 30° S to 40° S, in which the first vines were planted. Nearly all are in the eastern half of the continent, in New South Wales, Victoria and South Australia. The latter is responsible for 75 per cent of the crop, followed by New South Wales and Victoria, with 12 per cent and 8 per cent respectively. Both Queensland and Western Australia have their small, old-established vineyard region and between them provide the other 5 per cent of the crop.

Most Australian wines bear some indication on their label as to the district from which they come and the student can, at very little expense, embark on an interesting course of study of the characteristics and qualities of the various districts and grapes.

New South Wales. In the Hunter River area, Hunter Valley and Rooty Hill, Muswellbrook and Mudgee; and in the Murray River area, Murrumbidgee Valley, Swan Hill, Robinvale, are the best of the wine-producing regions.

Victoria. In the Murray River area, Murray Valley, Rutherglen, Wahgunyah, Corowa, Tahbilk, Shepparton, Glenrowan-Milawa; and in the south, Great Western.

South Australia. Southern Vales, Langhorne Creek, Coonawarra, Barossa Valley, Clare-Watervale, Adelaide-Metropolitan. The Murray River area extends into South Australia.

Western Australia. Swan Valley (near Perth).

Queensland. Roma (north-west of Brisbane).

The Hunter River growers pride themselves on their table wines, grown on the slopes of the surrounding hills, whilst the Murray River growers speak of their fortified wines, including the sherries, grown on their rather heavy, sandy soil, slightly lime-impregnated. The Tahbilk region, however, specializes in table wines. In general, the types of wines grown are carefully adapted to the soil, the moisture and the heat.

The first vines were imported from the Cape and from South America, but have since been largely reinforced by direct imports from Europe. According to the very informative booklet published annually by the Federal Wine and Brandy Producers Council of Australia, the grape delivered in the largest quantities to the wineries and distilleries is one known as Sultana, but this was in the exceptional year of 1962 and is not borne out in others. In general, Doradillo is more popular for white wine and Grenache for red. Doradillo is from Spain and the Grenache grape from the Rhône. The Syrah, again from the Rhône, comes next, in almost the same quantities as the Spanish sherry grape, Pedro Ximenez. Comparatively small quanties of the white Bordeaux Sémillion and Spanish Palomino, and very little of the classic light wine grapes, such as Riesling, Cabernet Sauvignon, Malbec, and Traminer, are recorded. A distinction is made between Rheinriesling and 'other type Riesling', as it is in many European vineyards. As the reader will already have discovered, the mutations of the vine are increasing and the names by which local varieties are known are often quite misleading and sometimes entirely inaccurate.

The industry is made up of large estates, of smallholders, and of cooperative wineries. The large estates grow, make and market their own wines, either under brand names or by vineyard names, combined often with grape names. Wholesalers who buy wine from those small estates that do not belong to cooperatives use the same method of naming their wines and so do the cooperatives, who market their own wines, except that they are not often able to give a vineyard name since the wine they make is a pressing of the grapes of various vineyards in their area. The vineyard name is usually replaced by a brand name in these cases. The export of wine is controlled by the Australian Wine Board, acting under the authority of a Wine Overseas Marketing Act and responsible to the Minister of State for Primary Industry. A high degree of quality has been attained, but it must be sought out and discovered by the individual drinker. Label descriptions are not enough, nor is price a safe guide. There are, for example, wines described as Rheinrieslings at lower prices than ordinary Rieslings and far less good in quality, and there are many examples of cheaper wines being better than more expensive wines of the same type. On price lists table wines are sometimes described as red, white dry, etc., with the name of a region, such as Murray Valley, but more often they are quoted by the evocative names of European vineyards, such as Chablis, Burgundy, hock or claret, which at least indicate to the public the type of wine to be expected, even if they have nothing in common with the character of the genuine wine.

Table wines are sold for between 60p and 90p per bottle, or at 90p for quart flagons in which some brands, although fewer and fewer nowadays, are bottled. The fortified wines sold in Britain are usually described as sherry, without qualification, or port type or style, since the description 'port' alone is protected in Britain under an old-standing treaty with Portugal. The descriptions do not, and of course are not intended, to deceive anyone who has an elementary knowledge of wine. They do, however, mislead and misinform the younger generation of the newcomer to wine, and yet it is difficult to maintain that the words 'sherry', or 'Burgundy' (not, I think, Chablis, to which white Burgundy is an adequate alternative), or 'claret' have not become generic names which indicate in this country a type of wine that it would be difficult to describe in any other way. In fact, legislation now requires that 'Australian' precedes the word 'sherry' on wines of this type and the name of the country of origin must be similarly used on wines made by the sherry method elsewhere than in Spain. It would seem desirable that this practice were extended to other types also.

A large range of port type, sherry type and the table wines, hock, Burgundy and claret type, are available in Great Britain. They are robust, well-made wines, with a satisfying fullness of flavour, and occasionally the subtlety and finesse that would enable them to improve their quality with time in bottle. With rare exceptions, the combination of soil and climatic conditions do not allow the more delicate flavours to develop and the wise Australians keep the few rarities at home.

New Zealand

On North Island there are about 2 square miles of vineyards, producing 850,000 gallons of wine – a yield per acre comparable with the Provençal area of France. All sorts of wines are made and drunk in the country, reinforced by imports amounting to another 130,000 gallons. Australian wine-growers are interesting themselves in New Zealand and it is possible that wine production may increase.

South Africa

The South African vineyards have trebled their area in the last forty years, but nevertheless are not very extensive compared with European ones. They covered 153,000 acres (240 square miles) in 1963 and produced 67 million gallons of wine, which is less than the Bordeaux area of France. They are, for the most part, situated in the extreme southern tip of the continent, within 150 miles of Cape Town, planted amongst the hills of the coastal region and those adjoining of the Little Karoo. Vineyards in the Transvaal are not included in the above figures, as they are not important to the South African wine production. They produce mostly table grapes.

According to the latest information in that comprehensive and well-produced document, the Report of the K.W.V. (Ko-Operative Wijnbouwers Vereniging, or Co-operative Wine Growers' Association), it is the coastal belt district of Stellenbosch and Paarl that produce most of the table wine, with the addition – for red wines – of Cape, and – for white wines – of Tulbagh. The better class of dry sherry-type wine is also produced here, as well as some port type, whilst the heavier wines come from Worcester, Robertson and Montagu, in the mountainous district immediately to the east of the coastal belt, known as the Little Karoo. This seems to be a natural classification, for the soil of the mountain slopes of the coastal belt is derived from Table Mountain and consists of sandstone, granite and shale, whilst that of the Little Karoo is a richer, more fertile clay and loam, compensated to some extent by the higher altitude of the vineyards. Many different types of wine are made, in fact every type, ranging from light red and white table wines to a kind of fortified grape juice, like the mistelles of France, called Jerepigo, largely used for making the intermediate sweet dessert wines, both red and white. There is a flourishing trade also in brandy, both on the home market and for export, but the general emphasis is on the fortified wines and sweet dessert wines, whilst the table wine trade is increasing.

The vines are nearly all French, mostly from the Rhône, Burgundy and Bordeaux, and from a grape called Steen, which is a natural adaptation of some of the early vines planted by the pioneers of South African viticulture three hundred years ago.

South African sherry is made from this grape and from the Frandsdruift (the Palomino of Spain), planted where possible on a calcium-rich soil. Although some of the grapes and the soil are different from those of Jerez, the vinification methods are, as far as possible, the same. The *flor* which is so necessary to the production of good dry sherry does not form naturally, at least not sufficiently freely to be relied upon, and is cultivated separately and introduced to suitable wines on which it then grows exactly as in Spain. The solera system of blending has also been established and is the accepted method of making South African sherry. The best qualities, which sell at prices as low as 95p per bottle, compare well with medium-quality Spanish wines at much higher prices, a fact that has been amply demonstrated by many 'blind' tastings held for the wine trade by the London agents. The cheaper categories, grown mostly in the Little Karoo area, are palatable wines, and can be bought for 85p per bottle.

All the well-known types of port are produced – tawny, ruby, vintage character – from grapes used in France in the Rhône and Châteauneuf-du-Pape areas. Recently a start has been made with Portuguese grapes from vines brought from the Douro Valley. The soil is different but the method of vinification is the same, broadly, as that used in Portugal. The wines are described in Britain as 'port type' or 'port style', because in Britain the description 'port' is reserved by treaty only for wines produced in Portugal. The South African wines are well made, good wines, with a flavour of their own, and can be bought for about 85p per bottle. Other dessert wines, made from both the red and white Muscat grape, are not much seen in Britain, except in the north of England and Scotland; even the famous Constantia wines from one of the oldest vineyards in all South Africa are seldom seen in the form in which they were originally known – as red and white dessert wines – although other wines from Constantia vineyards are sometimes available. All these fortified wines contain between 16 and 20 per cent of alcohol by volume.

The table wines are almost universally quoted on British wine lists. They are of two types, the red ones generally known as claret type or Burgundy type, although they are often offered on lists under their regional names without further qualification, as, for example, Red Stellenbosch. The white wines are very often described as South

African hock or South African Sauternes, and are bottled in the appropriate bottles. They are made from the aforementioned Steen grape and from the Riesling, and from the French Languedoc and Provence grape Clairette Blanche, whilst the red are made from the same Rhône and Burgundy grapes as the fortified wines, and also from the Bordeaux Cabernet. Their alcoholic strength varies from 11 to 13 per cent and they are made in the traditional French manner. The wines are not, however, expected to produce individual vineyard's characteristics as they do in France, but are blended by co-operatives or wholesalers to produce a regular character and quality and to be sold under brand names. Their prices vary from 55p to 75p per bottle. Most of the table wines are grown on comparatively poor, stony soil, on the slopes of the hills of the Stellenbosch and Constantia valleys and at Paarl, the right kind of soil for this type of wine. Sparkling wines are also made, both by the Champagne method and in closed vats, but they are not generally exported.

In addition to a well-established brandy industry, many types of liqueurs are made, the most famous being Van der Hum, said to be named after a sea captain who was particularly fond of it, in the early days of Cape history. It has a flavour of mandarins. Liqueurs vary in strength, just as brandies do according to the time and conditions under which they have been matured in wood. Both can contain from 30 to 45 per cent of alcohol, but the variation in liqueurs is due to manufacturing methods and not to maturation periods. Van der Hum is quoted in Britain at £3·10 per bottle.

South African brandy is distilled under strict excise control with a view to ensuring the best possible quality from grapes grown in Worcester, Montague and Robertson in the Little Karoo. The grapes are not the same as those used in Cognac, but are well suited to the production of clean brandy. The Muscatel grape previously used is now discarded for brandy production. The Government encourages the production of high-quality brandy by a rebate on the excise duty payable on all spirits for brandies which, after three years in cask, satisfy the requirements of the Government Brandy Board. Furthermore, any brandy sold in South Africa must contain at least 25 per cent of this so-called Rebate Brandy. No brandy may contain anything but grape spirit; in other words, it cannot be a blend of grape spirit and corn or potato spirit.

There is no pre-history period to the South African wine industry and its development, since the first vine was planted by Dutch settlers in 1655, forms an interesting potted version of the sort of conditions and considerations which have influenced the oldest European vineyards during the many centuries of their existence. The first vine was planted in 1655 and the first wine produced, according to the diary of the man who planted it, in 1659; the first fine wine was produced at Groot Constantia in 1679. Both initiators were governors of the Dutch settlements in Cape Province, the first Jan van Riebeeck, the second Simon van der Stel, and both obviously inspired by a true colonizing instinct. Then in 1688 French Huguenots arrived and set about planting new vineyards and improving the quality of those already existing, just as they did throughout the wine-growing belt from America to the Balkans, and South African wines began to be well known in Europe. By the end of the eighteenth century, even English households got to know the sweet, warming wines of Constantia. Then came the really big fillip to the trade, when in 1805 the British finally took over the Cape and found that the local wines served well at home to replace the French wines which were becoming scarce because of the Napoleonic Wars. The South African wines were allowed into England at lower duties than French wines and the trade in them became important, until in 1861 Gladstone abolished the preferential duties and French wines, which by then were not only available again but had greatly improved their quality since the custom of maturing them in bottle had become general, regained their popularity. The South African wine trade, at that time primarily export, withered, and twenty years later received what might easily have been its death blow when the Phylloxera wiped out most of its vineyards, as it did those of Europe at the same time. However, the vineyards were replanted with grafted vines, but export markets had been lost, mostly to Spain and Portugal, who had escaped the worst effects of Phylloxera, and serious over-production in South Africa was again a problem. The sturdy and practical wine-growers who had already survived a depression and still found the courage to replant their vineyards after the Phylloxera, formed themselves into cooperative societies and united these in the Co-operative Wine Growers' Association (the K.W.V.), to whom they gave authority to guide and control their industry.

The K.W.V. quickly grew in authority and power. A few years later, in 1924, it obtained government recognition and certain powers which were gradually increased, until in 1940, whilst still retaining its independence, it obtained full powers to act as government agent for the implementation of wise wine control laws, largely inspired and initiated by itself as representative of the growers. With preferential duties again in their favour, South African wines began to recapture their British market in 1926, and a few years later established the strong selling organization in this country which exists today under the K.W.V. The control exercised by the K.W.V. at home and in the export trade is impressive. Ranging from the fixing of minimum prices throughout all stages of distribution, the rationing of production based on needs of the home market, the control of and active participation in the disposal of the surplus and the particular responsibility for the export trade which it undertakes, it is an example of how a well-disciplined trade can solve its own problems and build its own prosperity in cooperation with a government that has the intelligence to consult the industry before making the laws, and entrust the industry with the responsibility for their application. The system is clearly explained and elaborated on in the report already mentioned – *A Survey of Wine Growing in South Africa* – published annually by the K.W.V. and obtainable from the South African Wine Farmers' Association and other South African wine agents in London.

The United Kingdom today takes 55 per cent of South African wines and brandy exports, which totalled 3,700,000 gallons in 1960. The other outlets are Holland, Canada and the Scandinavian countries, who are mainly interested in Constantia and brandy. Imports into the U.K. in 1960 amounted to 1,800,000 gallons of wine and 13,000 gallons of brandy, whilst Scandinavia took only 160,000 gallons of wine and 170,000 of brandy, and Canada a little more wine and a little less brandy. Most of the wine imported is dessert wine and fortified wines of sherry type. Consumption within the Union has doubled in the last twenty years and is still increasing. The increase is entirely due to the consumption of light table wines, which are over four times greater in 1961 than they were in 1945, whilst the figures for fortified wines have increased by only 10 per cent. The total in 1961, including sparkling wine (241,000 gallons), is 26 million gallons, which is about fifteen bottles per head of the whole population.

The final assessment of South African wine qualities must, as always, be a personal one, but anyone who wants to try them can be assured that he is tasting wines made with skill, care and the ambition to produce honest wine of good quality

Canada

Canadian wine will be of little practical interest to readers, because it is sufficient only for home needs and none is exported. It is interesting to the student, because of the well-documented experiments that are taking place in Ontario at the Vineland Horticultural Experimental Station. They range from long-term investigations into the best variety of vine for the Ontario Niagara Peninsula area, where most of the vineyards are, to artificial methods of producing the Jerez *flor* on the wines destined to make Canadian sherry. The whole concept of Canadian wine-making is progressive and bold.

Most of the grapes used are not of the traditional wine-making species at all, but either their own Concord grape – *Vitis labrusca* – or various Frency hybrids bred from varieties of *Vitis rupestris* and French *Vitis vinifera*. These are the hybrids which have made so much progress in France during the last fifty years and are mentioned and explained in the chapters on French wines. Hybrids, incidentally, are generally known by the name of their creator and a number: Seibel 1,000, Joannes Seyve 137,567, Seyve-Villard 10,319, etc. It will be remembered from the section on French wines that the big problem has been to breed a hybrid that did not produce in the wine the unpleasant 'foxy' taste, generally associated with grape species other than *vinifera*. The adventurous approach of the Canadian to his wine is suggested also by the amount of flavoured wines which are sold and the existence of British Columbia wineries, making wine from loganberries. Whether this has anything to do with efforts to get rid of the 'foxy' taste of hybrids, I do not know.

Altogether, about 8 million gallons of wine are produced by the 75 square miles of vineyards, a good half of the grapes being used for eating; almost all the vineyards are in the Niagara Peninsula in Ontario, but there are a few in British Columbia in the Okanaga Valley. Here, however, the wineries are allowed to import grapes from California, so that these and the loganberry wine are apt to falsify the production figures. As already mentioned, Canadian wine is not sold in the United Kingdom.

U.S.A.

The U.S.A. produces 200 million gallons of wine, and drinks nearly all itself. Practically nothing is exported, though some Californian wines are now available in Britain. Although vines in abundance grew in the Eastern states when America was discovered, none of them were of the wine-making species, *Vitis vinifera*, but belonged to those sturdy American species, *Vitis labrusca, rupestris,* etc , which later, as root stock for grafting, saved the European vineyards from destruction by the Phylloxera pest. The American wine-producing vineyards date only from the beginning of the nineteenth century, when missionaries, political refugees, disappointed gold prospectors and immigrants of all kinds from Europe's wine countries imported their native vines and planted them in California. Today, Californian vineyards cover some 470,000 acres (700 square miles) and represent 80 per cent of America's vineyard area. There is a large industry in raisins and eating grapes, and it is estimated that only 28 per cent of the vineyard area is used for wine-making. The original grape-growing areas of New York State and New Jersey now produce only about $7\frac{1}{2}$ million and $4\frac{1}{2}$ million gallons respectively, mostly from native, non-vinifera grape species and very different from the 'European juices' produced in California. Even in California the area under vines in 1969 was only about 80 per cent of what it was in 1927, half-way through the Prohibition period. In spite of this, the Americans are drinking more wine than in the 1930s; the consumption had reached nearly four bottles per head a year in 1960, about 50 per cent more than in the U.K. today, and rises steadily every year. The increased consumption is reflected in the import figures of European wine: 10,000,000 gallons in 1960, 24,000,000 gallons in 1969.

Broad lines of nomenclature and classification of types are recognized by the authorities, but I can trace no attempts at classifying quality. Five types are recognized: aperitifs, table red, table white, dessert and sparkling. There are three bases for naming wines. They may be described by a 'generic' name; not everyone agrees on what names have become generic, that is to say so much used that they have become part of the foreign language and acquired a meaning different from the one they had in their country of origin. A name such as 'Sauternes', for example, originated in France and to a Frenchman only a wine from the district of Sauternes has the right to be sold as such, and even then it must be of a certain type and of recognized quality. One of the essential qualities is that it should be sweet. To an Englishman Sauternes has become generic, and describes sweet wine from such countries as Spain, as well as sweet wines from France that do not necessarily come from the Sauternes district. Californian growers on the other hand have borrowed the name to describe their own wines – but strangely they use the word Sauternes for dry wines instead of for sweet wines! Such French names as Chablis, Burgundy, Claret and Champagne are also considered by most people, though not by the French, to have became generic and are freely used to describe wines that can be similar or vastly different to the original French product. Wines can also be described by their region of origin and/or by the grape from which they are made. The last is the method most used in California for home-grown wines, made from European grapes such as Cabernet, Barbera, Grignolino, Pinot Noir, Traminer, Riesling, Gamay and, most popular of all, Zinfandel. All these names will be familiar to the reader who has read the chapters on French, Italian and German wines – except the last, and most popular, Zinfandel. A book on American wines by Schoonmaker and Marvell, published in New York in 1941, explains that the origins of this true *vinifera* grape are unknown and gives a list of a few varieties from which it is *not* derived – despite belief to the contrary in some quarters. Whatever it may be, the same authorities describe it as a sensitive grape, which represents faithfully the characteristics of the soil on which it grows – nice praise for a wine-making grape. Northern California's Napa Valley, Sonoma, Livermore Valley, Santa Clara and Fresno all grow an immense variety of European grapes, but since good grape varieties will produce something quite different in one place to another, depending on soil and climatic conditions, the European grape variety on the label will not necessarily indicate that the wine will resemble a European wine made from the same grape. Another significant factor is that in the United States a wine only needs to contain 51 per cent of a particular grape in order to have the right to be sold under that name. The grape variety on the label is, alone, therefore, little indication of what can be expected in the bottle. But the American wine industry is organized on a more rational, if less romantic, basis than the European; the wines are made to a large extent by large wineries who maintain a regular type and quality for each of their labels and they thus become indentifiable by the public. One company's Sauvignon, for example, might be quite different from another's, and very different from a European Sauvignon, but each producer will maintain his particular style from one year to another.

This is facilitated by the ideal and regular climate of Northern California so that there are not the variations of quality which have to be overcome in Europe.

Outside California there are important vineyards, mainly of hybrid vines, in the Finger Lakes District of New York State, Ohio, Lake Erie and the Niagara Peninsula, whilst about 2 million gallons of wine are made in each of the States of Illinois and Michigan. Wine is also produced in Maryland and vineyards have recently been planted in Oregon and Washington State. All kinds of wines are produced, though the sparkling wines are perhaps the most successful.

Mexico

Forty-eight square miles of vineyards produce 1·3 million gallons of wine. The area under vines is increasing. Some Mexican wines are on sale in Britain – cheap categories of both red and white table wines and also spirits. They have so far made little impression in the 55p to 60p category in which they belong.

Argentina

The Argentine produces about the same amount of wine as Algeria, with whom it shares first place amongst non-European vineyards. It is amongst the five biggest wine-growing countries in the world. The vineyards, steadily increasing in area, cover about 243,000 hectares (1,000 square miles) in the northern part of the country, mostly amongst the mountains of the western borders, but also in Buenos Aires province. By far the greatest part are, however, in Mendoza province, San Juan, Rio Negro, La Rioja and Catamarca, and from amongst these provinces the following areas enjoy a form of Appellation Contrôlée: La Rioja, Saint Luis, Catamarca, Cordoba, Jujuy and Salta. Nearly half the area is planted with traditional European vines from France, Italy and Spain. The total production is about 34 million gallons, three-quarters of it red wine and most of it in the *vin ordinaire* category. Almost the whole of this quantity is consumed by the Argentinians themselves, whose average consumption per head is about six dozen bottles of wine per annum. There is very little wine exported, the only customer at present being Paraguay, and the imports into the country are sufficient only to offset this small export trade and annual vintage fluctuations. They come mostly from Chile and Brazil. The Argentinians cultivate the vine sensibly for their own enjoyment. They expect the production to increase by nearly 30 per cent during the next ten years, home consumption by about the same amount and the population by about 22 per cent. Though little would seem to be left for export some wines from the Argentine have recently been introduced to the British market and are likely to retail at from 75p to £1 per bottle, less for wines imported in bulk.

Brazil

The southern part of Brazil, between latitudes 20° and 30° S, produces about 23 million gallons of wine, nearly all of which is drunk in the country. Whilst the wine production is decreasing and in 1960 was only half that of 1957, the production of grapes is steadily increasing, as is the area of the vineyards and the cultivation of eating grapes.

The total area planted in 1961 was 65,000 hectares (250 square miles); by far the biggest area, that of Rio Grande do Sul in the extreme south, produced almost only grapes for the table. São Paulo is the biggest wine-producing area, followed by Santa Caterina, Paraña and Minas Gerais. The main grape used is one called Isobel, which accounts for over half the planted areas, and thereafter a grape named Herbemont. Only about 25 per cent of the area is planted with recognizable European wine-making grapes and the products of these are named by the grape name – Trebbiano, Malvasia, Riesling, Merlot, Barbera, Moscatel, etc. The industry is well regulated and controlled by a series of regulations directed towards the maintenance of a reasonable standard. About 60 per cent is made by cooperative societies. The home consumption is about the same as that in the U.K. – three bottles per head per annum. What little wine is exported goes to France and the Argentine. None is imported into Great Britain.

Chile

The wines of Chile are the only South American wines that are widely quoted in Britain. Viticulture is a peasant industry in Chile. Of 30,000 proprietors, 17,000 own vineyards of under one hectare (2·5 acres) and 9,000 between one and five hectares. The area under vines has increased by over 50 per cent in fifty years and now totals about 280,000 acres (430 square miles), producing about 88 million gallons of wine per year – about the same as the Bordeaux area of France. In spite of a home consumption of something over five dozen bottles a year per head, there is an over-production of wine, which the Chilean authorities seek to remedy by the facilitation and encouragement of exports. Most of the wine made is red table wine, of a character and quality well suited to the taste of northern countries.

Despite this, exports are not impressive, amounting to under 3 million gallons in 1960, compared with 66 million gallons consumed in the country. The surplus available for export is therefore substantial and is reflected in the low prices at which these excellent wines are available in Britain. The main provinces concerned lie in the central part of the country, in the same latitude as the vineyards of South Africa and Australia. Santiago, O'Higgins and Colchagua are the most important, and, with Talca just to the south, form the vineyard country. Coquimbo marks the northern limit.

The vines are all French varieties of *cépages nobles* from the Bordeaux area and from Burgundy; the soil varies from district to district and the climate in the latitude between 30° S and 40° S is equitable, unlike the arid region to the north and the wet region to the south.

Regulations governing the cultivation of the vines and of wine-making are strict and sometimes surprising. Vines, for example, must not be watered within a fortnight of the vintage, nor may they be planted on ground with a gradient of less than 6° – both measures intended to protect the quality of the wine. Sugaring of musts is also prohibited – a practice frequently authorized in France and even more frequently practised. The whole industry makes full use of French wine knowledge and experience; it is hoping to introduce an

Appellation Contrôlée law and is continually striving to impròve the quality of its wines.

The red wines are full-bodied, soft and well flavoured, with an alcoholic content similar to that of Burgundy, and the whites, varying from dry to sweet, have a fullness of flavour which many people find attractive. They are sold under either a grape name or place name, or combination of both, at 60p to 65p per bottle, and are well worth the attention of anyone looking for inexpensive table wines.

Peru

With only 25 square miles of vineyards, Peru produced 1·5 million gallons of wine in 1961 and imported four times this amount to make up her requirements for home consumption. Wines are made mainly in the areas of Chincha, Ica, Moquegna, Lunahuanca, Lacumba and Tacna.

Uruguay

About 16 million gallons of wine are produced annually from 70 square miles of vineyards. The area cultivated has nearly doubled in the last thirty years – it consists mostly of smallholdings producing grapes which are processed by big wholesale houses. The biggest production of wine is in the regions of Montevideo and Canelones, and to a much smaller extent in Colonia and San José, all on the southern shore, and even smaller quantities in the still southern province of Florida and a few isolated plots spread throughout the remaining provinces or states. None appear to be exported. The disposal of the crop is not clear. If it is all consumed in the country it would given an average of fifty bottles per head of the population per annum, but some home-produced wine is possibly destined for distillation. Uruguay wines are not on sale in the United Kingdom.

Venezuela

Venezuela produces 500,000 gallons of wine. There is no information available about the area of vines planted, nor an indication of the way in which the wine is disposed of. As the population of the country is over 3 million, it seems likely that the domestic wine production can be absorbed on the spot without any great difficulty. It works out at one bottle per head per annum.

China

Wines from China are available in London at about 90p per bottle from the Tsing Tao province. There are also Chinese spirits sold in Soho at varying concentrations of strength and at prices varying from £1·35 to £3·30 per bottle.

Japan

Forty square miles of vineyards produce 2·5 million gallons of wine of which, in 1958, 5,000 gallons were exported. The only wine available in Britain from Japan is the rice wine saki.

PART FOUR

RECENT VINTAGES

1945 Possibly the best of the century. Very big wines, mostly not yet ready. Very rare, as they disappeared in the post-war rush. Look at in 1975.

1947 Fine big full year. Difficulties at time of fermentation, leaving some with unpleasant acidity. Started with a fine reputation, which faded because of the stubborn acidity, but now improving again and likely to produce some outstanding wines in the 1970s.

1948 Good vintage. Unappreciated at first. Rather hard wines but of classic flavour. Drinking well now.

1949 A good amiable year. Mostly ready to drink now. Considerable variation in the quality of different bottles of the same wine are noticeable.

1950 Pleasant, graceful, easy wines, without any strong individuality. Ready to drink.

1952 Well-balanced, complete and true clarets, which have gained a great deal in character during the last two or three years and are now developing a refinement that adds greatly to their attraction. Can be drunk now but should improve for another three or four years.

1953 Started off with a winsome charm of character that gave them a higher reputation than they deserved. Seem to be changing now. In some cases taking on more durable characteristics, but generally tending to fade. A very pleasant vintage to drink now.

1955 A slow starter, always soft and pleasant, always correct, but in the beginning rather self-satisfied and smug. They have made great progress recently and are developing individuality and character. Can be drunk now.

1957 Another slow starter, but rather hard and aggressive, with a strong character. They are developing well now and are producing some fine wines.

1958 Light, pleasant drinking now. No great wines.

1959 Hailed by the press as the vintage of the century but deposed two years later on the arrival of the 1961s. At its best, a pleasant, well-balanced year of soft wines, likely to improve for another ten years. There is, however, a considerable variation in quality and there are some wines of this vintage which should be drunk within the next four or five years, others will last for many years.

1960 Despite unfavourably wet weather there are some wines of this large vintage which, although light in character, are both full in flavour and typical clarets. Their price is relatively low and they are excellent for immediate drinking.

1961 Very small quantity, about one-third of a normal crop, but superb in quality. Generous, well-balanced, individual wines of great subtlety, which will need twenty years to develop and demonstrate their full qualities.

1962 An abundant year and a ripe year. The wines have great balance and elegance and an unusual regularity of quality. Because of the size of crop the wines tend to be on the light side but are drinking well now and will be good for at least another five years.

1963 A poor year.

1964 Irregular. An exceptionally hot summer was followed by two weeks of rain during the harvest. Some were lucky in having picked at least part of their crop before the rain started, others picked all their grapes in the rain. Often the wines have body, but they lack elegance. Beginning to drink well now and the best should still be good, and perhaps better, in six to eight years' time.

1965 A few pleasant wines were made which should be drunk now. Generally a poor year.

1966 Similar to 1962, though perhaps with rather more body. After the exceptional 1961s almost certainly the best year of the decade. Very regular, great length and outstanding balance. Pity to drink them now, should be explored from 1974 onwards.

1967 Have now been in bottle two years and are developing well. At first it was feared they would be hard but they are developing into wines of considerable elegance and finesse. Prices were reasonable and the crop was large. A very useful vintage, drink from 1973 onwards and give 1966 full time to mature.

1968 A poor year, few wines worthy of a reputable château name.

1969 A small crop of wines that were starved of sun in the latter part of the summer. They tend to be 'mean' and are generally light but, as did 1967s, it is possible they will gain much elegance once in bottle. Because of the small crop, and the failure of 1968, prices extremely high and difficult to justify in comparison to relative quality, and prices, of previous vintages. Probably ready to drink from 1975.

1970 A 'dream' year for growers, merchants and consumers. Ideal conditions throughout the spring and summer produced a large quantity of excellent wine. The best vintage since 1966 and some may turn out to be even better than that very good year. They should of course not be drunk for at least two years, and the best will certainly live for at least twenty years.

1971 Bad weather in June resulted in a poor flowering and consequently a small crop. The rest of the summer was fine, and the quality is therefore good. The wines do not generally have the fruit and immediate charm of 1970, but many have great elegance and should develop well. Again a small crop resulted in a considerable price increase and the new level makes all previous prices – including 1969 – look reasonable.

BURGUNDY

1947 Two good vintages now rarely obtainable, but now just about at
1949 their best. The 1947s are more regular in their quality than the 1949s, but both vintages have produced good wines. In character the 1947s are more solid and the 1949s, when really successful, more charming.

1952 Excellent vintage for drinking now. Well-made, classic wines of the same type as the Bordeaux of this vintage.

1953 Even more advanced than the 1952s. Very attractive wines. Should be drunk now.

1955 A 'correct' vintage. Uninspiring, but true, pleasant Burgundies. Should be drunk now.

1957 Solid wines, a year more successful here than in Bordeaux. Good drinking now.

1959 Another year more successful in Burgundy than in Bordeaux. Exceptionally hot summers are always more rewarding in Burgundy. Excellent flavour and shape and often with all the richness associated with Burgundy. Now approaching their best.

1960 Some successful whites; they should be drunk now.

1961 Perhaps not as outstanding as in Bordeaux but well constituted wines with considerable character. The best should be given another three to four years though many can be enjoyed now.

1962 Light for Burgundy but great elegance and length. A good year for drinking now.

1963 A poor year.

1964 More regular here than in Bordeaux. Fat wines, perhaps lacking the shape and elegance of a great vintage but warm wines that will certainly be enjoyed. Approaching their best.

1965 Some successful white wines, but a poor year for red.

1966 Balanced wines with adequate body and great style. The kind of year growers would like to have more often – consumers too, no doubt. Developing extremely well in bottle, many can be enjoyed now, but the best should be given another two to three years.

1967 As in Bordeaux started life with a reputation well behind that of
     1966 but may surprise after a couple more years in bottle. Lighter
     than 1966 but often great finesse and elegance. Some particularly
     good white wines.

1968 As so often, a year that can be written off for quality red wine has
     produced some stylish light white wines of real character.

1969 Prices extremely high because of a very small crop, the wines have
     a good clean character and style but lack a little ripeness. A good
     vintage, but not a great vintage.

1970 A large crop. The white wines are outstanding. The reds some-
     times tend to be on the light side, but the best have great elegance
     and style and will certainly give great pleasure to all who look for
     something more than 'beef' in their Burgundy.

1971 Hail damage and poor weather for the flowering resulted in a
     small crop. Outstanding summer conditions produced grapes
     with the highest sugar content that can be remembered for many
     years. Such freak conditions make the actual wine making more
     difficult, but those growers who overcame these difficulties have
     made outstanding wine. An excellent year for Burgundy, but
     careful selection essential.

CHAMPAGNE

1947, 1949, 1952, 1953, 1955, 1959, 1961, 1962, 1964. These are likely
to be followed by 1966 and 1969. 1961 is outstanding and will remain
at its best for another three to four years.

PORT

Older vintages: 1942, 1935, 1934, 1927, 1923, 1922.
Recent vintages: 1963, 1960, 1958, 1955, 1954, 1950, 1948, 1947, 1945.
The war years of 1942 and 1945 were bottled in Oporto. This was
unheard-of up to that time, but the results were considered satisfactory
by some wine merchants and shippers and the practice has not been
entirely abandoned since the war.
For drinking now: 1945, 1947, 1950
For drinking from 1970 onwards: 1948, 1954
For drinking from 1975 onwards: 1955, 1960, 1963
For drinking from 1980 onwards: 1958, 1966, 1967

GERMANY

1952 Particularly good in *Spätlese* and *Auslese* qualities, owing to an
     effective 'Indian summer'.

1953 The best of all current vintages and the best since 1921.

1955 A medium-quality vintage, but variable in quality between 'fairly good' and 'rather poor'.

1957 Similar to 1955 with some slightly better wines.

1958 Very large quantity but quality similar to 1955 and 1957.

1959 A well-earned reputation for fine quality, with fewer highlights than 1953. Moselle and Rheingau particularly successful. The best, those with sufficient acidity, will continue to improve.

1960 Interesting mainly because it produced a record quantity, nearly double the average of the last ten years. Quality was pleasant and easy and the wines were drunk young.

1961/62 A fair quality, better than 1960.

1963 A few light wines suitable for quick consumption but a lot of poor wine as well.

1964 A very large crop, though not quite so large as 1960. Also a good year for quality with some particularly good *Spätleses* and *Ausleses*.

1965 Generally a poor year, producing wines high in acidity. Expert vinification did however enable some useful wines to be made.

1966 Comparatively small crop with the exception of the Moselle. Quality well above average, many fine wines made, especially in the Moselle, Saar and Ruwer. Vintage combined fruity acidity with body and elegance.

1967 Sound, pleasant wines. The presence of botrytis in the Palatinate and Rheingau produced some excellent *Auslese* and *Beerenauslese*. These are maturing rapidly.

1968 No top quality wines but generally well balanced and some useful wines, particularly in the middle price category.

1969 As elsewhere, a small crop resulting in high prices. Generally a good average quality, perhaps more successful on the Moselle than in the Rhine areas.

1970 A huge record vintage of pleasing average quality. Excellent value in the medium price ranges but few top wines.

1971 A really excellent year, beautifully balanced, the best vintage since 1953. Quantity was about average but there was a great preponderence of superb *Spätlese* and *Auslese* wines; the Palatinates outstanding.

FURTHER READING

GENERAL

A Guide to Good Wine (Chambers, 1952)
  The classic wines, described by members of the wine trade.
Wines and Spirits of the World: edited by Alec Gold (Virtue Publishing Co., 1968)
  Exactly what its title says, comprehensive and authoritative, by members of the wine trade, with copious maps and illustrations.
Wines of the World: edited by André Simon (McGraw-Hill, 1967)
  This incorporates in a single volume the principal specialized volumes separately published.
A Concise Encyclopaedia of Gastronomy: a guide to good food and wines: André Simon (Wine & Food Society, 1956)
  Also many other books by André Simon, the greatest authority on wine in the U.K. during his time.
Encyclopaedia of Wine: Frank Schoonmaker (Nelson, 1967)
  This standard work, originally published in the U.S.A., was edited for the U.K. by Hugh Johnson.
Encyclopaedia of Wines & Spirits: Alex Lichine (Cassell, 1967)
  There are controversial features as well as facts in this comprehensive book.
Winecraft: T. A. Layton (Harpers, 1935)
  This has been revised and brought up to date and provides a valuable addition to existing dictionaries of wine.
Wines and Spirits: L. W. Marrison (Penguin, 1957)
  Comprehensive and good on wine chemistry.
The Earnest Drinker: Oscar Mendelsohn (Allen & Unwin, 1950)
  Contains much varied, accurate and well-classified information.
A Man May Drink: Richard Serjeant (Putnam, 1964)
  Particularly good on the physiological effects.
An Alphabet of Choosing and Serving Wine (Herbert Jenkins, 1955) and *The Home Wine Cellar* (Herbert Jenkins, 1960): Raymond Postgate.
  Factual and easy to read for quick reference. Like any other books by this author, to be relied on for accuracy and balanced judgement.
A World Atlas of Wine: Hugh Johnson (Mitchell Beazley, 1971)
Wine: Hugh Johnson (Nelson, 1966, and Sphere Books)

Wines and Spirits: Pamela Vandyke Price (Corgi, 1972)

A Winelover's Handbook: Pamela Vandyke Price (Condé Nast and Collins, 1970)

Basic information for beginners.

The World of Wine: Creighton Churchill (Collier-Macmillan, 1967)

Wine: R. S. Don, M.W. (English Universities Press, Teach Yourself Series)

Essentials for the beginner, with helpful advice on shopping.

HISTORICAL AND ANECDOTAL

Gods, Men and Wine: William Younger (International Wine & Food Society, 1966)

Dionysus, a Social History of the Wine Vine: Edward Hyams (Thames & Hudson, 1965)

These two books, most beautifully illustrated, provide a detailed background to the whole history of wine drinking and making.

Notes on a Cellarbook: George Saintsbury (Macmillan, 1923)

The classic reminiscences of an enthusiast.

Stay Me With Flagons: Maurice Healy (Michael Joseph, 1930)

A frank assessment by a gifted amateur of classical wines.

A History of Wine: H. Warner Allen (Faber, 1961)

Recommended, like the many other books of this scholarly lover of wine: *Sherry and Port* (Constable, 1952), *White Wines and Cognac* (Constable, 1952), *Natural Red Wines* (Constable, 1951), *Through the Wine Glass* (Michael Joseph, 1954), *A Contemplation of Wine* (Michael Joseph, 1951).

The History of the Wine Trade in England: André L. Simon (Holland Press, 1965)

This, first published in 1906, has been reprinted, with an index.

Lafite: Cyril Ray (Peter Davies, 1968)

Bollinger: Cyril Ray (Peter Davies, 1971)

The next three books are specially for the traveller:

Vineyards of France: J. D. Scott (Hodder & Stoughton, 1950)

The French Vineyards: Denis Morris (Eyre & Spottiswoode, 1958)

Eating and Drinking in France Today: Pamela Vandyke Price (Tom Stacey, 1972)

SPECIALIZED

A Book of French Wines: H. Morton Shand (Jonathan Cape, 1928. Penguin edition, edited by Cyril Ray, 1964)

The Noble Grapes and the Great Wines of France: André L. Simon (Rainbird, 1957)

The Wines of Bordeaux: J.-R. Roger (André Deutsch, 1960)

The Wines of Bordeaux: Edmund Penning-Rowsell (International Wine & Food Society, 1969, rev. edn, 1971)

Comprehensive and authoritative, particularly on history and the technology of the properties.

The Wines of Burgundy: H. W. Yoxall (International Wine & Food Society, 1968)

Simply explicit on a complex subject, with additional useful information for the traveller.

The Wines of Burgundy: Pierre Poupon and Pierre Forgeot (Presses Universitaires de France, 1968)

Champagne, the wine, the land & the people: Patrick Forbes (Gollancz, 1967)

Perhaps the most valuable and detailed study of this great wine.

The History of Champagne: André L. Simon (Ebury Press, 1962)

Alsace and its Wine Gardens: S. H. Hallgarten (André Deutsch, 1957)

German Wines and Vines: Alfred Langenbach (Vista Books, 1962)

The Great Wines of Germany: André L. Simon and S. F. Hallgarten (Ebury Press, 1963)

German Wines: Frank Schoonmaker (Oldbourne, 1957)

The Wines of Italy: Cyril Ray (McGraw Hill, 1966, and Penguin, 1971)

Portuguese Wine: Raymond Postgate (Dent, 1969)

Port: Rupert Croft-Cooke (Putnam, 1957) and, by the same author, *Madeira* (Putnam, 1961)

Sherry: Julian Jeffs (Faber, rev. edn, 1971)

Sherry and the Wines of Spain: George Rainbird (Michael Joseph, 1966)

California Wines: John Melville (Nourse, 1955)

American Wines: Frank Schoonmaker and Tom Marvell (Duell, Sloane & Pearce, New York, 1941)

Classic Wines of Australia: Max Lake (Jacaranda Press, 1966)

The Wines of Australia: Harry Cox (Hodder & Stoughton, 1967)

Wine in Australia: Walter James (Georgian House, 1952)

Wine Tasting: J. M. Broadbent, M.W. (Wine & Spirit Publications, 1968)

The Wines of Central and South-Eastern Europe: R. E. H. Gunyon (Duckworth, 1971)

A scholarly study of wines of increasing importance for today's drinking.

PERIODICAL

Wine Magazine (Wine & Spirit Publications, South Bank House, Black Prince Road, London, S.E.1.)

GLOSSARY

CONTAINERS

Aum
German wine cask containing 30 gallons.

Barrique
French name for a cask. Not a universal measure. A Bordeaux barrique = 225 litres (50 gallons). A Burgundy barrique (generally called a *'pièce'*) = 215 litres (48 gallons). A Mâconnais barrique = 214 litres (48 gallons). The English translation for commercial purposes is 'hogshead'.

Bontemps
A small shallow wooden bowl used in Bordeaux cellars for the mixing of finings or other cellar purposes. It is also the name of a Bordeaux wine fraternity.

Bottle sizes
A normal bottle holds 72–75 centilitres, about 26 fluid ounces. A *magnum* is two bottles. A *jeroboam* is variously considered to take four or six bottles. A *rehoboam*, according to various authorities, is six or eight bottles. *Tappit-hen* (originally a Scottish pewter drinking vessel), *Methuselah*, *Nebuchadnezzar* and others are fancy names sometimes given to unusual-sized bottles and can vary in capacity from three bottles to twenty bottles. They are impractical from several points of view.

Butt
A Spanish cask containing 108 gallons of wine. In other countries the term is also sometimes used, but the capacity will vary according to local custom.

Carafe
This has the ordinary meaning of the word and is not a fixed measure. It is sometimes used by restaurants and bars to describe wines sold in open carafes straight from the cask.

Double Aum
German wine cask containing 60 gallons.

Feuillette
A small cask mostly used in Chablis, containing 136 litres (30 gallons). In other parts of France it varies from 112 litres to 144 litres.

Fillette
A small half bottle in Alsace and in some of the white-wine areas of Bordeaux.

Fuder
A Moselle cask containing 1,000 litres (220 gallons).

Hogshead	A cask. In Bordeaux a legal standard measure of 46 gallons.
Pipe	A standard port cask containing 115 gallons. A Madeira pipe contains 92 gallons. In France it is a cask varying in size – generally about 120–130 gallons – used for storing spirits.
Stück	A German cask containing 1,200 litres (270 gallons). A standard measure in the Rheingau district.
Tastevin	A small saucer with a handle, generally made of silver, used for tasting young wines from the cask. The Bordeaux *tastevin* has no handle.
Velinch	A long metal or glass pipette, used for drawing wine from the top of a cask or vat.

MEASURES OF WINE STRENGTH

Baumé	A measure of sugar in wine. One degree Baumé is roughly equivalent to 18 gm. of sugar per litre. A medium dry wine may have about 1° Baumé, a medium sweet about 2°. A sweet wine may have 3° and a rich table wine up to 5°. Fortified wines or specially made dessert wines can go much higher.
Gay Lussac	The French method of measuring the strength of alcoholic liquids, expressed in percentage of pure alcohol by volume.
Oechsle	A German scale for measurement of the sugar content of wine.
Proof	Proof spirit is a standard solution of pure spirit defined by the Customs authorities and used as the basic for the assessment of Customs and Excise duties. It is measured by a system known as Sykes (or Sikes). Roughly, 100 per cent proof means about 57 per cent pure alcohol by volume. Spirits sold as 30° U.P. (i.e. 30° under proof) therefore contain about 40 per cent pure alcohol by volume. Foreign wines paying the table wine duty are limited in strength to what is known as N.E. 25°, that is 'Not exceeding 25 per cent proof spirit', in other words containing a maximum of 14 per cent pure alcohol by volume.
Sykes (or Sikes)	The British method of measuring the alcoholic strength of liquids. See '*Proof*'.

WINE IMPORT DUTIES

(See also under 'Proof')

Duties in force after the Budget of April 1969 are as follows:

	Per gallon	Per dozen
Still foreign table wines imported in cask	32s. 3d. (app. £1·61½)	64s. 6d. (£3·22½)
Still foreign table wines imported in bottle	34s. 9d. (app. £1·74)	69s. 6d. (£2·47½)
Still foreign fortified wines imported in cask	54s. 3d. (app. £2·71½)	108s. 3d. (app. £5·41½)
Still foreign fortified wines imported in bottle	56s. 9d. (app. £2·84)	113s. 6d. (£5·67½)
Sparkling wines	44s. 9d. (app. £2·24)	89s. 6d. (£4·47½)

There is a preference of 2s. (10p) per gallon accorded to all light wines from the Commonwealth and from South Africa and Cyprus, and of 10s. (50p) per gallon on all fortified wines imported in cask. The preferential allowance on sparkling wines is 2s. (10p) per gallon and on other wines imported in bottle 3s. (15p) per gallon. The duty in excise on a bottle of whisky or brandy, etc., depends on the strength of the spirit. On the average bottle it amounts to about 44s. (£2·20).

TERMS USED IN THE PRODUCTION OF WINES

Fining	The process of clarifying a young wine during the period of development in cask.
Lees	The wine containing impurities left at the bottom of a cask after it has been clarified.
Rack	To draw the bright wine off the lees in the cask.
Viner (French)	To add alcohol to a wine.

DESCRIPTIONS OF WINE

Brut	A term used to describe natural Champagne which has not been sweetened.

Demi sec	Half dry.
Doux	Sweet.
Dry	Not sweet. The word has only a comparative significance when applied to wine.
Finesse	When applied to wine, denotes a subtlety of flavour.
Sec	Dry.
Sekt (German)	Sparkling wine.
Table wines	Unfortified wines with a maximum alcoholic content of about 14° and paying the lowest import duty.

OTHER FOREIGN WORDS USED IN CONNEXION WITH WINE

Caves	Underground cellars.
Cépage	Vine.
Chai	Ground-level wine-maturing stores, built of thick stone and without windows in order to maintain a cool temperature. The usual method of storing wines in Bordeaux and Cognac.
Chambrer	To 'room' a wine, that is to take the chill off red wine.
Chaptaliser	To add sugar to the unfermented grape must in order to increase the alcoholic degree of the eventual wine.
Clos	Literally, 'an enclosure'. Used to describe individual vineyards in areas such as Burgundy, where there are generally no château buildings as there are in the large Bordeaux properties.
Crémant	A sparkling wine with less than the usual degree of effervescence.
Cru	A named vineyard.
Cuve	Vat.
Cuvée	The wine from a vat; sometimes used to designate a special blend.
Eau-de-vie de marc	Brandy distilled in most wine-making areas from the residue of grape skins left after all the juice has been squeezed out to make wine.
Étampé	Stamped or branded. Generally on a cork.
Fass (German)	A cask.
Frappé	Iced.
Marc	The residue of grape skins left after all the juice has been extracted from the grapes by two or three pressings.

Nu	Literally 'naked'. A wine quoted without the price of the cask being included.
Pièce	A transportable wine cask.
Race	A French word used to denote breeding in a wine.

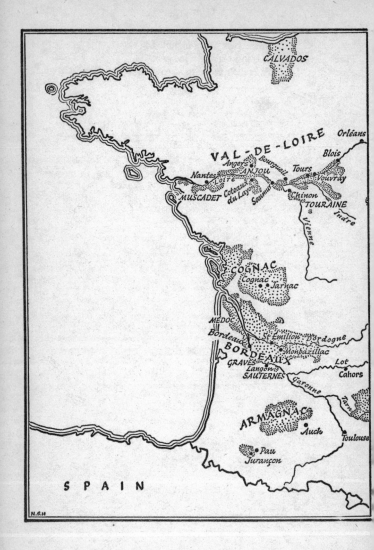

CALVADOS

VAL-DE-LOIRE

Orléans

Blois

Angers   Bourgueil   Tours

Nantes   ANJOU   Vouvray

Loire

MUSCADET   Coteaux   Chinon
du Layon   Saumur   TOURAINE

Indre

Vienne

COGNAC

Cognac   Jarnac

MEDOC

Bordeaux   St Emilion   Dordogne

BORDEAUX   Monbazillac

GRAVES

Langon   Lot
SAUTERNES   Cahors

Garonne

Tarn

ARMAGNAC

Auch   Toulouse

Pau
Jurançon

S P A I N

N.G.H

FRANCE

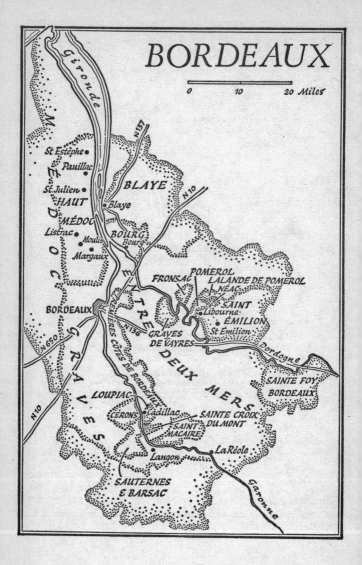

BORDEAUX

0   10   20 Miles

Gironde

N137

St Estèphe
Pauillac
St Julien
HAUT
MÉDOC
Listrac
Moulis
Margaux

MÉDOC

BLAYE
Blaye
N10

BOURG
Bourg

ENTRE

BORDEAUX

N650

GRAVES

PREMIÈRES CÔTES DE BORDEAUX

N136

FRONSAC
POMEROL
LALANDE DE POMEROL
NÉAC
SAINT
Libourne
ÉMILION
St Émilion

GRAVES
DE VAYRES

Dordogne

DEUX

MERS

SAINTE FOY
BORDEAUX

N10

LOUPIAC
CÉRONS
Cadillac
SAINT
MACAIRE
Langon

SAINTE CROIX
DU MONT

La Réole

SAUTERNES
E BARSAC

Garonne

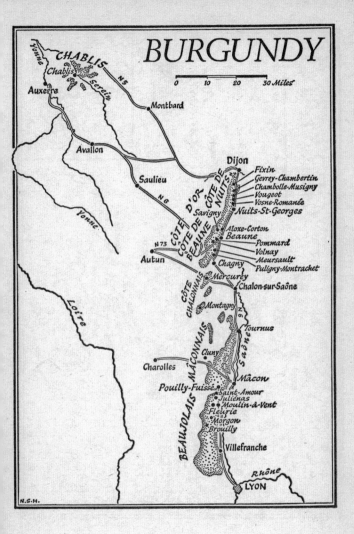

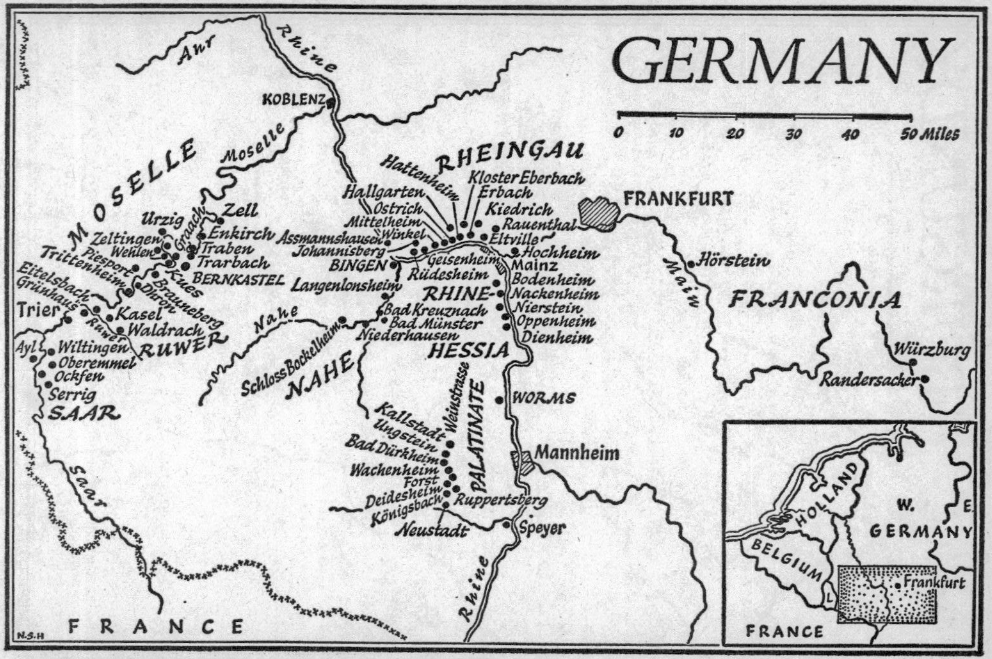
GERMANY
0 10 20 30 40 50 Miles
Ahr
Rhine
KOBLENZ
Moselle
MOSELLE
Zell
Urzig
Graach
Enkirch
Zeltingen
Wehlen
Traben
Piesport
Trarbach
Trittenheim
Kues
BERNKASTEL
Eitelsbach
Grünhaus
Brauneberg
Dhron
Trier
Kasel
Ruwer
Waldrach
RUWER
Ayl
Wiltingen
Oberemmel
Ockfen
Serrig
SAAR
Saar
FRANCE
N.S.H
RHEINGAU
Hattenheim
Kloster Eberbach
Hallgarten
Erbach
Ostrich
Kiedrich
Mittelheim
Rauenthal
Assmannshausen
Winkel
Eltville
Johannisberg
Hochheim
Geisenheim
BINGEN
Mainz
Rüdesheim
Bodenheim
Langenlonsheim
RHINE-
Nackenheim
Bad Kreuznach
Nierstein
Bad Münster
Oppenheim
Niederhausen
Dienheim
HESSIA
Nahe
Schloss Bockelheim
NAHE
FRANKFURT
Main
Hörstein
FRANCONIA
Würzburg
Randersacker
WORMS
Kallstadt
Weinstrasse
Ungstein
PALATINATE
Bad Dürkheim
Mannheim
Wachenheim
Forst
Deidesheim
Ruppertsberg
Königsbach
Neustadt
Speyer
Rhine
HOLLAND
W. GERMANY
E.
BELGIUM
L
Frankfurt
FRANCE

ITALY

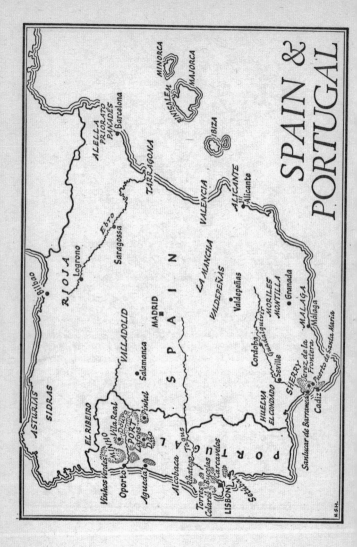

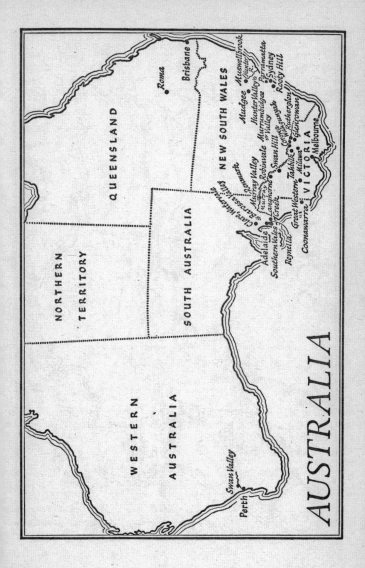

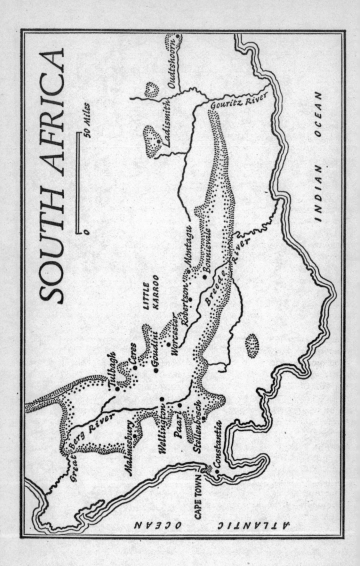

INDEX